Criminal Injustice

Criminal Injustice

An Evaluation of the Criminal Justice Process in Britain

Frank Belloni
Associate Professor of Political Science
Virginia Commonwealth University

and

Jacqueline Hodgson
Lecturer in Law
University of Warwick

First published in Great Britain 2000 by
MACMILLAN PRESS LTD
Houndmills, Basingstoke, Hampshire RG21 6XS and London
Companies and representatives throughout the world

A catalogue record for this book is available from the British Library.

ISBN 978-0-333-77883-8   ISBN 978-0-230-59976-5 (eBook)
DOI 10.1007/978-0-230-59976-5

First published in the United States of America 2000 by
ST. MARTIN'S PRESS, INC.,
Scholarly and Reference Division,
175 Fifth Avenue, New York, N.Y. 10010

ISBN 978-0-312-22620-6

Library of Congress Cataloging-in-Publication Data
Belloni, Frank P.
Criminal injustice : an evaluation of the criminal justice process
in Britain / Frank Belloni and Jacqueline Hodgson.
    p.   cm.
Includes bibliographical references and index.
ISBN 978-0-312-22620-6 (cloth)
1. Criminal justice, Administration of—Great Britain—Evaluation.
2. Criminal procedure—Great Britain—Evaluation.   3. Human rights–
–Great Britain.   I. Hodgson, Jacqueline.   II. Title.
HV9960.G7B45   1999
364.941—DC21   99–33856
                                                CIP

© Frank Belloni and Jacqueline Hodgson 2000

This book is printed on paper suitable for recycling and made from fully managed and sustained
forest sources. Logging, pulping and manufacturing processes are expected to conform to the
environmental regulations of the country of origin.

Transferred to digital printing 2001

Contents

'I don't think them people in there have got the intelligence or the honesty to spell the word justice, let alone dispense it. They're rotten.'

Paddy Hill (one of the Birmingham Six) outside the Court of Appeal on the day of his release, 14 March 1991

Preface

This book arose out of our astonishment and dismay at the report of the Royal Commission on Criminal Justice in 1993 and the subsequent legislation. Despite the catalogue of errors and malpractice uncovered in the miscarriage of justice cases, reform has centred upon the creation and maintenance of government populism on the strength of the 'law and order' card. Enhancing the rights of suspects and defendants is not a vote-winner. It is easier to 'talk tough' than to make the effort required to alter the climate of public opinion.

Reforms have been concerned with generating greater knowledge within the criminal process, not in a way that facilitates the due process rights of the accused, but in order to benefit the efficiency of the system itself. The trial represents the ultimate safeguard for the defendant, an opportunity to test out the strength of the evidence against her, in public, before an impartial tribunal. But the reforms of the last five years have sought to minimize what is considered to be the costly and unpredictable risk of cases going to trial, by making the pressures upon the defendant to plead guilty, almost irresistible. The new procedures distort the adversarial underpinnings of the criminal process and are the reverse of what one might expect after the revelations of the miscarriage cases. Confession evidence has been shown to be unreliable, yet the suspect's right to silence has been curtailed almost out of existence. Non-disclosure of prosecution evidence has led to wrongful convictions, yet the prosecution duty to disclose evidence has been reduced and made conditional upon a new requirement that the defence disclose its case. At the level of daily practice, safeguards against the abuse of police power have been overridden. The elasticity of the reasonable suspicion requirement has not constrained the police in stopping, searching and arresting people as they see fit, including in discriminatory ways. Yet, new stop and search powers have been introduced, which dispense with the requirement for reasonable suspicion in some circumstances.

There have been some positive initiatives such as the improved training requirements for defence lawyers advising suspects at the police station; or the higher place which racially motivated crimes now occupy on the criminal justice agenda; and the creation of the Criminal Cases Review Commission. But these are overshadowed by the dominant thrust of government reform which does violence to due process and which leaves us with a depressing criminal justice landscape.

The writing of this book has spanned births and deaths in our families, as well as moves between universities, houses and continents. Virginia Commonwealth University kindly granted Frank Belloni research leave which enabled him to come to Warwick as a visiting research fellow in the Law School from 1994 to 1996, where he benefited greatly from the facilities and academic exchange extended to him there. We are grateful for the support of the Law School at the University of Warwick, and in particular, to Mike McConville and the secretarial staff there, and to Roger Leng for reading and commenting on parts of the book. We are also indebted to the lawyers and others we interviewed, who took the time to express their views to us. But most of all, we thank our families who supported us in so many ways throughout this project. In particular, to Debra Chilton for her valuable IT assistance and to Mark Jackson, who undertook to cook for us all in the final run. Ella and Lotte will be glad to regain a parent from the quarantine of her study.

Birmingham   FRANK BELLONI
November 1998   JACQUELINE HODGSON

List of Cases

List of Statutes

List of Abbreviations

ACPO	Association of Chief Police Officers
CAA	Criminal Appeal Act 1968, 1995
CCRC	Criminal Cases Review Commission
CDA	Crime and Disorder Act 1998
CJA	Criminal Justice Act 1967, 1987, 1988
CJPOA	Criminal Justice and Public Order Act 1994
CJU	Criminal Justice Unit
CLRC	Criminal Law Revision Committee 1972
COP	Code of Practice
CPIA	Criminal Procedure and Investigations Act 1996
CPS	Crown Prosecution Service
DPP	Director of Public Prosecutions
ECHR	European Convention on Human Rights
FSS	Forensic Science Service
HRA	Human Rights Act 1998
PACE	Police and Criminal Evidence Act 1984
PCA	Police Complaints Authority
PDH	Plea and Directions Hearing
PII	Public Interest Immunity
POOA	Prosecution of Offences Act 1985
PTR	Pre-Trial Review
RCCJ	Royal Commission on Criminal Justice 1993
RCCP	Royal Commission on Criminal Procedure 1981
WMSCS	West Midlands Serious Crime Squad

1

The Criminal Justice System and Miscarriages of Justice in England and Wales

Introduction

This book examines the ways in which justice miscarries in the criminal justice process in England and Wales. The inquiry carries us through the various stages of the criminal justice process, beginning with the police constable's first contact with a 'suspect' on the street, on through to a possible arrest, trial and resolution of a case, including appeal (if initiated) following a conviction. We examine the recommendations of the 1993 Royal Commission on Criminal Justice and the wave of legislation that followed it. Critical evaluation of these, together with research findings on the functioning of the criminal process,[1] leads us to conclude that the occurrence of miscarriages of justice will continue, but the chances of detecting them will diminish. As the due process protections for suspects and defendants are systematically weakened, the very notion of injustice is redefined.

A miscarriage of justice refers to the failure of the criminal process to function in such a manner as to achieve outcomes which are considered 'just' from several different perspectives – that is, of those who directly experience it or are impacted by it; of those who are responsible for its operation; and of the community which is served by the process. Thus the scope of matters that might be considered a miscarriage of justice is quite broad.[2] Furthermore, while miscarriages of justice generally are seen as deriving from the criminal process, and it is with these that we are concerned here, defects in the criminal law itself might also be considered responsible. An example would be the difficulties encountered by abused women in raising the defence of provocation to a charge of murdering their partner.[3]

1

In this study the concept of miscarriage of justice is used mainly in the sense understood by those committed to the application of due process principles and procedures in the criminal justice system.[4] It refers not only to the wrongful conviction of innocent persons that results from the failed application of due process, but also to those who may be guilty, but who are convicted as a result of wrongful police practices. Otherwise, to condone convictions produced by malpractice undermines the rationale of the criminal process, the objective of which is (or should be) to ensure that only those against whom there is sufficiently strong evidence are prosecuted and convicted, thereby minimizing the prospect of innocent people being wrongly convicted.[5]

In seeking to understand the causes of these miscarriages, we uncover the ways in which the accused is disadvantaged throughout the criminal justice process: in her relationship with the police, the prosecution, the courts and even her own defence lawyer.

Routine injustice: on the street and in the magistrates' court

Before examining what lies behind some of the more high-profile miscarriages of justice, we will consider briefly two particular sources of injustice which receive scant attention, despite (or perhaps because of) their invisibility and the frequency with which they occur.

The way in which the police exercise their power to stop and search individuals results in 'invisible' injustices which are experienced by some people on a daily basis without their ever having been charged with a criminal offence or brought before the courts. In a review of research on ethnic minorities and the criminal justice system prepared for the Royal Commission on Criminal Justice, Marion Fitzgerald (1993) reports that Afro-Caribbean youth are still significantly more likely than whites to be stopped by police;[6] and a 1994 Policy Studies Institute survey of 2,400 youths from England's inner cities found that four out of 10 boys had been stopped in the previous year, and that for blacks the proportion stopped was over 50 per cent. Moreover, about one-fifth of those stopped reported that they had experienced 11 or more such incidents in a year. A national survey conducted by Statewatch (1999) found that black people are nearly eight times more likely to be stopped and searched than whites, and four times more likely to be arrested.

These data confirm what is widely known – that police exercise their power to stop and search in a discriminatory way against youth, especially black youth,[7] and various other target groups; but what is less often understood is that in stopping them the police may be carrying out a form of punitive 'street justice': as such, each instance of an unjustifiable stop or search or oppressive policing may constitute an injustice.[8]

The impact of race can also extend to police behaviour towards the victims of crime, as evidenced by the enquiry into the death of Stephen Lawrence. There have been allegations that the investigation was hamstrung from the very beginning by the institutional racism within the police. Other cases have now been re-opened (such as the deaths of Ricky Reel and Michael Menson), where the victim's family believe the death of their relative to have been both deliberate and racially motivated.[9]

For most, the spectre of miscarriages of justice conjures up images of the Birmingham Six and the Guildford Four: cases involving the most serious crimes, tried before a judge and jury in the Crown Court. Sheltered from the public's attention are the magistrates' courts, where the overwhelming majority of cases are tried, most of them ending in conviction. Here, too, injustices occur.[10] Yet, these are of less interest and are considered less important because of the notion that magistrates try only relatively minor matters. However, the lower courts also handle offences which are by no means trivial, such as wounding, indecent assault, burglary, the use and supply of controlled drugs and firearms offences; and the number of such offences is growing as a result of the 'reclassification' of hitherto indictable offences to summary offences. In addition, magistrates' courts often deal with serious offences which have been 'downgraded' in exchange for the willingness of defendants to plead guilty.

The RCCJ did not consider magistrates' courts to be a source of injustice. Without commissioning any research into the operation and outcomes of summary justice, they declared simply that the magistrates 'should' be trusted to try cases fairly, as they deal with over 93 per cent of all criminal business in the courts. However, a number of factors cast doubt upon the quality of justice received by those convicted in the magistrates' court. First, the prosecution of defendants is heavily reliant upon evidence provided by the police, who are keen to secure the conviction of those charged with offences. McConville *et al.* (1994: 237) report that 'in the overwhelming majority of summary trials, police evidence is essentially evidence of the police themselves, consisting of what they allege they saw the defendant do or heard the defendant say'. The legitimacy of this police evidence, they argue, derives from several factors: their skill in presentation, the 'authenticity' accorded their evidence via police notebooks, and corroboration by other police officer testimony (ibid.: 227–9).

Secondly, magistrates are very strongly disposed to believe and rely upon the integrity of the police and the veracity of their evidence. This was explained to us by a solicitor-advocate as follows:

> I think the police are more believable to the magistrates than the defendants. They think: 'The police don't have to come here and tell lies. On the other hand, the defendant comes here because he's in trouble and he might tell lies to get out of trouble.' I think they work on that basis too often: so it is an uphill struggle for us solicitors to persuade them otherwise. (Interview, February 1995)

Hedderman and Moxon (1992) found that the majority of both defendants and their solicitors believe that 'magistrates are on the side of the police';[11] and Gifford (1986: 36) asserts that the impression most often given by magistrates to defence solicitors 'is of total partiality towards the prosecution. The burden of proof seems to be reversed: if the police say you are guilty, you will be found guilty unless you can prove your innocence.' McConville *et al.* (1994) also gained the impression that in magistrates' courts 'there is a reverse onus of proof under which it is for the defendant to establish innocence rather than for the prosecution to prove guilt' (211–38). Thirdly, defence solicitors are often poorly prepared and disinclined to function in an adversarial capacity. According to McConville *et al.* (1994), they operate in a way which assumes the client's guilt. The extent to which defence lawyers share the values of magistrates in this respect is supported by a number of our own interviews with solicitor-advocates, as in the following example.

> My view is that probably 90-plus percent of defendants are guilty; and as you pointed out, about 95% of defendants get convicted, so it probably works out just about right – but whether for the right reasons I don't know. I suspect that the vast majority of people who are charged are guilty of an offence, and I think that's probably the view taken by most magistrates. ... Unlike jurors, I think magistrates tend to become ... perhaps the word isn't cynical, but hardened to a certain view. I think they probably expect and believe that most defendants are guilty. Their decisions, not always based upon the evidence, reflect that ... I think it's a rough-and-ready result that comes out [in magistrates' courts] at the end. But in most cases, happily, I think it is probably justified. However, the magistrates'

way of dealing with it doesn't necessarily equate with it being correct and unbiased. (Interview, February 1995)

McConville *et al.* (1994: 71) describe 'criminal defence practices as geared, in co-operation with other elements of the system, towards the routine production of guilty pleas'. The bulk of major defence service providers do not conceive of their role in adversarial terms. The exceptions, argue McConville and his associates, are just that – exceptional – and such lawyers are likely to face heavy counter-pressure from the police and, sometimes, the media. A solicitor strongly committed to the defence of his clients described the pressure in this way:

> After a day at the police station and in court, you'd come back to the office and have to restore your pride in what you're doing – having had everyone suggest that really the whole of society would be better off without you. You had to remind yourself that people are entitled to know what the law is and need to be advised; and remind yourself that some people are innocent and are entitled to have the prosecution case tested![12]

The consequence of most solicitors failing to act in this adversarial, client-centred way is that, inevitably, some defendants will be wrongly convicted.

Fourthly, in contrast to trials on indictment or offences triable-either-way, the defendant in summary trials is not entitled to full advance disclosure of the prosecution case; and finally, in certain kinds of cases, defendants tried in magistrates' courts may be refused Legal Aid.[13] Reinforcing the unfavourable image of magistrates' courts are the long delays for hearing contested cases, the inconsistencies in decision-making, and the fact that there are no transcripts of trials, thus making difficult any attempt to appeal.

Unofficial estimates made by JUSTICE, the Legal Action Group and Liberty suggest that the number of miscarriages of justice arising from summary trials is substantial. There is also some official evidence in the form of summary court convictions quashed by the Crown Court, which hears appeals on the sole ground of alleged miscarriage of justice.[14] Over 16,000 cases were appealed to the Crown Court in 1996–7. In 23 per cent the conviction was quashed and in 19 per cent the sentence was varied. But whatever the outcomes, the fraction of one per cent of magistrates' cases that is appealed to the higher courts is a mere drop in the ocean of cases processed by summary judgment;

and there is little doubt that in the daily summary processing of the huge and ever-growing volume of criminal cases, there is a level of routine injustice which attracts little media, and therefore public, attention because of the widespread perception that cases dealt with by magistrates involve only trivial offences.[15]

Miscarriages of justice: high-profile cases

Over a number of years, beginning in the late 1980s, there was a notable increase in the number of miscarriages of justice reported in the media.[16] Among the most prominent cases were those of the Guildford Four (murder caused by IRA pub bombings), the Birmingham Six (murder caused by IRA pub bombings), the Maguire Seven (possession of explosive substances), the Cardiff Three (murder of a prostitute), the Taylor sisters (murder of Alison Shaughnessy), the Darvell brothers (rape and murder of shop manageress), Stefan Kiszko (murder and sexual assault of schoolgirl), Jacqueline Fletcher (infanticide of her baby), Judith Ward (IRA M62 bombing in which 12 people were killed), Winston Silcott (murder of PC Keith Blakelock) and the Bridgewater Four (murder of the newspaper boy Carl Bridgewater).[17] The repetition of this ongoing phenomenon gradually led to widespread public concern about corruption, incompetence and partiality in the criminal justice system; and to the officially recognised need to restore public confidence in it.[18] In order to examine the nature of these miscarriage of justice cases, we will look at some of them in more detail.

The first three examples cited above are the most notorious. In October 1975, Paul Hill, Gerry Conlon, Patrick Armstrong and Carole Richardson were sentenced to life imprisonment after having been convicted of the murders of five people killed in the 1974 pub bombings in Guildford and Woolwich. These bombings were said to have been carried out at the behest of the IRA, and the Four had been convicted largely on the basis of the alleged confession of Armstrong. However, 14 years later, on 19 October 1989, the Guildford Four were released by the Court of Appeal following the discovery that police investigators had fabricated evidence against them. The discovery – a decade and a half after the convictions occurred – was of a rough set of typed notes with hand-written addenda, which matched Armstrong's supposedly contemporaneously recorded interview. On the basis of this post-scripted interview, the Lord Chief Justice, Lord Lane, concluded that the police officers involved in the investigation must have lied to the court.[19]

Despite the gravity of the Lord Chief Justice's conclusion, it took more than a year for the Director of Public Prosecutions to decide (in November 1990) that the police detectives involved in questioning the Guildford Four were to be prosecuted for conspiracy to pervert the course of justice; and thereafter, it took another three-and-a-half years to bring them to trial – at which they were duly acquitted (in May 1993).[20]

The 'Maguire Seven' were convicted in 1976, on the evidence of scientific tests, of possessing explosive substances. Leave to appeal was refused, but the case was referred to the Court of Appeal after the quashing of the conviction of the Guildford Four. After having spent thirteen years in prison (one of the seven having died there), the convictions were overturned. Additional scientific evidence had been withheld from the defence, as well as information showing that the traces of nitroglycerine could have originated from an innocent source.

Paddy Hill, Richard McIlkenny, Johnny Walker, Billy Power, Hugh Callaghan and Gerry Hunter were convicted in 1975 of the murder of 21 people in two pub bombings in Birmingham in 1974. The evidence consisted of forensic tests conducted by Dr Frank Skuse which suggested that Power and Hill had been in contact with explosive material (nitroglycerine), and of confessions made by four of the men. However, having been in prison for 16 years, and after having twice had their appeals dismissed, in March 1991 the Court of Appeal quashed the convictions of the Birmingham Six.[21] The Court found, first, that the evidence of Dr Skuse, the forensic expert for the prosecution, had been discredited: he had not disclosed the possibility that alleged traces of explosives could have come from innocent contamination – even from smoking cigarettes. Secondly, the Court learned that the supposedly contemporaneous record of McIlkenny's confession interview, critical to the conviction of the Six, had been written by the police after the fact.[22]

Following the release of the men, three West Midlands detectives were charged with perjury and conspiracy to pervert the course of justice (they were accused of having fabricated evidence against the Birmingham Six). However, the charges were dropped without a trial on the grounds that adverse publicity attending the case of the Birmingham Six made it impossible for the (by then) former police detectives to receive a fair trial. Mr Justice Garland, presiding at the Old Bailey (7 October 1993), argued that the 'volume and intensity' of media coverage following the Six's acquittal in 1991 made it impossible for the officers to have a fair trial.[23]

To the foregoing high-profile cases, there must be added the growing number of persons wrongly convicted as a result of deliberate police misconduct carried out over a number of years by members of the West Midlands Serious Crime Squad (SCS)[24] and Metropolitan Police officers based at Stoke Newington police station in Northeast London.[25] In August 1989 the SCS was actually disbanded following exposure of systematic malpractice by its police officers; but the quashing of wrongful convictions secured during its operation continues.[26]

Examination of one case will suffice to illustrate the cynical disregard for the law demonstrated by the West Midlands SCS. In 1983 Derek Treadaway was arrested on suspicion of armed robbery and subjected to police interrogation which the Birmingham High Court later characterized as 'systematic torture'. While he was detained at the police station, five members of the Squad, having first hand-cuffed the suspect, placed a plastic bag over his head in such a manner as to induce a degree of asphyxiation. He was then told to stamp his feet when he had 'had enough' and was ready to make a statement. This procedure was repeated several times. On the third occasion the suspect, Treadaway, passed out. When he regained consciousness, the bag was put over his head a fourth time, at which point he stamped his feet and agreed to sign a false confession.

On the same night, however, in a lengthy statement to his lawyer (Ewan Smith), Treadaway described in detail the treatment he received at the hands of the police; he repeated his allegations at his trial a year later, where he pleaded not guilty to all charges. Despite his denial and his allegations of police abuse, the confession extracted by the police was accepted. He was convicted by a majority vote of the jury at Leicester Crown Court and sentenced to 15 years imprisonment. He appealed against his conviction but lost, and ended by serving nine years in prison.[27]

In 1985 Treadaway initiated a civil action against four police officers,[28] but in 1989, after two unsuccessful attempts, the police succeeded in persuading a Birmingham judge to strike out the action on the grounds that too much time had elapsed to secure a fair trial. Treadaway persisted, appealing twice against the court's decision to strike his action: in 1991 he failed, but in 1992 the Court of Appeal ruled in his favour.

At the end of seven days of testimony in the civil action for assault, Mr Justice Stuart McKinnon, on a standard of proof normally required only for a criminal trial,[29] concluded that he was satisfied that Derek Treadaway had, as he had claimed for 12 years, been assaulted by five members of the West Midlands Serious Crime Squad. 'What happened to him', the judge stated, 'amounted to nothing less than torture. The police officers concerned had shown contempt for the Plaintiff and thus for the rule of law.'[30] Justice McKinnon ordered the police to pay damages of £50,000.

Despite the High Court ruling in the civil suit, the CPS decided against prosecuting the police officers who had tortured Treadaway; and there the matter remained until 31 July 1997, when the High Court once again dealt with the case. Responding to Treadaway's appeal against the decision of the CPS, two senior judges ruled that the decision not to prosecute detectives from the West Midlands SCS was one which 'no reasonable Crown Prosecutor could have reached'. In quashing the decision, the judges held that the reasons given by the CPS demonstrated a 'flawed approach', and they ordered the then Director of Public Prosecutions, Barbara Mills, to reconsider it.[31]

These cases are illustrative of the types of malpractice which have led to many miscarriages – the fabrication of evidence, especially confession evidence; the production of partial and misleading scientific evidence; the failure to disclose information to the defence. They also demonstrate the sheer determination required to take a case to the Court of Appeal or to bring a civil action for damages. In each of these cases of miscarriage of justice, those falsely convicted spent years maintaining their innocence in the face of steadfast disbelief, or at least expressions of disbelief, by judicial authorities before finally securing relief from the long sentences that had been imposed. Moreover, it was not the officials of the criminal justice system – the police and prosecution, the courts, responsible government ministers – who recognized the miscarriages and initiated steps to correct them. It was, instead, the victims themselves, along with their supporters, who finally succeeded in forcing reluctant and resistant officials to take corrective action. In most cases the media have also played a crucial role. As Chris Mullin has noted, 'it remains an unhappy fact that a victim of a miscarriage of justice is far more likely to successfully overturn a conviction if he or she can first attract the attention of a television company, rather than a lawyer' (Mullin, 1991: para 6).

Whilst acknowledging the wrongdoing committed in these cases, many are quick to point out that they pre-date the Police and Criminal Evidence Act (PACE) 1984, and so are unlikely to be repeated.[32] Measures such as the tape-recording of interviews, or the provision of custodial legal advice, for example, make it unlikely that confessions can be concocted. However, miscarriage cases have not ceased with the passing of PACE. The 'Cardiff Three', for example, were convicted in

1990 of the murder of a Cardiff prostitute. Miller, one of the appellants, benefited from having his interview tape-recorded as well as having a solicitor present. Yet this in no way deterred the police from conducting an oppressive interrogation, which the Court of Appeal held should not have been admitted in evidence. The judges were shocked at what they heard.

> Miller was bullied and hectored. The officers ... were not questioning him so much as shouting at him ... Short of physical violence, it is hard to conceive of a more hostile and intimidating approach by officers to a suspect. It is impossible to convey on the printed page the pace, force and menace of the officer's delivery.[33]

Miller's solicitor was also criticized for sitting passively by while his client was bullied and intimidated.

In another case, in 1994, the Court of Appeal quashed the conviction of Ivan Fergus, a 13-year-old boy who had been convicted of attempted robbery. The case revealed a string of errors from virtually all parties involved in the case. The police had refused to interview four alibi witnesses, despite repeated requests from the Crown Prosecution Service. The defence were at fault in preparing the case and, in particular, in failing to call key witnesses or to submit that there was no case to answer. The trial judge failed to warn the jury of the dangers of convicting on identification evidence alone. And it was only when Fergus' mother went to a third firm of solicitors that she was properly advised as to how to obtain legal aid and a transcript of the trial in order to appeal.

Whilst legislation such as PACE has prevented specific police malpractices, such as the outright fabrication of signed confessions, it has failed to transform the operation of the criminal justice process in fundamental ways. In subsequent chapters, we will discuss the importance in shaping daily practice of both the structural relationships between actors in the criminal process and of their occupational cultures. We will also examine the range of measures introduced since PACE, which have systematically weakened the position of the accused.

Damage from miscarriages of justice

Before turning to the more general context in which many of these cases have occurred, it is important to note the damage that results from miscarriages of justice. For those most directly involved – the innocents who are wrongfully convicted and imprisoned – there is the traumatic denial of liberty and the deprivation associated with incarceration: separation from family and friends and the loss of reputation, job and home. The drastic psychological effects which may result are described by Dr Adrian Grounds, consultant psychiatrist, who conducted extensive interviews with four of the 'Birmingham Six' and their families. He told the *Guardian* newspaper, 'Three years after release they were suffering from persistent and disabling post-traumatic stress syndromes ... These are similar clinical symptoms of brain damaged people. I have found the same in the victims of war crimes and other people with post-traumatic stress disorder'.[34] In addition, the family of the wrongfully imprisoned may suffer in both a material and psychological sense.

Secondly, the victims of the original crime are made to suffer again, with the realization that the real offenders have not been caught. When Stefan Kiszko's conviction for the murder of Lesley Molseed was quashed after sixteen years, her father said 'For us, it is just like Lesley had been murdered last week.'[35] Society also suffers in that the guilty parties may remain at liberty and in a position to offend again. Finally, and of special relevance to this inquiry, frequent and serious miscarriages of justice discredit the integrity of the criminal justice process and undermine respect and support for it among the general public.[36] And this may be harmful to the political system as a whole. As the Runciman Commission noted, 'For a person to be deprived of his or her liberty, perhaps for many years, on account of a crime which was in fact committed by someone else, is both an individual tragedy and an affront to the standards of a civilised society' (1993: 2).

General causes

There are a number of general causes of miscarriages of justice in England and Wales – no doubt beginning with the unintentional mistakes and errors that may be expected in a large and complex operation such as the criminal justice process.[37] Beyond this, however, one can point to an insufficient commitment throughout the system to the basic legal rights of the individual. These must include a systematic adherence to due process protection against the denial of liberty. At the operational level, the problem begins with the police tendency to characterize certain individuals, even whole subsets of the population, as 'suspects' whose rights can be ignored;[38] and it is compounded by the failure of prosecutors to adequately screen cases which are prosecuted,[39] and the insufficiently adversarial posture adopted by many defence lawyers, whose practices, instead, are structured towards obtaining a guilty plea. Capping these is the reluctance of judges to question the integrity of police and their evidence, and the frequent failure of the contemporary judiciary to insist on maintaining high standards of proof for conviction.

Those in power are similarly uncommitted to due process values. Successive governments have traded rights and safeguards through populist (and repressive) legislation. We do not have a 'rights culture' within our criminal process. Rights are residual and used to justify further encroachment on the position of the accused. Nothing is regarded as 'fundamental', such that it cannot be 'exchanged' for something else. A recurring theme in modern criminal justice policy discourse is that of 'balance'.[40] Typically, new repressive measures are introduced to 'redress' the balance of the criminal process, which police and politicians perceive of as tilted too far in favour of the accused.[41] The suspect's right to custodial legal advice, in particular, has been used in this way.[42] The RCCJ made liberal use of this 'balancing' device, and their report illustrates the dangers in doing so. They made no attempt to define the weight that should be attached to the interests and values they so readily placed in the scales. The result is an absence of any clear framework, where concepts such as 'a fair trial' have no certainty. The following example illustrates their confusion:

> there is a potential conflict between the interests of justice on the one hand and the requirement of fair and reasonable treatment for everyone involved, suspects and defendants included, on the other ... But we are satisfied that ... our recommendations serve the interests of justice without diminishing the individual's right to fair and reasonable treatment. (RCCJ, 1993: 8)

It is of extreme concern that the Commission seemed to think that fair and reasonable treatment of suspects and defendants would not be in the interests of justice: one can only wonder at what they would consider to be in the interests of justice.

The refusal of the courts to enforce systematically the rights and safeguards provided for in legislation such as PACE is also justified in this way. Section 58 PACE provided suspects with a right to custodial legal advice. As well as being a necessary feature of any fair pre-trial process, the provision was intended to go some way to redress the increased police powers enacted in PACE. Despite the early Court of

Appeal decision in *Samuel* describing access to custodial legal advice as a 'fundamental right of a citizen',[43] the later decision of *Dunford*[44] held that a confession obtained in the absence of a lawyer need not be excluded. The appellant's previous criminal experience, reasoned the court, tipped the balance away from him requiring this 'fundamental right'. In the case of *Dunn*, the police failed to make a contemporaneous note of the defendant's admission, but the presence of a legal adviser again 'tipped the balance in favour of admitting the evidence'.[45]

A second cause of miscarriages is that the machinery to remedy mistakes in the criminal justice system when they occur is inadequate.[46] We will return to this issue in more detail in Chapter 9, which examines the role of the Court of Appeal, the Home Secretary and now the Criminal Cases Review Commission, in dealing with allegations of wrongful conviction.

A third, perhaps intermediate, cause has been the climate of political and public opinion that emerged in the 1980s in reaction to the conflict over Northern Ireland. The growing incidence of political terrorism attributed to the IRA was paralleled by an equal rise in demands for retribution against those believed to be the perpetrators. As the public and political crescendo for action grew, the police, prosecution and courts responded with arrests and with convictions, some of which were carried out with less than due regard for the normal protections of the criminal process. As a result,

> terrible mistakes were made in the Irish cases, the [most notorious] miscarriages of justice cases. What happened was that you had a reaction to the terrorism inflicted on England [by the IRA]. That was reflected right through the criminal justice process: the police, the apprehension, the detention, the torture, the dishonesty, the forged statements and what have you. That was all acceptable to the judicial system, which at the time failed miserably to take a proper stance ... There is then this period of shock and horror that this was allowed to happen under our supposedly Rolls Royce criminal justice system.[47]

Unfortunately, the lessons learned from the policing experience in Northern Ireland, as well as police awareness that the public and politicians were more tolerant of tactics which violate due process principles when employed against a category of suspects viewed with special scorn, tended to be carried over to normal policing practices. Whilst the threat of terrorism has receded from the public consciousness, this has been replaced in part by a more general fear of crime, and an emphasis on ensuring the conviction of the guilty rather than the acquittal of the innocent.

Official assessments of the problem

The response of those responsible for the functioning of the criminal justice process will determine what action is taken to ensure that such miscarriages of justice do not continue to take place. Most government officials and judges portrayed the miscarriage cases as aberrational and the RCCJ was not established to analyse the causes of these injustices and to make recommendations designed to prevent their reoccurrence. Instead, it was asked 'to examine the effectiveness of the criminal justice system in England and Wales in securing the conviction of those guilty of criminal offences and the acquittal of those who are innocent, having regard to the efficient use of resources' (RCCJ, 1993: iii).

Official explanations often attribute injustices to the unusual circumstances of a particular case. For instance, those associated with emotionally charged crimes (such as acts of terrorism, the murder of a child or elderly person) that produce strong public reactions and undue pressure on the police to find the culprits and secure their conviction.[48] Such crimes become the subject of widespread media coverage which excites or exacerbates public emotions and fears. Enormous pressures arise for quick investigative results, and the police, who assume tacit public and political approval, allow themselves to take investigative shortcuts or to bolster their case in improper ways. The results are: grave charges are made which are supported solely by confessional evidence and/or, in some cases, dubious scientific material. This may be followed at trial by the failure of prosecution (and perhaps by the defence as well) to evaluate evidence properly, and their failure or unwillingness to disclose highly relevant materials which run counter to their case.[49]

The results have occurred most visibly (and some would argue are most likely to occur) when the police are under pressure to deliver 'results', as they clearly were following the IRA pub bombings of the 1970s. In his Final Report on the factors which contributed to the wrongful convictions arising out of the bomb attacks in Guildford and Woolwich in 1974, Sir John May noted that

> against the background of a terrorist bombing campaign such as there was in 1974/5, and the consequent public demand for the

arrest and conviction of those responsible, there may be pressure on the police to induce suspects to confess to the offence by means of conduct which is not acceptable. (1994: 307)

Defenders of the criminal justice system (not necessarily those connected with it) argue that these anomalies and imperfections are an inevitable part of any system, the negative effects of which can be minimized by correcting 'bad procedures' or 'over-zealous conduct' on the part of the police. Thus, argued Michael Zander (a member of the Runciman Commission):

[T]he high profile miscarriages of justice were in the main the result of human factors, such as police officers who fabricated evidence, scientists who made mistakes or suppressed evidence. No system is, or could ever be (fully) proof against human error or human wickedness – although, of course, one should do what one can to set up checks and balances and controls to reduce the risk as much as is practicable.[50]

And the Commission itself, in its official report, suggested that 'police malpractice, where it occurs, may often be motivated by an over-zealous determination to secure the conviction of suspects believed to be guilty in the face of rules and procedures which seem to those charged with the investigation to be weighted in favour of the defence'.[51]

As well as portraying the cases of wrongful conviction as aberrational, there is an unwillingness to take 'corrective' action against any of its components or in favour of those who may have been wrongfully convicted and imprisoned by the system.[52] This applies not only to government authorities but also to high-ranking members of the judiciary.[53] Most judges are staunch defenders of the criminal justice system. Michael Mansfield illustrates the typically negative reaction of judges to challenges to police integrity by defence counsel, with the following example. Mansfield appeared in a case with John Platts-Mills, who suspected the police of planting a fingerprint and asked the police witness if this was technically possible to do. The latter replied that with very specialist equipment and under laboratory conditions it might be possible, but that it was a complicated procedure. At this point,

Platts-Mills produced a role of Sellotape and two glasses and asked if this was the specialist equipment to which the officer was referring. He then asked the officer to place his fingerprint on one of the glasses. Platts-Mills then took a piece of the tape, placed it over the fingerprint, raised the tape and stuck it on the second glass. He then removed the tape and showed the court that he had successfully transferred the policeman's fingerprint from one glass to another.[54]

Although Platts-Mills had proved his point beyond a doubt, the judge was far from pleased, and he 'made it clear that this was reprehensible conduct by the Bar and that all counsel associated with it would have their fees reduced for the time taken in making these allegations against the police' (ibid.).

Bennett (1993: 5–15) reports that following release of the Guildford Four there appears to have been a 'whispering campaign' in the form of off-the-record briefings to journalists which were designed to influence attitudes towards the case. This included members of the judiciary, who insisted – usually in private (but not always) – that despite the release of the Four, they were in fact guilty. In the face of criticism of the criminal justice system following the release of the Guildford Four, the Lord Chancellor himself publicly defended it – albeit in a way that seems to damn it at the same time. In response to a BBC TV interviewer's observation that 'they have had the wrong people for 15 years', Lord Hailsham replied: 'We don't say that. We say that [the police and prosecution] obtained convictions by *wrongful means* ... [and to say otherwise is] wholly indefensible and it lowers confidence in the judicial system.'[55]

However, the most striking illustration of high-level judicial resistance to corrective action against probable injustices in the criminal justice system, and the most cynical attitude toward those who suffer the consequences, was offered by Lord Denning. In halting the Birmingham Six's civil action against the police for assault in 1980, Denning, then Master of the Rolls and one of the most powerful judges in the country, said:

> If the six men win, it will mean that the police were guilty of perjury, that they were guilty of violence and threats and that the convictions were erroneous. That would mean that the Home Secretary would have to recommend they should be pardoned or remit the case to the Court of Appeal. This is such an appalling vista that every person in the land would say: 'It cannot be right that these actions should go any further.' ([1980] 2 WLR 609, at 706)

Denning elaborated on his view in an interview in *The Spectator*, where he argued that it would have been better if the Birmingham Six had been hanged so as to avoid all the damaging campaigns in support of guilty men and against the criminal justice system (Hillyard, 1994: 74). And in 1988, again in reference to the Birmingham Six and the growing demand for their release, he asserted that 'It is better that some innocent men remain in jail than that the integrity of the English judicial system should be impugned' (quoted in Mansfield and Wardle, 1993: 261).

Nor was his view an aberration from the norm in the judiciary, asserts Helena Kennedy, QC: 'It was shared by many less vocal (judicial) colleagues' (1992: 8). The reason for this, the Society of Black Lawyers told the RCCJ, is that

> Allowing an appeal may be seen by some as constituting an implied criticism of their colleagues. At times professional loyalty and loyalty to other criminal justice personnel appears to outweigh the commitment to carry out a critical evaluation of the original decision to convict. (Thornton, 1993: 930–1)

In the view of Chris Mullin, MP, this illustrates the perspective of some people in authority that whatever misconduct may have occurred in cases like the Birmingham Six and the Guildford Four, 'it should be swept under the carpet in order not to undermine public confidence in the police and the judicial system'.[56]

The impact this judicial behaviour has upon other actors in the criminal process should not be underestimated. As one solicitor-advocate observed:

> Looking at our system from the outside you must wonder how it is possible to have miscarriages like the Guilford Four, the Birmingham Six and all the others. And although these convictions have been overturned it should also be stated that the judges privately believe those appeals should never have been allowed. As far as they are concerned, those who had been convicted are guilty: and if they weren't guilty of the charges for which they were convicted then they were guilty of something else. You meet judges socially and they will say, 'Bloody Irishmen, if they weren't guilty of that, they must have been guilty of something else.' And that's the common talk from judges who should know better. But when you get senior judges like Denning actually saying, articulating things like that publicly, it reflects a judicial culture that puts an emphasis on expediency in securing convictions ... But this culture pervades

all the way down the system, so that now the police feel they have all this latitude in having evidence admitted, even though it is unfairly and improperly obtained. So the judicial culture at the moment, and the atmosphere in the criminal judicial system, is to secure convictions for political end.[57]

Moreover, while nearly every month of the early 1990s brought forth another example of 'prisoners who had spent years maintaining their innocence in the face of disbelief, those who criticise the judiciary, however tepidly, continue to be rounded upon by the legal establishment as wreckers and iconoclasts' (Kennedy, 1992: 9). Conversely, many in the legal establishment rallied in support of the (then) Lord Chief Justice, Geoffrey Lane, who had for two years borne the brunt of growing public concern.[58] Responding to criticism of their own possible role in miscarriages, barristers and judges pronounced themselves blameless, having done no more than believe in the honesty of police, the reliability of forensic scientists and the rationality of defendants, who, after all, ought not be expected to confess to crimes they had not committed.

As a final defence, the finger of blame is pointed at the jury. Thus Lord Ackner, in absolving his colleagues on the Bench of any responsibility for 'certain notorious miscarriages of justice', observed that a 'judge does not try an accused: the jury does that'; and that the 'judge's function is [no more than] that of an umpire'.[59] Yet the record of serious miscarriages suggests that judges do bear a heavy responsibility for what happens. In the Birmingham Six case, for example, the trial judge (Lord Bridge) alone took the crucial decision to admit the confessions in evidence; and in an appeal of the Guildford Four case, which was effectively a re-trial, Lord Justices Roskill and Lawton and Mr Justice Boreham ruled out a jury trial (ibid.: paras. 46 and 47). Furthermore, while a jury makes the final determination of innocence or guilt, its decision is certainly influenced by the role of the judge during the trial and summing up. Thus, in the Birmingham Six trial, Lord Bridge frequently intervened, openly sharing with the jury his clearly biased view of the defendants' guilt.[60]

Miscarriages of justice: the need for collective responsibility

All of these explanations seek to blame particular aspects of the criminal justice process: whether it be the police, the prosecution, those providing expert evidence, even the jury, who are confronted with the task of having to evaluate the case which has been so carefully constructed against the accused. Yet, it is not possible to compartmentalize the criminal justice system in this way. For good or ill the police, prosecution agents and the courts are all parts of an inclusive structure, with the judges at the apex and the police constituting the foundation.[61] For 150 years the police have seen themselves as the central force in the maintenance of law and order. This view has been shared by the 'better classes' in society who look to the police as front-line defenders of the system: they are the 'thin blue line' that stands as a bulwark against the large, potentially criminal, element in society. The police role, as Manning (1977) puts it, 'conveys a sense of sacredness or awesome power that lies at the root of political order, and authority, the claims a state makes upon its people for deference to rules, laws, and norms'.[62]

Backing up the police in the criminal justice system are the prosecution agencies and the courts, who enforce and legitimize what the police do in the name of law and order.[63] Even when judges are persuaded that the police may have manipulated the evidence or have attempted to mislead the court, they cannot be relied upon to take corrective action because of their entrenched view of the police as their law and order partners. As Helena Kennedy, QC, argues, in 'accepting the judicial role, many judges come to see themselves ... as joined with the police in the battle against crime'.[64] Moreover, in viewing themselves as allies of the police in the protection of good order against anarchy, the judges tend to surrender their impartiality – which makes it difficult for them to be staunch guarantors of the due process rights of citizens (McConville *et al.*, 1991: 173–90).

In light of this, any discussion of high-profile miscarriages of justice has to recognise that the roles played by the different components of the criminal justice process are linked in such a manner as to make it difficult to restrict criticism to only certain parts of the system. The actions of each are not and cannot be separated from the remainder. Indeed, research studies carried out for the Royal Commission make it evident that criminal justice is a *system*, and the Commission's recommendations urge that it be made even more systematic.[65]

In the chapters that follow, we argue that the behaviour of legal actors at all stages of the criminal justice process is relevant in understanding the ways in which miscarriages of justice can occur. This includes the broad discretion afforded officers to stop, search and arrest individuals; the circumstances in which confession evidence is obtained; the disclosure (or non-disclosure) of evidence; the trial; and the appeal process itself. We examine the limits of the legal framework, the power it provides and the protections it affords, as well as the daily practices of those who work in, and (therefore) in one sense constitute, the criminal process.

Summary

This study examines the ways in which the criminal justice process in England and Wales produces and deals with miscarriages of justice. Many officials within the process argue that the abuses identified by high-profile cases, such as that of the Birmingham Six, are exceptional, and that it is indeed a credit to the system of criminal justice that they were brought to light and rectified. In their view, any further remedial action which might be required can be provided by legislative reform. Indeed some go further in claiming that the suspect/defendant is now protected excessively, preventing the thorough investigation and prosecution of crime.

In contrast to this, we argue that wrongful convictions are neither exceptional nor the result of isolated human error. Awful though the 'celebrated' cases are, the malpractice of police and prosecution and the incompetence of the many defence lawyers who produced them are not confined to these cases, but are typical of the routine processing of criminal defendants which has been well documented by an array of empirical studies over the past twenty years – from police encounters with citizens on the street through to trial and conviction. While the celebrated cases concern offences of the most serious nature, where evidence and procedure is potentially subjected to the most rigorous scrutiny, the majority of cases tried in our courts are of a far less serious character and come, not before a judge or jury, but before a bench of lay magistrates. Yet the same practices of obtaining confessions, fabricating and failing to disclose evidence and poor defence preparation, together with the greater credibility afforded the evidence of the police than that of the defendant, occur just as – if not more – easily in the mundane surroundings of the magistrates' court. The difference is the lack of scrutiny in these settings, as well as lack of public attention and the absence of academic discussion that attends lower court proceedings.[66]

Furthermore, whilst legal rules are an important constraint, of greater significance are the operational practices of actors within the criminal justice process – overzealous police and prosecutors, passive and conviction-oriented defence lawyers and a judiciary which is reluctant to delve into that which might damage the reputation of the process as a whole.[67]

Like any debate surrounding political issues, the terms in which discussion of the criminal justice process are couched are neither universally defined nor accepted. There has been a great deal of discussion about citizens' rights and the balance to be struck between the liberties of those citizens and the need to investigate and prosecute crime. Yet the nature and extent of the individual's rights in the face of state power exercised by the police remains unclear. Even less clear is the degree to which they can be traded-off against other competing interests, whether these be framed in terms of crime control, surveillance system rights or system efficiency.[68] The European Convention on Human Rights may be one starting-point, but in the end the weight given to different interests will ultimately depend upon the objectives and values of those regulating and operating the criminal justice process.

2
Policing on the Ground: Gathering Evidence

The context: police culture

'The seeds of almost all miscarriages of justice', writes Chris Mullin, 'are sown within a few days, and sometimes hours, of the suspect's arrest' (Testimony to RCCJ, 1991: para. 13). This view is shared by the Legal Action Group, which asserts that the bulk of miscarriages are traceable to the initial actions of police in carrying out their functions (LAG, 1993b: 8). Once the police suspect a person of having committed a criminal offence, whether their suspicion is correct or not, a process is initiated that is strongly tilted toward the confirmation of this first judgment. According to Ashworth (1998: 93), 'What remains fairly constant ... is the high significance of judgements made at this early stage. As the case against a particular person begins to take shape, so (in most cases) does the investigator's belief that that person is guilty.' And what the investigator believes goes a long way toward structuring the perceptions of other official actors in the criminal justice process.[1]

An explanation of why and how this occurs is multifaceted: it begins with both the historical status and contemporary role of the police in British society. The police are a deeply-rooted institution, having an existence that extends back more than 150 years. The roots of the unique constitutional status of the police are to be found in the gradual evolution of the common law system of parish constables, and the first organized 'police force' was authorized in London under the Metropolitan Police Act 1829. Outside London, local authorities were empowered to establish police forces in the boroughs by the Municipal Corporations Act 1835 and in the counties by the County Police Act 1839. The organization of the modern police is expressed in the Police Act 1964. Apart from the London Metropolitan Service, there are presently 43 forces supervised by individual chief constables (who are operationally independent), local police authorities and the Home Office, which functions as an overarching regulatory and supervisory authority.

The police have been the central mechanism in the maintenance of law and order, and thus at the forefront of the criminal justice system. With the passage of time they increasingly came to dominate the process (Reiner, 1992). Moreover, throughout history they have exercised their power with a remarkable degree of autonomy: under the doctrine of 'constabulary independence', they have the legal right to enforce the law as they see fit. Thus, although the chief constable has overall responsibility for his force, virtually all operational decisions are independently made by on-duty police officers. This is because the powers that the law gives to the police are largely vested directly in the individual constable.[2] Thus, regardless of the orders of superior officers, even the least experienced constable makes decisions which impinge on the rights and liberties of citizens.[3]

The discretion possessed by the constable is an important contributor to her independence,[4] covering as it does the decisions and actions she takes in controlling crime and maintaining order on the street. In the process, police officers may stop and question suspects and witnesses, make arrests or otherwise detain those suspected of an offence. However, once a suspect has been brought to the police station, the responsibility for deciding whether to detain her further is taken by the 'custody officer', a police officer not below the rank of sergeant whose responsibilities include ensuring that anyone held in custody at a station is being lawfully detained, and recording all matters relating to detained persons required by PACE.[5] As will be shown, this role definition of the police constable, and the wide discretion that accompanies it, have profound consequences for the operation of the criminal justice process.

Ordinary police officers also carry out investigations of offences and although s. 37 of PACE states that it is the custody officer's responsibility to determine whether there is sufficient evidence to charge an arrested person with an offence, she usually relies on the account given by the arresting officer.[6] To a considerable extent, police investigations focus heavily on interrogation of suspects in an effort to secure a confession or incriminating statements. In this activity, also, they are largely immune from direct control or supervision. Interviews are tape-recorded and the suspect may have her lawyer present, but this has not inhibited the police from using overbearing and even oppressive tactics. The recording of the interview is seldom listened to by defence lawyers, supervising officers or the court.[7]

In addition to having considerable power and independence, the occupational culture of the police permeates all levels of practice – in particular, the exercise of discretion. It is heavily defensive and views the society outside as being permanently on the brink of chaos and disorder.[8] According to Sanders and Young (1995: 33) the related elements of 'cop culture' are the 'danger' of the job;[9] the need to uphold 'authority' in order to maintain the law; the need to produce 'results'; and the sense of a mission to prevent 'them' from ruining things for 'us'. Thus, operating behind a rhetoric of their own choosing the police do what they see as necessary to deal not only with threats to social order, but also with challenges to their own authority. Moreover, whatever the police decide to do 'becomes, by definition, in the interests of "law and order" and therefore of "society" too. Whoever opposes them is, equally by definition, "anti-police" and thus hostile to "law and order" and therefore hostile to "society"' (Kettle, 1980: 59).

However, the police tend to view threats to law and order as coming mainly from certain types of 'suspect' groups and individuals. The most likely candidates are young working-class males, especially black males; but the suspect category includes immigrants, the Irish, pickets, demonstrators, squatters, gays, feminists, etc.[10] What makes someone a 'suspect' is made clear in the research of McConville *et al.* (1991). As they explain, 'the suspect population is constructed' on the basis of the experience, perceptions and discretion of the police, who operate in a legal and situational context which imposes few constraints on how they use their powers.[11] Primary to their view of the policing function is the containment of threats emanating from the suspect population, and this is done by a discretionary mixture of control or removal of 'threatening' persons from the streets.[12] Their approach to 'disorderliness' is an example. The police will tolerate it only if it ceases on their arrival – which it usually does. If it continues, it will be interpreted by the police as an attack on their authority, and arrest powers will be used to crush the disorder.[13]

The policing of suspect groups is facilitated also by the police's open-ended power to stop and search, arrest and detain 'suspicious' persons. Once a suspect is arrested and charged with an offence, the police are strongly oriented toward securing her conviction; but if the suspect is not actually caught committing or attempting to commit a criminal act, the police must find evidence sufficient to secure conviction. However, whether or not they are successful, the police's goals may be served by merely cautioning the suspect or releasing her with no further action. Thus, even when they do not expect to be able to convict, the police still may arrest and detain as a 'control device' or a means of 'teaching the suspect a lesson'. Thus, the 'aims of stops and arrests are often not to enforce the law *per se*, but to secure broader objectives: the imposition of order, the assertion of authority, the acquisition of information'.[14] What happens to the suspect population in any given situation is the decision of the police – to charge, caution or take no further action.[15]

To a large extent, the police 'see their role as involving a determination of guilt or innocence *at the outset*'; and this determination defines for them whether an incident (e.g. even a 'bad attitude' on the part of someone they stop) is a crime or not; or whether it should be transformed into an offence, such as 'breach of the peace', or 'obstructing a police officer in the course of his duties', which should be prosecuted. If they decide it should, evidence in support of their decision will have to be created.[16] In all this a form of 'low visibility discretion is exercised by the police directly involved, and this discretion increases as one moves *down* the police hierarchy to the officer on the street as a function of the principle of constabulary independence.[17]

The research findings of McConville and his colleagues are supported by evidence from two barristers with broad experience in criminal cases. In discussing the police's contribution to wrongful convictions, they both observe that it begins with the police's attitude at the time of arrest, and then with their disposition and behaviour thereafter in the investigative process. According to our first respondent:

> The underlying problem with the police, both before and after PACE, is not so much police corruption as such, although that has existed and in some forces almost took over, but rather a sort of tunnel vision, where the police don't arrest somebody unless they believe they've 'done it'. And once they've arrested someone they genuinely believe they've got the right person, and all that is necessary is for them [the police] to ask the question as many times as it takes, or maybe hit the person about the head a bit as in the olden days, or whatever.[18]

A similar view is expressed by our second respondent, who argues that the police approach to crime, once they have identified a suspect, is to secure the evidence needed to convict – meanwhile ignoring all evidence that points in a different direction.

The police see themselves as judge and jury. Typically in a police investigation, they think of who the likely suspect is and then fit the bill: that is, they aim to collect all the evidence that would suggest the guilt of the person that they suspect; and ignore any evidence that may point in somebody else's direction. They do not openly and impartially investigate. Now I don't want to tar them all with the same brush, but an all too common occurrence is that they think of Freddie, and then they get the evidence which would implicate Freddie, and if there is any other inconvenient evidence that points in a different direction they ignore it.

Now their role, technically, is to investigate. It's not their role to limit themselves to getting only evidence that may tend to implicate one particular accused suspect as opposed to another particular suspect, but they take on that role in practice.[19]

This approach also applies to serious offences, especially those that attract a great deal of media and public attention, as happened in the high-profile miscarriages. They started out as shocking cases which put police under great pressure to find the culprits. Thus,

as a common denominator in the big miscarriages of justice I think you will often find that the police are under a lot of pressure. They want to get someone. They want to get the media off their backs. They want a result. They are under huge public pressure to get a result, so they go for it; and if somebody gets trammelled en route and it happens to be the wrong person, well that's tough. Birmingham and Guildford are classic examples, but it goes right across the board. Tottenham Three, huge pressure there to get somebody. (Ibid.)

In addition to incriminating statements which may be obtained from suspect interrogation,[20] other possible sources of evidence that the police can use to construct their case against the suspect include physical clues, suspect identification and information from witnesses. In their search for suspects, as well as the evidence with which to convict them, legislation such as PACE and the Codes of Practice, and the CJPOA provide the police with considerable latitude. However, in their efforts to build a case against suspects the police may make mistakes, or may be tempted to engage deliberately in unacceptable or illegitimate tactics in the pursuit of evidence which, if they are not countered at another stage in the criminal justice process, can lead to a miscarriage of justice. As we shall see, the lack of independent scrutiny of police-generated evidence means that these errors may be compounded rather than corrected. Given their strong orientation towards establishing guilt and securing conviction the police may, for example, through psychological or physical pressure, attempt to extract a confession from a suspect; or use protracted or abusive questioning to at least secure damaging statements from suspects.[21] Although interviews with suspects are tape-recorded, they are rarely listened to;[22] reliance is placed, instead, upon police summaries which tend to favour the police account.[23] Witness evidence may also be tainted where individuals are encouraged to exaggerate their account[24] and in producing a written statement, the police interpret what has been said in ways which support the prosecution and overlook or exclude evidence that does not point to the suspect's guilt.[25]

We will focus here upon the individual's initial encounter with the police, through stop and search and arrest, as it is the exercise of power at this early stage which places the suspect in the 'revolving door of police suspicion', where efforts are mobilized towards the confirmation of that suspicion.

The legal regulation of police powers

Although the powers of the police have accumulated over time, their present stipulation is set forth for the most part in the Police and Criminal Evidence Act 1984 (or PACE), which largely replaced (and extended) the mix of statutory and common law rules that previously regulated the police. PACE is supplemented by 'Codes of Practice' (generated by the Home Secretary under the Act), which are intended to govern police conduct in dealing with those who are suspected of, or charged with, criminal offences. Further powers are provided for in the Criminal Justice and Public Order Act 1994, or CJPOA.

As a counter to police mistakes and malpractice, PACE (1984) and the Codes of Practice were aimed at protecting suspects and accused persons by providing certain safeguards. For those detained in police custody, these included the establishment of the custody officer, access to counsel at the station and during interrogation, the tape-recording of interviews and time-limits on detention before charge (see Chapter 3). In relation to stop and search powers, recording procedures were introduced in order to permit supervision and monitoring of police activity. Furthermore, under s. 78 of PACE, failure to observe the Codes may lead to the exclusion of any evidence if the court, taking into account the circumstances in which the evidence was obtained, considers it unfair to admit it.

It seems clear, however, that PACE and the Codes have not been wholly effective in altering the conduct of police in important areas of policing. Some changes have been introduced in recording practices (stop and search forms, custody sheets, etc.) and the tape-recording of interviews of suspects is virtually universal,[26] but in a number of areas PACE has not yet had the intended impact on police practice. PACE regulations are viewed by officers as inhibiting their policing activity, and in order to get on with their policing functions they have learned to 'get around' some of the obstacles placed in their path by PACE, to exploit the gaps in the regime.

Stop and search

Under PACE s. 1, police officers may stop and search a person only if they have reasonable grounds for suspecting that she may have committed an offence or that articles unlawfully obtained or possessed are being carried.[27] Code A para. 1.6 stipulates that the existence of reasonable grounds for suspicion will depend on the circumstances in each case but 'there must be some objective basis for it': that is, it cannot be limited to personal factors alone (such as colour, age, sex or dress) or to stereotyped images of certain persons or groups as more likely to be committing offences.[28] In addition, a police officer has no power to stop or detain a person against her will 'in order to find grounds for a search' (para. 2.1); however, this is not to be construed as affecting 'the ability of an officer to speak to, or question, a person in the ordinary course of his duties (even in the absence of reasonable suspicion) without detaining him or exercising any element of compulsion' (Note 1B). Nor does the code prevent an officer from searching a person in the street 'with his consent' where no search power exists (Note 1D(b)).

In addition, the police officer is obliged to first give the person stopped an opportunity to provide an explanation that may obviate the need for a search (para. 2.2). If no satisfactory answer is offered the officer must, before making a search, provide her name and that of her police station to the suspect, as well as state the object sought and the grounds for making the search (para. 2.4). She must also say she is making a record of the stop-search (unless she decides it 'will not be practicable to make a record of the search'), and that the suspect is entitled to a copy of the record (para. 2.6).

Altogether the aim of these powers and constraints is to ensure that the police have sufficient power to detect crime, yet to inhibit them from stopping and searching indiscriminately or in discriminatory ways.[29] In practice, however, individual police constables exercise a great deal of discretion in deciding when and who to stop and search, and in determining what amounts to 'reasonable grounds' for suspicion. The difficulty in defining reasonable suspicion means that it does not operate as an effective constraint since its meaning and application are subject to varying interpretations (even by courts),[30] and it is almost impossible for people to know whether they are being searched lawfully, or whether they might justifiably resist.[31]

One result of the elasticity of the 'reasonable suspicion' criterion is that it has allowed police officers to identify certain categories of the population as more suspicious than others. Thus despite the PACE Code provision which proscribes the adequacy of ascriptive or personal criteria (see above), these factors continue to influence the behaviour of the police. Race,[32] for example, remains a significant factor in post-PACE stop and search activity,[33] as does social class:[34] most convicted criminals are working class.[35] There is thus a general process that involves police stereotyping, whereby judgments are made about people on the basis of a very rapid assessment of visible indicators (e.g., 'inappropriate' dress or the 'wrong colour' for a particular area). This corresponds closely to the approach of the police found in the pre-PACE study of Smith and Gray; and further support is offered by McConville *et al.* (1991), who found that despite the gradual impact of PACE on some of the cultural attitudes of police, their working practices appear to rely on 'instincts' as much as ever.[36] Dixon *et al.* (1989) discuss the use of incongruity procedure in street policing, whereby individuals who do not 'fit in' are suspicious. They argue that this is more complex than a process of crude stereotyping, but the two are inseparable. Incongruity procedure will operate to the disadvantage of blacks, who are narrowly stereotyped and therefore viewed as inherently more suspicious. In a police world-view that is white, they are more likely to be viewed as out of place or engaged in suspicious activity. There are, of course, dangers that any form of stereotyping becomes self-fulfilling. The more blacks who are stopped, for example, the more will be arrested and charged: so the police stereotype appears to be justified. There is no incentive to change behaviour patterns as certain groups become over-represented in the police constructed criminal population.

A number of research studies demonstrate that stop-search activity is a particular source of injustice for ethnic minorities, especially Afro-Caribbeans, who are the subjects of discriminatory stops by the police;[37] and similar discriminatory reactions by other agents in the criminal justice process are likely to follow. Thus once having been stopped, minorities are more likely than whites to be searched (between four and eight times more likely)[38] and arrested;[39] and once in the criminal justice process the trajectory of ethnic minorities through the system to the point of imprisonment is markedly different from that of whites. Again, this is especially true of Afro-Caribbeans. According to Fitzgerald (1993), they are less likely to be cautioned and more likely to be referred for prosecution; more likely to be charged with indictable-only offences and to be remanded in custody; and more likely to receive more severe sentences (pp. 32–36). Fitzgerald concludes that there 'is an obvious inference that Afro-Caribbeans have disproportionately been brought into the criminal justice system and carried through to its end-point without due process cause'; and that 'it cannot be assumed that magistrates, judges and juries will rectify injustices which have occurred earlier in the system' (ibid.).

The discriminatory approach of police towards ethnic minorities is also evident where the latter are the victims of crime, as demonstrated in their approach to the death in April 1993 of a young black man Stephen Lawrence. In a public inquiry before a High Court judge, the conduct of the police was severely criticized and John Newing, chief constable of Derbyshire and chair of the new race relations task force set up by ACPO, stated that he believed that racism played a part in the string of police errors in the case.[40] Greater Manchester's Chief Constable, David Wilmot, also acknowledged that institutional racism existed within his force, including stereotyping and police attitudes in dealing with incidents on the street: 'we still have some way to go internally within the force – what you'd call canteen culture'.[41] There has been disagreement over the meaning of 'institutional racism' – whether it is part of the occupational culture of the police, an internalised set of values which includes the negative stereotyping of ethnic minorities, or something more overt. Sir Herman Ouseley, chair of the Commission for Racial Equality defines it in a way which synthesizes these definitions: it is 'organisational structures, policies, processes and practices which result in the ethnic minorities being treated unfairly and less equally, often without intention or knowledge'.[42]

The PACE requirement to make records of searches is designed to facilitate the monitoring and supervision of what is otherwise a 'low visibility' exercise of police power. However, the value of this has been undermined in several ways. Firstly, stop and search activity is not closely supervised. Dixon *et al.* (1989: 185) report that over three-quarters of the constables and sergeants they interviewed said that their stops were not generally supervised, and the Royal Commission also expressed concern that records of stops and searches were not properly reviewed (1993: 20). Maguire and Norris (1993) found that most officers' views of 'supervision' centred on checking paperwork, ensuring the equitable allocation of work and checking expense claims, rather than ensuring that suspects' rights have been respected and that investigations have been conducted thoroughly. Supervisors are also subject to the same pressure to produce 'results' in the form of clear-up rates and identifiable activity such as arrests, making it difficult for them to stand back and focus upon the quality of officers' work.[43]

Secondly, a large number of searches are classed as 'consent' searches, and so are not recorded and cannot be subject to scrutiny. This is an example of McBarnet's (1983) criticism of the permissive way in which the law is fashioned, providing maximum discretion to the police: alongside the clear recording requirements set out by PACE, the COP provisions allow these to be bypassed where a search is conducted by consent. Dixon *et al.* (1990) found that consent searches were not exceptional to the regime set out in PACE, but operated as standard practice – indeed, refusal of consent was itself a ground for suspicion. Searching by consent was considered more straightforward and records were kept only if a check was likely to be made – for example, where an arrest followed. McConville *et al.* (1991) report the same findings. They were told by one officer 'I've always got their consent ... I tell people, "Why make life difficult on yourself?"' (p. 94). The notion of individuals consenting to searches, however, is illusory. Most will either not know that they can refuse or can require reasons to be given and a written record to be made, or they will feel unable to challenge the police's authority to conduct a search. The police, for their part, do not consider it appropriate that those whom they consider to be suspicious should enjoy 'rights' such as these. 'As one officer put it starkly, "PACE was meant to protect decent people, but we don't deal with decent people"' (Dixon *et al.*, 1990: 352).

The use of largely unrecorded 'consent' searches is an important context in which to understand the figures of recorded searches and resulting arrests. The number of searches recorded declined between 1981 and 1986, but this is as likely to be attributable to the new recording procedures as to an actual decline in searches. Since then, the numbers have increased rapidly – from 109,800 in 1986 to over one million in 1997–8. The proportion leading to arrest has declined from 17 per cent to 10 per cent in the same period (Home Office, 1999). Given the number of unrecorded searches, the actual proportion leading to arrest is even lower, suggesting that the police widely overuse their power in this area. The value of street stops to officers, however, goes beyond the possibility of an arrest and a crime cleared up. Police objectives extend beyond simple law enforcement, to 'order maintenance' (Dixon *et al.*, 1990: 352), the production of knowledge for the management of suspect populations (Ericson and Haggerty, 1997) and '*social control*, targeted against specific *communities* ... frequently prompted by the desire of the police to impose their *authority* on groups who are seen to challenge "respectable" notions of normality.' (Singh, 1994: 172; original emphasis) Together with the absence of careful supervision and monitoring, the requirement for 'reasonable suspicion' does not inhibit police officers from conducting searches which may satisfy a range of police objectives: a resulting arrest, the collection of useful information, or simply the assertion of police authority over suspect groups.

As with other police powers over the citizen, where a stop-search is legally questionable, PACE provides no remedies: it neither makes it a crime nor a tort to stop and search someone unlawfully, or to fail to provide information, or to make a record of it afterwards.[44] While common law makes detention unlawful if the reason for it was not provided, any suspect who might think of challenging stops in court would be faced with the difficult task of trying to prove the police officer lacked 'reasonable suspicion' or failed to give information prior to a search. Indeed, even where specific remedies exist to deal with alleged misuse or abuse of police power the odds are strongly tilted against the complainant.[45] For example, there has only been one reported case of evidence being excluded after an unlawful stop and search.[46]

As well as ordinary searches of vehicles and persons under s. 1 of PACE, a suspect (under s. 55 PACE) may be subjected to what is euphemistically called an 'intimate' search. This involves a physical search of the body orifices and requires reasonable grounds for believing that an arrested person in police detention may have concealed on them anything which might cause physical injury; or, in the case of suspected couriers or dealers only, a Class A drug. Only a suitably qualified person may search for drugs, but in the instance of harmful articles, where this is not practicable, a constable will carry out the search. Clearly, a degrading and humiliating search of this kind should only be carried out in exceptional circumstances. With the exception of 1993, when fewer such searches were recorded, the number has remained fairly constant at around 70 per year. In 1996, however, it rose dramatically to 132 and then again to 224 in 1997/8, a nearly four-fold increase from the 64 recorded in 1995. Almost all of the increase over both periods is accounted for by searches for drugs – from 52 searches in 1995 to 197 in 1997/8. However, this increase in the number of searches has not been matched by an increase in the numbers resulting in drugs being found. Class A drugs were found in 15 per cent of instances in 1995 and 1996, but in only 9 per cent in 1997/8. Whilst the number of searches almost doubled, drugs were found in only 17 cases in both periods. The requirement of a reasonable belief that drugs are being concealed does not appear to be an effective constraint upon police power under this section. Given the invasive nature of these searches and the affront to a person's dignity that they represent, it is unacceptable that 91 per cent turn out to be unfounded.

Despite the failure of PACE to inhibit or control police activity, police powers have been widened further under the CJPOA. But while PACE complemented these with some new protections for those subject to police power,[47] the CJPOA did not. The police view that existing protections for suspects have already tipped the balance too far in favour of criminals, thus hamstringing the police's ability to do their job, has prevailed. In this view, they had the backing of Michael Howard, a Home Secretary whose crime control orientation was so excessive that it provoked sharp criticism from the higher judiciary, including Lord Donaldson, the former Master of the Rolls.[48]

The new power under s. 60 CJPOA is extremely broad. In anticipation of violence, a police officer may now stop and search any pedestrian, or stop and search any vehicle and its occupants, for offensive weapons or dangerous instruments, 'whether or not he has any grounds for suspecting that the person or vehicle is carrying weapons or articles of that kind'. Authorisation to conduct such searches over a 24 hour period and in a specified locality, may be provided by a superintendent (or, if unavailable, an inspector) who reasonably believes that the measure is expedient to prevent the occurrence of serious violence. In addition, pursuant to the prevention of terrorism, police authorities now have discretion to authorize, for a period up to 28 days (with further 28-day period extensions permissible), any constable to stop any pedestrian or any vehicle, its driver or any passenger, and search for articles which might be used in the 'commission, preparation or instigation of acts of terrorism'; again, she may do so 'whether or not he has any grounds for suspecting that the vehicle or person in question is carrying articles of that kind'.[49]

The new police powers provided under the CJPOA 1994 appear similar to those the police exercised under the 'sus' laws that existed in the past.[50] They have been opposed by the Law Society as counter-productive, being seen as likely to increase street harassment by the police of ethnic minorities and other 'suspect groups', thereby worsening relations with the very communities the police must depend upon as sources of information and cooperation. As explained by a London defence solicitor of 15 years' experience,

> The Law Society was opposed to the new stop and search powers on the basis that it was just likely to alienate the police from the public. The fact that the police can stop and search without having to justify the reason we saw as giving officers who dislike certain sections of the community a perfect opportunity to exploit their prejudices. Given that relations between the police and the public are fragile anyway, and that they are particularly fragile between the police and certain ethnic communities; and given that the police depend upon the public for information and need the public in terms of detecting crime, this is something which was going to cause more problems than it would alleviate.[51]

Clearly, the use of s. 60 will hinge on the interpretation given by the police to the phrase 'in anticipation of violence': the power has already been used widely, with nearly 8,000 searches recorded both in 1996 and 1997/8, only 5 per cent of which resulted in arrest (Home Office, 1999).

Arrest

Just as the police enjoy broad discretion in the use of stop and search, the power of arrest is also broadly framed. The police[52] may arrest a person whom they reasonably suspect to be about to commit, to be committing, or to have committed an arrestable offence (s. 24 PACE). An arrestable offence is one that would attract a maximum prison sentence of five years or more, together with several other listed offences.[53] Under s. 25, the police may arrest a person who is committing or has committed a non-arrestable offence if service of a summons is impractical or inappropriate – for example, if the suspect's name or address is not known.[54] Arrest deprives the individual of her liberty and so is coercive, and for that reason the RCCP advocated the use of a 'necessity principle' to restrict the use of arrest – recommending that the use of summons be the preferred procedure. Despite this recommendation, PACE widened police powers in this area and arrest is used routinely in order to detain and question a suspect – an approach which has been endorsed by the courts.[55]

There is considerable overlap between arrest, and stop and search, in terms of the grounds required and arrest has been described as the beginning of imprisonment.[56] If the police suspect that a person is carrying an offensive weapon, for example, they might stop and search the person, or arrest them (and possibly search them under s. 32(2) PACE, avoiding the safeguards set out in ss. 2 and 3 PACE). Thus, the constable's discretion is wide – whether to stop, to search or to arrest and it is the exercise of this discretion which permeates the whole of policing practice. As with stop and search, arrest is used disproportionately against ethnic minorities, especially blacks. In the Phillips and Brown study (1998), 13 per cent of all arrests in the sample were of black people and even allowing for arrestees who did not live locally, the numbers hugely exceed the proportion in the local population.[57] In addition, fewer police officers believed there to be sufficient evidence to charge in arrests of ethnic minority suspects, compared to whites.[58] Legal regulation operates as a baseline over which the police should not step, but it does not prevent them from exercising their powers in ways which they see fit – to acquire information, to assert their authority over certain groups, or to 'teach people a lesson'.[59]

The suspect must be told the reason for the arrest, otherwise it is unlawful and may be resisted with a reasonable degree of force.[60] Once arrested, suspects should be questioned at the police station, where their treatment and detention can be monitored by the custody officer and interviews can be recorded once the suspect has received legal advice. However, conversations which occur prior to reaching the station may also be admissible as evidence. The new caution,[61] which has been widely criticized as pressuring suspects to answer questions,[62] warns that the accused's defence may be harmed if she seeks to rely in court on anything not mentioned when questioned. This means that adverse inferences may be drawn at trial if it would have been reasonable to expect the accused to mention when questioned, something relied upon at trial. Although the expectation is that this questioning should take place in a formal interview, questioning outside the police station is not excluded.[63]

Furthermore, under s. 36 CJPOA, where an accused fails or refuses to account for objects, substances or marks found on her person, clothing or in her possession, or in the place where she is arrested, which are believed to be connected to a committed offence, a court or jury may draw adverse inferences. Similarly, under s. 37, where an arrested person is found by a constable at a place where, or at a time when, an offence is alleged to have been committed, and the person fails or refuses to account for her presence, inferences may be drawn.[64] For these provisions to take effect, the suspect must be under arrest and the police must explain in everyday language why the question is being put and what the possible consequences of silence might be.[65] However, unlike silence when questioned, these provisions do not require a defence to be raised in court before an adverse inference can be drawn. Bucke and Brown (1997) found that 5 per cent of suspects[66] were given either a s. 36 or s. 37 warning and most refused to provide an account.[67]

The collection of body samples

In addition to the foregoing, other changes in CJPOA 1994 include new provisions on the taking of body samples.[68] Despite uncertainties about the use of DNA evidence,[69] the provisions clearly point to an expanded role for DNA profiling in the investigation and prosecution of criminal offences. Under the Act, the police are given new powers to take body samples and to store new forms of information acquired from them about the population they police.[70] These provisions were sanctioned by the Royal Commission, despite widespread criticism that to oblige suspects to provide samples of breath, blood or other body fluids violates the principle that persons should not be required to incriminate themselves.[71]

The RCCJ recommended extending police power to extract samples from suspects, without their consent if necessary (RCCJ, 1993: 14–15). The CJPOA (ss. 54–9) amends ss. 62–5 PACE and the police are authorized (for the purpose of DNA profiling) to take non-intimate body samples, without the consent of a person in police detention.[72] Saliva and mouth swabs have been reclassified as non-intimate, in order that samples may be taken by force if necessary. The RCCJ recommended that burglary and assault be classed as serious arrestable offences for the purpose of taking non-intimate samples, but the CJPOA goes further and extends the powers to all recordable offences.[73] In addition, by allowing samples to be taken after the decision to charge has been made, sampling becomes a tool for DNA profiling and intelligence gathering, rather than simply forensic evidence in establishing guilt or innocence in the immediate case. Bucke and Brown (1997) found that non-intimate samples were taken from 7 per cent of detainees. About three-quarters of these were mouth or body swabs – 10 per cent of which were taken without consent. Only 18 per cent of these samples were to ascertain involvement in an offence: the rest were for the DNA database.

Similarly, an intimate sample (blood, semen or other tissue fluid, urine or pubic hair; dental impressions; swabs taken from a person's body other than the mouth)[74] is no longer restricted to serious arrestable offences, but can now be taken from any person detained at a police station for whom the police have reasonable grounds for 'suspecting' her involvement in a recordable offence;[75] or from a person not in police detention but from whom at least two non-intimate samples have already been taken during an investigation which, however, have proved 'unsuitable or insufficient' for the purpose for which they were taken. In all such cases, the taking of intimate samples requires the suspect's written consent, but if such consent is refused 'adverse inferences may be drawn by a court'.[76] Creaton (1994: 212) has argued that drawing inferences from refusal amounts to unacceptable pressure and 'Convictions based on inference rather than probative evidence are likely to increase the risks of miscarriages of justice'. Bucke and Brown (1997) found that very few intimate samples were taken – 40 instances out of 10,496 suspects – and the sample taken was blood in 70 per cent of the cases. Twenty-three suspects were warned that adverse inferences may result from refusal to provide a sample, three of whom still refused their consent.

Information that results from the DNA profiles may be checked against DNA profiles derived from other crime scenes and from other criminal justice samples, as well as against existing records, in a speculative search to see if the person has been involved in some other unsolved offence.[77] Noteworthy here is that previous regulations (s. 64 of PACE) required the destruction of all samples taken from those who were acquitted, not proceeded against or dealt with by way of a caution, or who were not themselves suspected of having committed an offence but were merely sampled in connection with an investigation, once the samples had fulfilled the purpose for which they were taken. But, under the new law such destruction is no longer required.[78] According to a Home Office interpretation of the regulations governing the disposition of DNA samples, which was produced in consultation with the Association of Chief Police Officers, 'Even though the Act says only that samples "need not be destroyed", samples should not be destroyed in these circumstances'. Also

'Information derived from samples (including DNA profiles) does not need to be destroyed'.[79] Finally, there is no statutory requirement to destroy samples of persons detained in cases that fall under the Prevention of Terrorism Act 1989.[80] Therefore, the Home Office advises that profiles from terrorist suspects will 'be retained in a searchable form on the DNA database *irrespective* of the outcome of detention'.[81]

The Royal Commission's Report also encouraged the creation of DNA databases, using samples (including non-intimate samples extracted without consent) taken from all persons arrested for serious criminal offences, whether or not DNA evidence is relevant to the offence in question and even if the suspects are not convicted (RCCJ, 1993: 15). Critics see this development as an unwarranted use of police power, and as heralding gross violations of civil liberties. However, the police have strongly supported DNA profiling, which they see as crucial for the future of crime investigation; and in response to their demand, the government, following the Commission Report, agreed to establish a DNA Database, with testing to be introduced by the police in April 1995. The goal is to create a single, consolidated, central database of DNA samples,[82] with details taken from persons 'suspected, cautioned and convicted of a recordable offence'.[83]

The operational plan for the first year of the Database called for its scope to be restricted to those involved in offences against the person, including serious assault and sexual offences as well as all burglaries. This was expected to limit the number of samples for 1995 (the first year of the Database) to about 135,000 persons, at an estimated cost of £5.4 million. The projected figure for new offender records is 130,000 per year; however, it is anticipated that the offence scope will widen annually to maintain submission levels. Ultimately, the intent is to secure DNA samples from everyone convicted of or cautioned about a recordable offence, and it is expected that the national DNA Database will include details on 5 million samples.[84] The costs will rise accordingly.[85] John Wadham of Liberty is not only staggered at the number of people likely to be eligible for DNA sampling, but concerned that samples will be taken even when it is not necessary – for example, from persons charged with an offence but found not guilty.[86]

Summary

The actions of the police are crucial in shaping the case against the accused and the origins of most miscarriages of justice can be traced to the early stages of the police investigation. To better understand the causes of miscarriage cases and other types of criminal injustice, it is necessary to examine the nature of the legal powers exercised by officers, together with the ways in which they are carried out in practice.

The police enjoy a high degree of autonomy in their work and their legal powers are framed in such a way as to provide wide discretion in their exercise. This applies to the operational discretion of the chief constable, but more importantly, to the daily work of constables carrying out stops, searches and arrests. This means that those at the lowest levels in the police hierarchy regularly make decisions which impact upon the rights and liberties of individual citizens. As well as a wide discretion in defining who or what is suspicious, infusing police practice at all levels is what has been described as a 'cop culture' where the values of the police become, by definition, in the interests of law and order. Those opposing the police, or failing to accept their authority, are thus seen as posing a 'threat' to the accepted social order. Class and race are of particular significance in the definition of such 'suspect' groups. Police activity is not always concerned simply with law enforcement, but also 'to secure broader objectives: the imposition of order, the assertion of authority, the acquisition of information'.[87] The law is used as a control device, facilitating the arrest of those whom officers consider need to be arrested.

A further feature of the investigation and prosecution of criminal offences is the way in which evidence is assembled. Leads tending to undermine the initial police suspicion are not followed up; in some instances, they are suppressed. Crime does not represent an objective reality waiting to be discovered, but, rather, consists of a case which is constructed against the suspect.

PACE and the COP form a legal framework within which most police powers are contained, but they have failed to inhibit police behaviour, including malpractice. Procedures can be circumvented and internal hierarchical supervision is inadequate, with senior officers facing many of the same pressures which lead those under their charge to bend the rules and engage in bad practice. Despite this, under the last Major administration (and more importantly, under the careful shepherding of the Home Secretary Michael Howard), a host of new and coercive police powers were introduced. These included the power to stop and search without reasonable suspicion (s. 60 CJPOA 1994) and the threat of adverse inferences for suspects not answering questions put to them after caution (s. 34 CJPOA 1994). Despite doubts as to the reliability of DNA evidence and the way in which it is presented to and subsequently interpreted by the jury (see e.g. Redmayne 1995), much emphasis has been placed, by both the RCCJ and the government, on the collection of forensic evidence from the suspect. The circumstances under which body samples may be obtained have been extended under ss. 54–9 CJPOA 1994, in many cases to circumstances as broad as for the taking of fingerprints. In the case of intimate samples (such as blood, semen or pubic hair), adverse inferences may be drawn if the suspect refuses to give written consent, and saliva and mouth swabs have been reclassified as non-intimate, in order that they might be taken by force in some circumstances.

The law does not operate as a significant constraint upon the exercise of police powers, in part because the police enjoy sufficient autonomy and authority to flout requirements such as reasonable suspicion and in part, because the law is framed in terms broad enough to allow officers to pursue a range of objectives around the maintenance of social order. As Reiner (1992) comments, the police see themselves as 'the thin blue line' between the respectable and the undeserving.

3
The Suspect at the Police Station

Fabricated or false confessions have been at the root of a number of miscarriages of justice. Given the centrality of confession evidence in the prosecution case against the accused, it is important to examine the context in which confessions are obtained, and the safeguards against unreliable admissions which are in place. The significance of the suspect's silence during interrogation will be examined briefly and is discussed in greater detail in Chapter 5.

The impact of PACE: police, defence lawyers and suspects

PACE allows suspects held in police custody to consult a lawyer at any time, free of charge; to have someone informed of their detention; and to consult the codes of practice which set out in detail the way in which the detention period should be conducted.[1] The custody officer (a police officer of at least the rank of sergeant but unconnected with the case) is responsible for keeping the custody record and for the suspect's welfare whilst in custody.[2] She is the linchpin of many of the regulatory provisions and acts as a gatekeeper to the rights of those detained. She must inform the suspect of her right to legal advice, for example, and if this is declined, she must ask and note on the custody record, the reasons why.[3] Additional safeguards, such as periodic detention reviews and the tape-recording of interviews, also promise to regulate better the time spent in custody by suspects. Detention itself must be authorized independently by the custody officer and the reasons justifying detention noted on the custody record.[4] Those held on suspicion of committing serious arrestable or terrorist offences may be detained longer, and may have their right to have someone informed of their arrest, or to receive legal advice, delayed. In the case of vulnerable suspects (juveniles, 'mentally handicapped' or those appearing to be suffering from a mental disorder), the custody officer must also inform an appropriate adult and ask them to come to the station.[5]

The provisions of PACE and the COP provide a clearer regime for the conduct of detention periods than was formerly the case and, in particular, place the suspect's right to legal advice on a statutory footing, marking a significant improvement over the previous uncertainty. This has meant that increasing numbers of suspects have access to legal advice. Zander's (1972) pre-PACE study found that less than half of the suspects interviewed had asked to see a lawyer; Baldwin and McConville (1979) reported that only one-third of their Crown Court sample of defendants requested legal advice; and Softley (1980) found the figure to be even lower, at around one in ten. Refusal rates were high – one-third in Softley's study and three-quarters in both the Zander and the Baldwin and McConville studies. Access to legal advice has gradually increased since PACE, and Bucke and Brown (1997) report request rates to be around 40 per cent, with 34 per cent of suspects actually receiving legal advice either by telephone (18 per cent) or at the police station (82 per cent).[6] Nevertheless, this still leaves two-thirds of suspects detained in police custody declining the option of free legal advice.

It is important to be clear about the context in which custodial legal advice became a statutory entitlement, as it has been used repeatedly (and doubtless will continue to be used) to justify further coercion of the suspect – most notably in the recent curtailment of the right to silence. In its 1981 report, the RCCP, recognised the disadvantaged position of those detained by the police and their need for proper legal advice:

> [The suspect] is unlikely to be properly aware of the legal intricacies of the situation, to understand, for example, the legal concept of intent or the application of the laws of evidence to his case, of the full implications or desirability of exercising his right to silence, or to know what the penalty is likely to be for the offence for which he is suspected. Only an experienced lawyer can give him this kind of information and advise him how best to proceed.[7]

The mere fact of being detained in police custody makes the suspect isolated and vulnerable and in need of proper legal advice in order that she can make meaningful decisions on how best to respond to the allegations made against her. The RCCP's recommendation that suspects have access to legal advice was intended to go some way towards counterbalancing the proposed, and later enacted, increased police powers. Yet, couched in a discourse of 'balancing of interests' between those of the suspect and those of an effective investigation, the availability of legal advice continues to be weighed in the scales by the courts, police and policy-makers to justify further encroachment upon the suspect's position. For example, breaches of PACE and the COP which might otherwise result in the exclusion of evidence are deemed not to have harmed the suspect's interests to the same degree if there is a lawyer present.[8] Most recently, it has been forcefully used to argue that suspects are adequately protected at the police station (even though at that time the evidence was that they were not),[9] so justifying the curtailment of the right to silence. This discourse of 'balance', so favoured by successive governments, is misleading. First, any balance which was struck between custodial legal advice and other interests was done so by PACE, and access to a lawyer cannot properly be used repeatedly against the interests of the suspect without providing further safeguards. It is fanciful to suggest that PACE 'tips the balance' in favour of the accused. The police enjoy the upper hand as accusers rather than accused; in their authority as state agents preparing the case for 'The Crown'; and through physical, territorial and information control. In addition, the significance of police interrogations of suspects must be understood in the context of the wider criminal process and, in particular, the importance of admissions 'within a system whose ethos is that of partisanship and competitiveness, in which the surest way to "victory" is aborting formal combat – the trial – by obtaining the other side's "surrender" – a guilty plea or at least a confession.' (Lustgarten, 1986: 9). Secondly, this discourse assumes that any exercise by suspects of their rights will have a negative impact upon the investigation of the case.[10] To view these interests as inherently conflicting is unhelpful. If the presence of a lawyer, for example, inhibits police malpractice, the quality of the investigation is enhanced rather than diminished.

In what ways have the provisions of PACE and COP been effective in regulating the detention of suspects? When JUSTICE researched some of the cases that depended upon disputed admissions, it found some improvement in the behaviour of the police post-PACE:

> And that is partly because there are more safeguards in police stations now, because everything is done on tape and you remove immediately the argument about whether the person did or didn't say something.

There is better access to lawyers, and obviously any ill-treatment can or should be caught at that point. What we saw from those cases was that the sort of very blatant misbehaviour of police that previously existed has largely been corrected in that way.[11]

The Secretary of the Law Society's Criminal Law Committee, Roger Ede, believes that whilst progress has been made among the police officers who are responsible for training and for setting policy, it will be much harder to alter the behaviour of the rank-and-file officers:

it will be some considerable time before the street-wise officer who is conducting an investigation actually believes what the policy-makers tell him or her is the approach they should adopt. They tend to come back on tried and tested methods, which very often are brow-beating someone to the extent that the person then agrees with what the officer is putting forward.[12]

Research, too, indicates that the provisions of PACE have failed to guarantee suspects' rights or to transform police practice. Firstly, the law itself is fashioned in a way which is problematic. A variety of research studies have shown that the primary objective of the police investigation is to assemble a case against the suspect in order to obtain a conviction and that once somebody becomes a suspect, all efforts are mobilized to that end. The role of the custody officer is central to many of the provisions, but expecting a fellow police officer, albeit independent of the case, to act as gatekeeper to the suspect's rights and to place obstacles in the path of her colleagues' investigation by questioning the decision to arrest and detain is perhaps unrealistic. It is unsurprising, therefore, that a variety of research studies have found custody officers reluctant to challenge the initial decisions of officers to arrest and that detention has been granted routinely.[13] Secondly, and following from this first point, relevant legal actors have translated the legal provisions into practice in a way which subverts the objectives of PACE and the preceding RCCP. Custody officers have sought to prevent or delay suspects' access to lawyers; detention has not been actively reviewed; custody records have not been kept accurately; and interviews with suspects are seldom listened to by lawyers or the court.[14] Instead, reliance is placed upon summaries of interview prepared by the police. Yet, these often represent an account which is biased towards the police version of events and their construction of the case against the accused.[15] Lawyers, for their part, have failed to respond to the task of custodial legal advice in a strategic and professional way. Widespread use has been made of unqualified and inexperienced clerks – including former police officers – and the quality of advice from advisers, whatever their status, has been generally poor.

Given that interrogation evidence is often the determining issue in cases and has been at the heart of so many miscarriages of justice, both before and since PACE, the ability to regulate interrogation and detention is crucial. The enactment of new legislation alone, however, cannot change the behaviour of individuals. The working culture in which they operate, and their practices and ideologies, are more powerful and sustained. Research has demonstrated that, unless addressed directly, these factors are likely to transcend mere changes in the rules. The primary purpose of arrest and detention is the interrogation of the suspect in order to obtain a confession.[16] Whether or not it is placed on a statutory footing, the presence of a legal adviser is likely to be seen by the police as an impediment to their legitimate efforts to secure an admission from the suspect (Hodgson, 1994: 91–2). Empirically, this scepticism has been shown to be misplaced. Advisers are unlikely to advise suspects to remain silent (both before and since the right to silence restrictions introduced under the CPJOA 1994) and until recently, most have adopted a passive role during interrogation. Stephen Miller's police interrogation continued despite more than 300 denials on his part and his solicitor was described as 'being gravely at fault for sitting passively through this travesty of [a police] interview'.[17]

However, police opposition to defence lawyers is more fundamental. Even if the solicitor does not advise silence, her very presence is viewed by the police as an impediment to the creation and maintenance of an atmosphere in which the suspect is more likely to cooperate in the interrogation process (McConville and Hodgson, 1993: 51–2). Quite simply, defence lawyers are seen as being on the side of the suspect and unless there is some functional benefit to the police, there is no incentive for officers to assist them in any way and every reason to obstruct them. It is perhaps surprising then, that recent research conducted for the Home Office (Bucke and Brown, 1997; Phillips and Brown, 1998) found virtually no instances of custody officers delaying the suspect's access to legal advice. In their 1998 study, Bridges and Choongh report that custody officers are now also more willing to provide case-related information to defence lawyers. Dixon and others who claim that PACE has altered police practice and ushered in 'a new professionalism' may interpret this as the impact of PACE on officers rising through the ranks.[18] However, it is more likely a result of the new provisions in the CJPOA 1994 and to be motivated by a desire not to provide the defendant with any excuse for remaining silent, where inferences might not then be drawn. Dixon (1997: 161) has criticized accounts of the power of police culture and their commitment to crime control values as overstating 'the commitment of many to anything, and to understate the extent to which policing is a job, in which other more profane concerns (having a good time, getting to the end of the day/night without trouble, etc.) are as important.' Yet, it is just these concerns which feed into a shared working culture in which defence lawyers are antithetical to police objectives – whether representing the monitoring of detention procedures which then hinder the course of the investigation, or a restriction to the general behaviour of officers. It is Dixon who overstates the case. Police culture is not an overt commitment to explicit values, but a drift into, and absorption of, general working practice and objectives, many of which serve to make the police officer's job more tolerable.

The impact of PACE upon defence lawyers has also been by no means immediate. Universal access to custodial legal advice was greeted enthusiastically by criminal defence firms, but for most this was not seen as an opportunity to influence the course of the investigation at an early stage, but as an additional category of work available to them and a means of securing clients. Duty Solicitor schemes were established and legal aid made available to all those detained in police custody. Whilst some formal level of skill was required to participate in the former, the provision of advice from 'own solicitors' was not monitored in any way. As professionals, solicitors were trusted to organize their own work in a way which best served the interests of their clients rather than their profits. Given the determining influence of the police interrogation upon the case and the importance to the accused of the later charge and bail procedure, an experienced and legally qualified adviser is required. As one experienced solicitor-advocate explained,

> Experience makes a hell of a difference because providing legal advice at the earliest possible moment is tremendously important. It's at the very start of the process, that point in the police station when you first interview an accused person, where maybe you can stop the conviction. But once you've passed that point it's probably too late.[19]

As well as legal skills, the adviser needs to be confident in dealing with the police, as another experienced criminal solicitor explained,

Obviously if the police are getting what they want then they are relatively friendly. And there are some very decent policemen who play by the rules, and whatever you say they will treat you with respect. But there's an awful lot more who don't; and if you let them, they can walk all over you. Some police are very rude and aggressive. In fact, if you advise your client to shut up and say nothing a large percentage of the police become very aggressive indeed. So you've got to be pretty tough at the police station and behave to them in the same way. If they behave badly then you have to make a complaint about it; and if there is anything like abuse, you have to go to the custody officer and report it.[20]

McConville *et al.*'s (1994) large-scale study of the organization and practices of criminal defence lawyers found that qualified and experienced lawyers were engaged predominantly in magistrates' court advocacy. Firms were heavily reliant upon non-legally qualified staff for much fee-paying work and to operate a system geared very much towards guilty pleas. In stark contrast to the police mythologies of highly adversarial lawyers concocting defences and priming witnesses, they found that most lawyers lacked any kind of adversarial ideology and viewed the majority of their clients as undeserving. Their primary operative mode is the 'effective management of clients towards a guilty plea' (Hodgson 1994: 95). McConville and Hodgson's (1993) Royal Commission study focused upon the provision of custodial legal advice and found this to be a microcosm of the wider culture of defence practice. Heavy use was made of non-qualified[21] and often inexperienced staff who were overawed by the police and unable to offer 'advice' of any meaningful sort,[22] with solicitors providing advice in only one quarter of cases. Silence was rarely advised, and where it was, this was often as a safety measure to avoid *the adviser* getting into deep water. Work was organized from within firms such that there was no delegation by senior to more junior staff in any meaningful way: it was never contemplated that a solicitor would attend clients in custody. Police station work was seen as low grade, conducted in unpleasant surroundings and often at anti-social hours. For this reason, former police officers were considered to be ideal, as they were very much on home territory.[23] The fundamental 'transition' from police to defence work did not seem to concern solicitors unduly. In the majority of cases, the professional rhetoric of high levels of expertise and commitment to the interests of the client, justifying self-regulation and potentially high levels of remuneration, does not seem to have shaped criminal defence lawyering in a desirable way. By way of contrast, there are a minority of firms who have managed to provide a high standard of custodial legal advice to their clients, using either solicitors or trained and experienced paralegals. These firms, operating under the same constraints of legal aid, have different lawyering objectives and tend to attract staff who are highly motivated and often have a political commitment to their role as defence lawyers.

The Royal Commission on Criminal Justice (1993) was critical of the standards of custodial legal advice and this added weight to the move to regulate those who should properly be able to provide such advice.[24] An accreditation scheme has been set up under a joint Law Society/Legal Aid Board initiative, which requires non-solicitors advising suspects held at the police station to pass a written exam as well as to gain supervised experience of custodial legal advice. The profession has shown itself unable to ensure high standards in this crucial area of legal work and it is significant that the accreditation scheme is backed by financial sanctions: only those who are, or are registered to be, accredited, will be paid for police station advice work. Bucke and Brown's (1997) study shows a decline in the use of non-qualified advisers since the beginning of the accreditation scheme in February 1995 – from 26 per cent in 1993–4 to 16 per cent in 1995–6. A comparison between Bridges and Choongh's (1998) evaluation of the scheme in its first years and McConville and Hodgson's earlier study suggests that it has had a considerable impact in many areas. More time is spent in client consultation and a better understanding of the client's version of events is obtained; only rarely will suspects enter interrogation with no strategy having been agreed; investigating officers are more likely to be asked for case-related information; and advisers are more likely to intervene during interrogation. However, high proportions of observed advisers were still failing to discuss the case with the custody officer and especially her intention re charge. In only 31 per cent of cases were clients asked about their treatment in custody. Although the scheme seems to have led to improvements, including the work of solicitors (who are not subject to the scheme), Bridges and Choongh (1998) point to the generally low rate of success (only 27 per cent by February 1998) and the failures of those who have been engaged in police station advice for many years.

The positive changes are to be welcomed and it is hoped that these will pave the way for improved training within the profession generally. However, it is important to remember the context in which this shift has taken place – one in which lawyers have been shown to provide a poor quality of service and to be uncommitted to the interests of their clients' defence – as well as the changing legal environment in which lawyers operate. Recent academic attention[25] has brought the role of the defence lawyer into the spotlight, highlighting the dangers of an inadequate defence. An adversarial system requires the defence to actively engage in defending the accused. If they do not, the process is distorted, the accused unprotected and the risk of justice miscarrying great – as illustrated by cases such as those of Stefan Kiszko and Stephen Miller. As mentioned above, the courts take account of the legal representation of the suspect in assessing the impact of breaches of PACE and the COP. An inadequate defence adviser disadvantages the accused, who is credited with a benefit which, effectively, she has never had. The sentiments of the RCCP (para. 4.89), set out above, are as relevant today as they were in 1981 and recent improvements through the accreditation scheme leave no room for complacency. The role of the custodial legal adviser is becoming yet more important as the period of detention at the police station becomes an increasingly significant part of the process of investigation and the construction of the case against the accused.

Firstly, the curtailment of the right to silence under the CJPOA 1994 means that the court may now draw adverse inferences from a suspect's silence.[26] This will happen if the accused mentions something in court which it would have been reasonable to expect her to mention when questioned by the police. The strategy employed during police interrogation, therefore, may impact upon the trial in strengthening the case against the accused. A decision to remain silent will have to be justified in order to avoid adverse inferences being drawn; and advancing a version of events which is later contradicted at trial has obvious dangers in terms of credibility before the magistrates or jury.

Secondly, defence advisers must be prepared to enter into active negotiation with the custody officer, whose decisions have an increasing impact upon the fate of the accused. Under s. 27 CJPOA 1994, the custody officer is now empowered to grant conditional bail after charge.[27] The RCCJ recommended this extension of power as an efficiency measure on the grounds that, frequently, 'suspects are brought before the courts to make applications for bail even though the police might be willing to grant bail themselves' (p. 73). However, granting bail is not simply an administrative task and this reform represents a shift of power from the judiciary to the executive and an additional lever of authority over the suspect, enjoyed by the police. Preliminary research suggests that the new power has not achieved the savings in time and resources anticipated (Raine and Willson, 1997). There is extra work for the police in deciding conditions and for both police and lawyers in negotiating bail; staffing levels at the station and for transporting prisoners to courts is unaffected; and some courts are concerned to 'review vigorously' either excessive or inadequate police-imposed conditions. Unsurprisingly, the new power has not been directed simply at those who would otherwise have been held overnight (detention rates fell by 2.5 per cent in 1994–5) but, more significantly, to impose conditions on those who would have been bailed unconditionally (unconditional bail fell by nearly 10 per cent). The authors of the research conclude that the judiciary is better equipped to decide on the liberty of the accused, as they are able 'to bring a measure of independence to the process of decision and to provide a check against abuse' (Raine and Willson, 1997: 606).

The government are also considering implementation of the proposal[28] that routine cases be dealt with speedily and are prepared for disposal the following day by a 'Criminal Justice Unit' made up of CPS and police civilian staff. This is likely to diminish the value of the CPS review of the charge preferred.[29] Lawyers will have to be prepared to make representations as to charge at the police station, since the custody officer's decision is more likely to be final and so of greater significance, leaving less scope for negotiation at court. This was one of the areas of weakness highlighted by Bridges and Choongh (1998), with three-quarters of advisers failing to discuss the custody officer's intentions re charge either before or after the interrogation.

Thus, each reform introduced strengthens the hand of the police, placing increasing pressure on the accused to capitulate to police demands and requiring defence lawyers to be both effective at the police station and to have one eye on the impact which the accused's responses will have on the trial. The accreditation scheme has gone some way to improving the quality of advice provided, but there is still some way to go. Only a quarter of those registered passed the scheme and those who fail may continue to provide advice for six months.[30] Bridges and Choongh (1998) express some concern that firms may continue to use unqualified staff by consistently registering people for accreditation who never go on to qualify. McConville and Hodgson's (1993) study found that poor quality legal advice was not limited to unqualified clerks; clients were often poorly served by solicitors too, but the Royal Commission recommendation that 'own' solicitors be included in the scheme was not acted upon. In this respect, it has served the profession's own interests to focus upon those outside its membership as being in need of additional training. However, substantive areas of weakness remain. Advisers are not engaging with the custody officer directly, nor asking clients about their treatment by the police. In addition, McConville *et al.* (1994) pointed out that most firms failed to provide continuity of representation for clients. Those undertaking police station work did not advise clients later in their case and typically, there was a split between magistrates' and Crown Court work. Given the increasing significance at trial of what the accused says whilst in police custody, improvements in the provision of custodial legal advice do not go far enough. The challenges to the legal profession created by the new reforms require defence lawyers to undergo a more thorough transformation of training and practice.

In concentrating attention on the police, it is not only defence lawyers who were, until recently, rarely scrutinized. What of those suspects detained in custody who are, after all, most directly affected by the reforms? How do they behave in the exercise of their rights under PACE? The majority of suspects detained in police custody do not seek legal advice (60 per cent) and do answer police questions (94 per cent) and around half make a full confession to the police (Bucke and Brown, 1997). Within police culture suspects are described as 'crafty crooks' who receive 'off-the-peg' defences from their lawyers and exploit procedural loopholes in order to escape conviction. McConville and Hodgson (1993), however, found suspects to be undemanding and even passive in their resignation to police control. Accounts of inducements or physical violence on the part of the police were reported by clients to their lawyers without surprise or complaint. In most cases the possibility of remaining silent in interrogation was never discussed: both the adviser and the suspect proceeded on the assumption that questions would be answered. Although defence lawyers were accepted as 'the experts' by most suspects, if silence was advised, many were reluctant to adopt it as a strategy, concerned at the negative way in which it might be viewed. Of those that began a 'no comment' strategy, many began answering within minutes of the interrogation. Others required advice in the strongest terms to prevent misleading self-incrimination, as the following example in an allegation of rape makes clear:

> Client: Do I say Guilty?
> Lawyer: No.
> Client: But I...
> Lawyer: (interrupting) Do you understand what rape is?
> Client: Having sex with a woman.

> (Quoted in McConville and Hodgson 1993: 94)

Clear and persistent advice is required to displace the existing police influence over the suspect. 'The defence adviser faces a huge task to secure the trust and confidence of the client in order that she will then behave in a way which may openly conflict with police demands. All pressures around the client are to capitulate to the expectations of those detaining her.' (Hodgson, 1994: 90) In this sense, all suspects are vulnerable and experience a sense of powerlessness which is heightened through the use of interrogation. A substantial body of research has drawn attention to the interrogative suggestibility of suspects – much of it deriving from the detention environment and the use of police authority and control. More specifically, problematic styles and forms of police questioning may lead to the production of unreliable evidence.[31] Restrictions on the right to silence further weaken the position of suspects by increasing the already strong expectation that they should answer police questions.

Whilst all suspects experience vulnerability through police detention, some individuals are considered especially vulnerable and studies have shown that given the pressure of even properly conducted police questioning, such people may be persuaded – or may persuade themselves – to make false confessions in order to liberate themselves from the interrogation environment.[32] As a result, a number of miscarriages of justice in both the pre- and post-PACE era have concerned vulnerable individuals. The RCCP was itself established in the wake of the now infamous Confait case in which three youths, two of whom were juveniles and the third had a mental age of eight, were wrongly convicted of the killing of Maxwell Confait. Aware of the climate of concern which surrounded the case, the RCCP's proposals formed the basis of the appropriate adult scheme now in place. However, the effectiveness of the appropriate adult provisions are doubtful and in the period since PACE, a number of high-profile miscarriages have occurred concerning vulnerable people – for example, those involving Engin Raghip and Stephen Miller. Yet, the problem of vulnerable suspects received scant attention from the RCCJ.

An appropriate adult must be contacted and asked to come to the station if the suspect is a juvenile, 'mentally handicapped' or appears to be suffering from a mental disorder (COP C para. 3.9). The Code describes the purposes of the presence of an appropriate adult as 'first, to advise the person being questioned and to observe whether or not the interview is being conducted properly and fairly, and secondly, to facilitate communication with the person being interviewed'.[33] Special care should be taken in interrogation and corroborating evidence obtained wherever possible.[34] This protection extends to the trial in the case of mentally handicapped persons, where, under s. 77 PACE, juries are warned of the dangers of convicting if the prosecution case rests wholly or substantially on confession evidence and no independent person was present.[35] However, there are a number of problems associated with the implementation of this scheme. Firstly, the custody officer is responsible for identifying a suspect as vulnerable. This may be relatively straightforward in the case of juveniles – but those with a mental illness or learning disability are less apparent and the custody officer has no medical or psychiatric training.[36] One recent research sample found that an appropriate adult was required in between 15 and 20 per cent of cases, but was requested in only 5 per cent.[37] Another study found that in a sample of 20,805 cases, appropriate adults were called in only 38 instances, whereas researchers considered they were required in a further 446 cases.[38] These figures suggest that substantial numbers of suspects requiring an appropriate adult do not have one present and that potentially, s. 77 warnings are not given in a sufficient number of cases.[39]

A second problem is that of locating an appropriate adult. Juveniles are expected to be attended by a parent or social worker. For others, it may be a relative, guardian or other person looking after the individual. In practice, it may be difficult to find someone to attend, as there has been no formal duty scheme along the lines of that in place for the provision of custodial legal advice.[40] As part of their duty to secure the availability of youth justice services under the Crime and Disorder Act 1998 s. 38, local authorities must now ensure that an appropriate adult scheme is available for juveniles. This still leaves a gap in provision for other vulnerable suspects. The role of the appropriate adult is onerous and requires both confidence and assertiveness as well as some knowledge of legal procedure and standards of fairness in interview. For the parent attending their child, this role is almost impossible. They are often as intimidated as the suspect and may even join with the police in pressing for admissions.[41] Those attended by social workers may fare little better. Although considered criminal justice professionals and therefore potentially better situated to advise, there is no formal training requirement for social workers to carry out this role and many are more accustomed to working alongside, rather than independently of, the police – for example, in child protection cases. This creates a serious danger of role conflict – the appropriate adult may become complicit in the police investigation, rather than protecting the interests of the vulnerable suspect.[42]

Furthermore, who is capable of acting as an appropriate adult, what is required of her and the degree to which she should intervene in an adversarial capacity is unclear. The case-law provides some guidance: some degree of empathy is required[43] and the person should be capable of giving advice.[44] But what kind of advice should be provided? And how is she to determine whether the interview is fair? If she considers that it is not, what action can be taken? Does assisting communication allow her to answer on behalf of the suspect? These are difficult questions which may have to be resolved in the tense atmosphere of interrogation, by someone with no legal training. Given the inherently coercive nature of police interrogations and the often inadequate protection provided by the defence adviser, the appropriate adult role is of great importance for vulnerable suspects who may be more easily pressured into making unreliable admissions. In addition, the recent curtailment of the right to silence places suspects under even greater pressure to speak, representing a high risk for those who are especially suggestible. The RCCJ was mindful of this in recommending retention of the right to silence: 'It is the less experienced and more vulnerable suspects against whom the threat of adverse comment would be likely to be more damaging.' (1993: 54) The reform of the right to silence made provision for vulnerable individuals only in relation to juveniles testifying at trial, where, ironically, the defendant will be under less intense pressure and will have had time to reflect and be advised upon her case. Under s. 35 of the Crime and Disorder Act 1998, juveniles are no longer protected from adverse inferences should they fail to give evidence at trial.[45] Despite the high-profile miscarriages in cases such as Stephen Miller and the uncertainty surrounding the effectiveness of appropriate adult provision, curtailment of the right to silence has placed vulnerable suspects at even greater risk of being pressed into making a confession which may not be reliable.

The reliability of confession evidence

[I]n a certain set of circumstances and in the particular environment of a police station, there are many people who will end up saying they have done something that they haven't done just to get out of that situation. And you are not necessarily talking about people you might call vulnerable because they have a mental problem or are especially suggestible. They are simply ¬eople who are made vulnerable by the set of circumstances they re in ... So being aware of the danger of resting convictions on onfessions is very important.[46]

Interrogation is the principal investigative tool employed by the police and Maguire and Norris (1993) describe confession evidence as forming the 'central plank' of the majority of prosecution cases. As the exposure of miscarriages has made clear, despite PACE and the codes, convictions based on allegedly false confessions remain an unresolved problem. A number of safeguards have been proposed, such as the requirement that the confession be tape-recorded or made in the presence of a solicitor or be corroborated by independent evidence. These were rejected by the Commission, which considered the benefit that these may afford accused persons to be outweighed by the risk of loss of evidence. The tape-recording of interviews is a requirement under Code C of PACE. It is now a nationwide practice,[47] and a failure to record *may* lead to the exclusion of a confession, or other incriminating evidence, that might result from the interview. However, the courts do not automatically exclude non-taped admissions made by suspects in the patrol car[48] or those made outside the interview room in the police station.[49] Furthermore, the police have proven willing to engage in oppressive interrogation *even* when the interview was being taped.[50] Given the police's hostility to due process protections and their clear preference for a regime which imposes the minimum of restriction upon evidence gathering, the Royal Commission, predictably, refused to recommend an absolute rule that a confession should be automatically inadmissible unless tape-recorded, on the grounds that some reliable confessions might be lost. In particular, this would exclude 'spontaneous remarks uttered upon arrest' which the Commission believed 'are often the most truthful' (p. 61).

The requirement that a solicitor be present in order for a confession to be admissible in court was also rejected. This was not thought to be a practical suggestion, as most suspects do not have a lawyer present at interview. Even where an adviser does attend, this neither guarantees the fairness of the interview, nor prevents the application of improper pressure upon the suspect beforehand.[51]

Two research studies, carried out at the request of the RCCJ, found that very few cases would be affected by a requirement for supporting evidence.[52] Yet, the Commission was not prepared to countenance the risk of even a small reduction in convictions. They argued that

the number of cases in which the police might or might not be able to find supporting evidence is less important than the prospect that the introduction of a requirement to do so would lead to some defendants walking free who would rightly be found guilty under the present rules. (1993: 65)

They were not persuaded that a corroboration requirement might also prevent wrongful convictions. They focused not upon the improvement to police investigative practice that this might bring about, but on the fact that such a rule 'would not by itself prevent miscarriages of justice resulting from fabricated confessions and the production of supporting evidence obtained by improper means' (p. 65). The fact that the police abuse their powers seems to have led, ironically, to the conclusion that there is no point trying to kerb that power.

Another safeguard against unreliable admissions is to put the confession evidence to the accused in the presence of an examining magistrate. This was provided for under s. 6(1) of the Magistrates' Court Act 1980. Most committals, however, were formalities, where the accused was committed to the Crown Court solely on the basis of written statements. The RCCJ noted that committal proceedings did not prevent weak cases from reaching the Crown Court and, in addition, that they were costly, cumbersome to administer and time-consuming for the court and its personnel. Therefore, they recommended that committals should be abolished. This was enacted in the CJPOA 1994, but later modified by the CPIA 1996.[53] Under s. 51 of the Crime and Disorder Act 1998, adults charged with indictable-only offences will be sent straight to the Crown Court for trial. The 1996 amended committal proceedings now apply to either-way offences only – and in some circumstances, these may also be dealt with directly by the Crown Court.[54] The new procedure diminishes the value of committal as an opportunity for the scrutiny of evidence, because oral evidence cannot be presented. A full committal is limited to the reading of witness statements and even the accused herself may not testify.

However, the Commission did acknowledge the tendency of police to jump too quickly to the conclusion that they have arrested the offender,[55] and that this often leads the police to abandon further investigation and to exert undue pressure on the suspect in an effort to secure a confession; and that the result can be the conviction of an innocent person while the guilty party goes free. Albeit in an understated form, the Commission here identifies the primary critique of modern policing and the root of many miscarriages of justice. Yet, it afforded it only superficial treatment, refusing to grasp the nettle and consider fundamental change. Any accountability or supervision of the police from outside their ranks (for example by the CPS) was roundly rejected without any real evaluation of the possible advantages.[56] Instead, the Royal Commission urged more 'thorough' investigations, although this was not made as a formal recommendation, nor (typically) was consideration given to the means by which this change in police philosophy and practice might be brought about. Greater follow-through, the Commission argued, would not only reduce instances in which 'guilty people are acquitted' because the evidence against them proves inadequate in court, but it would also help to exonerate innocent suspects (RCCJ, 1993: 10).

Despite its reference to exonerating the innocent, the tilt of the Commission here was clearly toward conviction of the 'guilty'. This was apparent in its unwillingness to take a firm stance against 'informal' interviewing. Despite the intent of Code C of PACE to restrict the interviewing of suspects to the police station,[57] the Commission actually recommended regularizing the current police practice of questioning suspects en route to the station – that is, under circumstances in which they clearly lack the benefit of the safeguards set out under PACE, including legal advice (RCCJ, 1993: 28). It argued, however, that this change could benefit the accused, if accompanied by safeguards such as the tape-recording of interviews outside the station and putting the admission to the accused at the start of the police station interview. Leng (1994: 179) suggests, however, that the defendant 'who contests the confession at trial may be prejudiced by the dramatic impact of the alleged confession at the beginning of the interview'.

The Royal Commission's proposal was made in the face of research showing the considerable scope already available for the police to bring pressure to bear on suspects while outside the formal interview situation as a means of securing incriminating statements. According to Leng (1994), all of the major post-PACE studies have found substantial evidence that informal interactions between officers and suspects have a significant role in police investigations. Moston and Stephenson (1993) have noted that such interactions may occur both prior to the suspect's arrival at the police station: at the crime scene (60 per cent); in/on the street (5.5 per cent); at home during a post-arrest search; and (although rarely) in the car;[58] and at the station: in informal cell visits; 'off the record' pre-interviewing; and in the interview room before tape-recording starts.[59] Contrary to its purpose, the custody record does not serve as a protection against such behaviour at the station. By logging conversations in the cells as 'welfare visits', the custody officer who is responsible for ensuring that suspect protections are enforced, may actually cooperate in the efforts of her colleagues to circumvent PACE by providing a covering record.[60] In this way, custody records validate rather than constrain police behaviour. 'They enable the police both to treat suspects as they wish (within certain self-imposed boundaries) *and* to justify their actions afterwards, thus creating perfect conditions for constructing cases on the most unshakeable foundations' (McConville *et al.*, 1991: 49; original emphasis). Among other purposes, police may use these informal contacts to gain the confidence of the suspect, to offer inducements or threats, to suggest, and to secure evidence – particularly confessions or other incriminating statements (Leng, 1994: 174).

Any spontaneous utterances made by suspects in the course of an exchange with the police continue to be a legitimate source of evidence, providing a record has been made in accordance with the rules of PACE and its Codes.[61] The pay-off for the police appears to be considerable. In their 1993 study of interviews outside the police station, Moston and Stephenson found that 74.5 per cent of the outcomes involved some form of admission (i.e. full confessions, admission of incriminating facts and other damaging admissions);[62] this compared with 58.8 per cent for interviews inside the police station (ibid.: Table 12, p. 34)

Given such outcomes, and despite the rules of PACE and the Codes, the scope for securing false admissions in the course of informal exchanges remains considerable. And Moston and Stephenson found a high correlation (82 per cent) between interviews outside the station and admissions made in formal interviews (ibid.: Table 14, p. 35). As a result of such findings, the Commission was urged to make inadmissible any 'evidence' derived in this manner. However, despite its recognition of the 'risk of invented confessions' (RCCJ, 1993: 26), it did not accept proposals which called for making inadmissible as evidence admissions made by suspects while in the police car or otherwise away from the police station. As discussed earlier, the Commission argued that 'spontaneous remarks uttered on arrest are often the most truthful' and that 'some genuine admissions' are made by suspects on the journey to the police station (RCCJ, 1993: 61 and 26). The Commission did propose that at the beginning of the first tape-recorded interview at the station, a suspect, after taking legal advice, be invited by the station custody officer to repeat admissions allegedly made to the police outside the station (RCCJ, 1993: 28, 61). It went on to say, however, that if the suspect, 'on having the confession put to him or her, does not confirm the confession on tape, it should not automatically be inadmissible'. In the Commission's view, the evidence should be allowed to go before a jury to be weighed-up (ibid.). The due process rights of the accused are considered subordinate to the wider interest of system efficiency in the production of knowledge.

As noted above, the Commission also recommended further exploration of the potential use of portable tape-recorders outside the police station.[63] The Commission was of the view that tape-recording outside the station would reduce opportunities for the police to influence the suspect to make admissions and to prescribe the content of the formal interview at the station. It also suggested that tapes would enable supervisors to monitor the conduct of officers on the street. However, this seems unlikely given that police internal supervision has failed to regulate behaviour at a number of levels – from the monitoring of stops and searches to the authorization of detention.[64]

Apart from the influence of informal exchanges between officers and suspects outside the station, a number of problems associated with exchanges between officers and suspects within the station itself have already been identified. These include informal questioning in interview rooms prior to switching on tape-recording equipment, as well as in cells and elsewhere in the station. The Commission took a step toward dealing with part of the problem by recommending continuous video-recording of the corridors of custody suites, but it did not extend its recommendation to interview rooms or to individual cells.[65] Although widely supported by the police,[66] the video-taping of formal interrogations may disadvantage the suspect and encourage juries to view the interrogation out of context: having 'seen' the interrogation, jurors may be increasingly unlikely to give weight to the influence of events occurring beyond the interrogation room. As Moston and Stephenson (1993: 45) have noted, a suspect's eventual statement inside the station is not determined only by the content and style of the interview in the station, but also by what has gone before. The previous history of the police–suspect relationship may also be relevant to the suspect's response (Singh, 1994).

Protection of suspects against unacceptable police practices that may produce unreliable incriminating admissions is not assured by the presence of legal advisers, the tape-recording of interviews or the video-recording of proceedings in the station. For example, McConville and Hodgson (1993: table 9.1, p. 158) found that in 78 per cent of the interviews they observed, legal advisers did not intervene. This was the case even when police questioning was thought to be overbearing or aggressive. Thus:

Despite the fact that the police might resort to overt psychological manipulation, accusation and abuse, and might lose their temper with the suspect, legal advisers usually continue to act as spectators and make no attempt to alter the interrogation dynamics. (Ibid.: 157)

Bridges and Choongh (1998) report an improvement in the willingness of advisers to intervene, but the impact this may have on police interviewing is as yet unclear. The current safeguards have not deterred the police in their use of pressure tactics in order to secure an incriminating admission from a suspect. In a case examined by Gudjonsson and MacKeith (1990), a 17-year-old suspect falsely confessed to two murders committed in 1987. Having retracted a confession first extracted by the police in the absence of legal representation, the youth was subjected to further interrogation characterized by repeated and persistent pressure, including accusations and psychological manipulation. To escape the intolerable pressure exerted on him, the youth, for a second time, finally made a full (and false) confession which was recorded in the presence of a duty solicitor. Nor should the role of the court be overlooked. In contrast to the Court of Appeal's strong condemnation, it should be remembered that the trial court judge in the Stephen Miller case did not consider the interrogation (over 300 denials through 19 interrogations lasting a total of 14 hours) to be oppressive, and admitted it in evidence.

Drawing upon a Home Office study conducted by Baldwin (1992), the Royal Commission cited certain methods used by the police in interviewing suspects – including repetitious and irrelevant questioning for prolonged periods without adequate breaks – which it characterized as bullying or harassment (RCCJ, 1993: 12). This treatment leads to suspect fatigue and thus tends to increase suggestibility and the likelihood that the suspect will make statements that are damaging to her defence. Yet, having correctly diagnosed the problem, the Commission offered little by way of a remedy. Apart from endorsing recent police efforts to improve their interview skills, it merely suggested that Code C of PACE, which also covers acceptable lengths of interviews, be re-examined with an eye to possible changes in the specified minimum length of breaks between interviews of a suspect (RCCJ, 1993: 13).

The statements made by witnesses and recorded by the police have also been found to be unreliable. Maguire and Norris (1993) identified witness statements as a weak spot in investigations.[67] Witnesses may be persuaded to exaggerate accounts in order to strengthen the police case

– especially if they are facing criminal charges themselves, when they may co-operate in the hope of receiving more lenient treatment. Police witnesses may also be tempted to 'gild the lily' and supervising officers admitted that there was little they could do to prevent this other than to encourage it to be viewed as deviant and unacceptable behaviour. In writing up witness statements, they may be interpreted in ways that provide supporting evidence for the prosecution, and the police may overlook or exclude statements that run counter to their presumption of the suspect's guilt. In one of the few studies of this problem, Maxwell McLean, an Inspector with the West Yorkshire police, compared tape-recordings of 16 police witness interviews with the subsequent written statements by the police. He found that the number of items omitted from the written accounts of interviews ranged from four to 38, the average being 14. Moreover, despite all the statements having been signed as a true record, on four occasions the officer wrote down a 'fact' that squarely contradicted what the witness had actually said. In each case the 'error' strengthened the case for the prosecution.[68]

Furthermore, the Commission recommended the removal of long-standing restrictions on post-charge questioning. This would allow the police to question suspects in custody at any time after they are charged (presently not allowed) until the full file is given to the Crown Prosecution Service (RCCJ, 1993: 16–17). This practice would, of course, be subject to the usual 'caution' being repeated, and to the right of the accused to have the opportunity to consult a legal adviser. However, prolonging custodial questioning (and, therefore, detention) increases the pressure upon suspects to confess. As for the protection of suspects' rights, it must be seen as a step backwards. At the time of the recommendation the availability of legal advice even for pre-charge interrogations had been shown to be inadequate (McConville and Hodgson, 1993) and even now, improvements are not universal (Bridges and Choongh, 1998). The proposed change would worsen the situation because defence solicitors would have to be available at police stations for the prolonged questioning of suspects. Since existing legal resources preclude satisfaction of the new demand, the change would increase the chances of wrongful convictions due to false confessions (LAG, 1993: 8). In addition, once the suspect has been charged, it is the court who should examine the evidence and try the defendant. Post-charge questioning increases the emphasis upon the detention period as the major case determinant.

There are additional complications here. For example, PACE rules require that a person suspected of an offence must be cautioned before any questions are put to her regarding her possible involvement in that offence (Code C, para. 10.1); but in trying to discover whether, or by whom, an offence has been committed, a constable may put questions to any person she thinks might provide information (Code A, Note, 1B) without cautioning the person. Beyond this, there is really nothing to prevent the constable from questioning a person she does suspect without suggesting to the suspect that she is under suspicion of having committed an offence. Having not been told she is under suspicion, the suspect may make statements in response to questions which justify her arrest, for which she may then be taken to the police station and there be persuaded to repeat in a tape-recorded interview the damaging statements made before or at the time of arrest – as well as any made in the car en route to the station.[69]

In summarizing their findings, Sanders and Bridges (1990) do not suggest that unlawful interrogation occurs in the majority of cases; only that the police may be expected to resort to such tactics whenever they feel the need to circumvent legal advisers and other controls – that is, when they are convinced of the suspect's guilt and are intent on securing a confession. The result has been a number of alleged wrongful convictions based on disputed confessions. As JUSTICE reports, a lot of the cases they examined depended on admissions made in the gaps within the PACE framework.

> For example, an amazing number of people suddenly seem to have been moved to confess in the police car, and then as soon as the tape was running they didn't want to say anything anymore. Or else there would be damaging admissions in the cell. The accused would have been questioned in the formal interview session with their lawyer present; the lawyer goes home, the guy is taken back to the cell, and all of a sudden it's come over him that he needs to tell somebody everything. So he summons the police and he makes a full breast of everything, and confesses that he's completely guilty.[70]

In short, the police may overcome the potential impediments represented by PACE and the Code provisions by following them in only a cynical or half-hearted way. In practice, rather than rejecting them outright, the police have simply interpreted and adapted them in ways which minimize their impact on their long-standing *modus operandi*. As one officer put it, 'we manipulate [PACE] in a way that it doesn't affect (us) much'.[71] More serious than this adaptive approach is the deliberate violation of PACE provisions by the police and (not infrequently) the condonation of this by chief constables and police superintendents.[72]

In short, while it is clear that both before and since PACE, 'police mal-practice has been at the heart of the majority of miscarriage of justice cases',[73] the expectations that PACE would change police behaviour in a positive way have been disappointed. Police behaviour definitely has been altered by the legal requirements introduced by PACE: but it has not occurred in the way intended. Moreover, it has been accompanied by some results that are both unintended and unfortunate. As Sanders and Bridges (1990: 507) conclude:

> Police malpractice has probably not been reduced but it has been made less overt, and hence more difficult to detect and control. In giving the false impression of complete police compliance with the law, unduly great faith in the police will not be encouraged. Thus PACE may, inadvertently, have made matters worse rather than better.

Summary

Once arrested, the suspect will be taken to the police station for ques-tioning. This is the most crucial stage in evidence-gathering. While suspect behaviour or the carrying of prohibited articles may provide a reason for the arrest, it is the interrogation of the suspect which stands to bear the most fruit in the investigation, in the form of a confession. Admissions form the central plank of the prosecution case against the suspect in the majority of instances.

As with stop, search and arrest, PACE and the COP form the legal framework which sets out a number of safeguards for suspects detained in police custody – access to legal advice; taped interviews; periodic deten-tion reviews; and a custody officer independent of the investigation whose role is to ensure that the detention is properly conducted. However, a decade of empirical research has demonstrated the inability of legal structures to transform police working practices and culture. Whilst PACE and the COP may have curbed some of the worst excesses of police malpractice, they have failed to re-define police objectives and behaviour and have not served to inhibit police practices. The presence of legal advisers have, until recently, been mistrusted and discouraged, and recording practices considered bureaucratic obstacles to effective invest-igation. The courts, for their part, have steadfastly refused to interfere, concerning themselves only with issues of the fairness of the trial, which they define as largely separate from issues of police investigative methods.

However, if PACE has not radically altered police practice, it has pro-vided the suspect with a number of statutory guarantees, most notably that of access to legal advice (s. 58). The right to have a lawyer present both before and during interrogation has been given greater effect by the universal provision of Legal Aid for custodial legal advice. Unfortunately the profession has not responded adequately to the possibility of pre-charge involvement in the investigation. Until recently, the majority of legal advisers were neither qualified nor trained. Most were clerks of some form or other, with little or no knowledge of criminal law and procedure. Even solicitors themselves were generally passive and cursory in their dealings with suspects. Clearly, custodial legal advice has been considered routine and mundane work for which non-qualified individuals might inexpensively be employed. Recent initiatives to improve the quality of service provided are the result of financial sanctions for those failing to comply, rather than conscious standard-raising by lawyers themselves. Recent reforms such as curtailment of the right to silence mean that non-adversarial defence lawyering, both at the police station and during case preparation, has a greater impact upon the construction and running of the defence case.

The provision of appropriate adults to vulnerable suspects was also intended to protect suspects. In this instance, no 24-hour cover was provided and no professional group presented itself as suitable to take on the job. Instead, appropriate adult provision is variable, ranging from intimidated parents to social workers and carers. Training is scarce and, as with defence lawyers, suspects are left rather less well protected than anticipated by statute. This, of course, is of especial concern in the case of vulnerable suspects, who are most in danger of succumbing to police pressure – or even simply expectations – to confess. The 1998 Crime and Disorder Act requires local authorities to provide appropriate adults for juveniles, which may result in more uniform training and provision across the country.

The police station is the key site in the construction of the case against the accused and is therefore central in understanding and tackling some of the major causes in miscarriages of justice. As we will see throughout the accounts in this book, despite the evidence of independent research and numerous wrongful convictions, legislative preference has been given to policing concerns and crime control objectives, rather than due process and greater reliability of evidence presented at court. Most notable is the virtual abolition of the right to silence, discussed in detail in Chapter 5 below.

4

Remedies for Police Misconduct

Introduction

There are a number of remedies available to the victim of police misconduct, aside from appealing against the decision of the court. Evidence may be excluded at trial, ensuring that a conviction does not result from improperly obtained evidence. This may act as a deterrent to officers tempted to act unlawfully, as well as providing a clear signal to the CPS regarding the standard of evidence required. In addition, the integrity of the criminal process is protected, by avoiding the conviction of an individual by wrongful means. A second remedy available is that of making a formal complaint. This does not form any part of the trial process, but focuses upon action being taken against the offending officer. Thirdly, an aggrieved individual may bring a civil action against the police – for false imprisonment or assault, for example. The successful plaintiff will be awarded damages in compensation, but this will not necessarily lead to any action being taken against the offending officer, or a conviction being overturned.

Judicial exclusion of evidence

Various types of evidence may be excluded at trial for a range of reasons: the fruits of an unlawful search; a confession obtained by oppression; a confession where a vulnerable suspect has not been attended by an appropriate adult; alleged admissions where no contemporaneous record has been made; admissions made where legal advice has been wrongly withheld. Confession evidence is of particular interest here, as it is both especially persuasive and potentially unreliable as a form of evidence – as evidenced by a number of miscarriage cases.[1] The courts, potentially, have a powerful role to play in sanctioning non-compliance with statutory police controls and upholding the rights of the accused during the pre-trial process.

One rationale for excluding evidence may reflect a strict due process approach, intolerant of breaches of procedure. Judges would exclude on the basis of the breach regardless of the motivation of officers or the impact upon the individual defendant. This would protect all accused persons in the same way and recognise preservation of the integrity of the pre-trial process as an interest to be protected. It would also set clear standards for future acceptable behaviour.

Alternatively, judges and magistrates may take into account a range of other factors in deciding whether to exclude evidence, such as the motivation of the officers (did they act in bad faith – or simply make an error?) and the impact of the breach upon the defendant. Under this approach, the integrity of the process is not an overriding value, only coming into play in instances of the most flagrant breaches. Crime control values dominate as apparently guilty defendants are not allowed to benefit from prosecution error.

The first of these rationales has never won approval in the English system, except in relation to 'vulnerable' defendants, who are seen as needing greater protection.[2] The dominant jurisprudence, both before and after PACE, reflects more closely the second approach. The Court of Appeal has produced a complex set of decisions which leave maximum scope for individual judicial discretion:

> the decision of a judge whether or not to exclude evidence ... is made as a result of the exercise by him of a discretion ... The circumstances of each case are almost always different, and judges may well take different views in the proper exercise of their discretion even when the circumstances are similar. This is not an apt field for hard case law and well-founded distinctions between cases.[3]

However, despite the complexity and sometimes inconsistency, of these decisions, general trends can be noted.

Before examining these in detail, we should bear in mind the context of judicial exclusion of evidence. Obviously, the question of exclusion only arises in trials, where the defendant has entered a plea of not guilty. In the vast majority of cases where the accused pleads guilty, whether or not there has been any impropriety on the part of the police, there will be no challenge to any prosecution evidence. This is significant, as much police malpractice may be masked by an apparent acceptance of the whole of the prosecution case. Secondly, a challenge to the admissibility of evidence relies upon the defence identifying the procedural breach and being prepared to argue at trial for the exclusion of the evidence obtained.[4] Given what we know of the poor quality of defence case preparation and the unwillingness of defence lawyers to adopt an adversarial posture, challenges to prosecution evidence are likely to be rare (McConville *et al.*, 1994). Many firms employ non-legally qualified staff to prepare cases for Crown Court with the result that they may fail to include legally relevant information in proofs of evidence, leaving counsel ignorant of admissibility issues. Firms are structured towards the production of guilty pleas and recent reforms offering sentence discounts for early guilty pleas will only serve to increase the pressure on defendants to capitulate and to accept the prosecution case. Finally, there is the problem of demonstrating that the breach took place. If the defendant mentions that, for example, she was threatened prior to the formal interview and the defence lawyer is prepared to argue at trial that this renders unreliable any subsequent admissions, it is likely to be the word of the defendant against that of the police. It is easy to anticipate how the accused (who may be seen as having every reason to lie) would fare against the police in the courtroom hierarchy of credibility.

Some, such as McBarnet (1983), are hostile to the provision of judicial discretion within the criminal justice process, while others see it as a necessary regulator, providing the flexibility needed to take account of a range of potential scenarios. However, it is the way in which the judges choose to exercise that discretion which is crucial in determining the degree to which the rights of the accused are upheld; the messages which are sent to the police concerning the acceptability of practices; and the maintenance of the integrity of the criminal process. One experienced solicitor we interviewed had no doubts about the way in which judges decided issues of evidence admissibility:

> There's an English disease, and that is that the moment you think you've got a line in the sand, they give the judges a discretion: and that really is saying to the judges, 'You can undermine this piece of legislation.' And in my view the judges have set out to do just that. What the judges now basically do is to say in all but the actual words, 'The end justifies the means: if this evidence is capable of resulting in a conviction, by and large, we will admit it.'[5]

The approach of the courts

Judicial regulation of the admissibility of evidence is dealt with principally by ss. 76 and 78 of PACE.[6] Section 76 *requires* the judge to exclude confession evidence if it was obtained by oppression or anything said or done which is likely to make it unreliable. This test replaced the common law standard of voluntariness.[7] Discretion exists in the determination of what amounts to oppression or when a confession is unreliable, but once either test is satisfied (by the prosecution beyond reasonable doubt), exclusion is mandatory. The value of this as a deterrent to police malpractice is limited by s. 76(5), which excludes from the coverage of the section evidence obtained as a by-product of an oppressive confession. Thus, for example, stolen goods found on the basis of information obtained during an interview deemed to be oppressive under s. 76, would not be inadmissible.

Section 78 applies to all types of evidence and gives the court a far wider discretion. Evidence may be excluded if, having regard to all the circumstances, including those in which the evidence was obtained, admitting the evidence would have such an adverse effect on the fairness of the proceedings that the court ought not to admit it. The judge here must determine not only the fairness of admitting the evidence, but also what weight to attach to which circumstances in making that assessment. In addition, the court may now be called upon to direct the jury to decide whether the absence of evidence may be admissible against the accused under the silence provisions in the CJPOA 1994[8] and the disclosure provisions in the CPIA 1996.[9]

Although s. 76 PACE applies to confession evidence, admissions are more frequently excluded under s. 78. Establishing oppression has proved a difficult hurdle to overcome and in practice, either the alternative ground of unreliability is often argued, or exclusion under s. 78. This was the case even in the extreme circumstances of the Miller case, where the Court of Appeal commented, 'Short of physical violence, it is hard to conceive of a more hostile and intimidatory approach by officers to a suspect.'[10] Less extreme cases of hectoring, hostile or aggressive interrogation have been held not to be oppressive nor to render admissions unreliable.[11] The Court of Appeal in *Fulling* (1987) gave oppression its 'ordinary dictionary meaning': the exercise of power in a tyrannical manner; cruel treatment; the imposition of unjust burden. This definition, however, relates to the behaviour of the police (and would probably require serious misconduct), rather than the psychological pressures of interrogation experienced by suspects.

Rather than relying upon oppression, most commonly this section has been used to exclude the confessions of vulnerable suspects, where breaches of PACE and the Codes have been causally linked to the unreliability of admissions. These decisions have been couched, not in terms of disciplining the police for wrongful behaviour (indeed the court specifically absolved the police from allegations of wrongdoing in some instances)[12] but protecting the accused, who by virtue of their vulnerability are seen as 'deserving' of due process protections. In the Miller case, the borderline mental state of the accused was an important consideration in the Court of Appeal's decision.[13] Sharpe (1998: 128) has argued that this subjective due process approach to excluding evidence has worked against defendants perceived to be 'undeserving'. The admissions of drug addicts suffering withdrawal, for example, are unlikely to be deemed unreliable. The court has applied the reasoning that the operative cause of the unreliability is the accused's own state of withdrawal, whereas the statute contemplates some external cause: some words or acts on the part of the police which are likely to induce unreliable confessions.[14] Yet, in other cases of 'deserving' suspects, the mental state of the suspect has been held to be part of the 'circumstances' relevant in considering unreliability[15] and evidence has been excluded without the need even, to show any impropriety on the part of the police.[16]

The things 'said or done' which make a confession unreliable may include breaches of PACE or the Codes of Practice. It is clear that not all breaches will result in exclusion – there will generally have to be several and again, many of these cases concern vulnerable suspects,[17] but not all. Questioning before allowing access to a solicitor, and failing to show a note of the exchange to the accused or her lawyer, for example, resulted in excluding the admission in the case of *Chung*.[18] Failing to caution the suspect, to maintain a proper interview record or to show it to the accused made the confession in *Doolan*[19] unreliable. Although excluded under s. 76, the grounds were similar to those in a number of s. 78 cases.

Any evidence may be excluded under s. 78 PACE, if its admission would have such an adverse effect on the fairness of the proceedings that it ought not to be admitted. The courts have required that any breaches of PACE and the Codes of Practice should be significant and substantial[20] before they will result in the exclusion of evidence. This may include confessions where there has been a failure to caution the suspect or make a contemporaneous record, for example, or where access to legal advice has been unlawfully denied. Evidence resulting from an unlawful search may also be excluded, though in practice, this is rare.[21] In principle, the court is not concerned with the manner in which evidence is acquired, but in its relevance to the matters in issue. This was affirmed by Lord Goddard CJ in *Jeffrey v. Black*: 'I have not the least doubt that we must firmly accept the proposition that an irregularity in obtaining evidence does not render the evidence inadmissible.'[22] Although this pronouncement was made before PACE (and the general widening of police powers contained therein), the courts have continued to be guided by it. Yet, this is not an inevitable feature of s. 78, which specifically directs the judge to consider the circumstances in which the evidence was obtained – which may include breaches of PACE (or the Codes of Practice) relating to search, seizure, arrest, detention, questioning or identification. It would be quite open to the courts to hold as 'unfair' any serious breach of PACE or the Codes of Practice, on the grounds that it undermines the statutory regime laid down for the conduct of pre-trial investigation.

Instead, the courts have sought to restrict the circumstances in which evidence will be excluded. Interestingly, this seems to have been anticipated by the government in introducing s. 78 into the Act. It was the result of a last-minute amendment to replace Lord Scarman's clause which would have placed the onus upon the prosecution to show that evidence was lawfully obtained. Instead, in the interests of efficiency in the criminal process, s. 78 shifted the onus onto the defendant. As Sharpe (1998: 85) comments, 'It can be assumed therefore that there was a belief that the judiciary, given an open textured section, would apply it narrowly and promote prosecution interests.' Although s. 78 is phrased in terms quite different from s. 76, the courts have tended to equate fairness with reliability, which is a narrowing of the definition. If evidence has been improperly obtained, but is nevertheless considered reliable, it is regarded as fair and admitted at trial. This crime control stance has a number of consequences. Firstly, it enables the police to profit from breaches of the rules and offers no protection to the accused in the instant case. More generally, by failing to censure unlawful acts, it offers no disincentive to officers to break the rules in future investigations.[23] The retrospective reasoning that an unlawful search is justified because it yields evidence of a crime is flawed; by definition, the court is unlikely to learn of searches unless they have a 'successful' outcome and so their experience of police practice is distorted. Unlawful searches yielding no relevant evidence go unnoticed and unsanctioned.[24]

The wide discretion provided for under PACE affords the judiciary the opportunity for independent scrutiny of the exercise of police power over citizens. The judges are ideally placed to ensure that statutory safeguards are not undermined. Instead, they have recast the terms of their role, and their function is not, say the judges, to 'discipline police officers'.[25] Yet the intentions of officers are considered relevant in determining whether to exclude evidence.[26] Where the police have knowingly exceeded their powers, evidence is more likely to be excluded. In *Mason*, confession evidence was excluded after the suspect's solicitor was deliberately misled as to the existence of incriminating evidence and in *Canale*, there were deliberate and flagrant breaches of Code of Practice C. Focussing upon police intention, however, does not take account of the effect of the breach upon defendants. Denial of access to legal advice, for example, does not impact less upon the suspect by virtue of the fact that it is not deliberate.

Another feature of appeal court decisions in this area, as with the operation of s. 76, has been to view some accused persons as more in need of due process protection than others. As with the treatment of cumulative breaches of PACE and the Codes, this serves to maintain the appearance of protecting the integrity of the process by excluding evidence in the most serious cases. This has been especially evident in the court's treatment of one of the most important safeguards for the accused, legal advice. So, for example, in *Alladice*,[27] there had been a breach of s. 58 PACE and the accused had been wrongly denied legal advice. The Court of Appeal decided, however, that there was no need to exclude the confession as the suspect understood the caution (as evidenced by the fact that he had exercised his right to silence on occasions) and knew his rights. The presence of a solicitor would have added nothing. The same conclusion was reached in *Dunford*[28] and *Oliphant*.[29] The logic of these decisions is that unlawful denial of access to legal advice results in unfairness only if it is deliberate, or if the accused does not have previous convictions. This is wrong in principle and ignores the empirical reality of custodial legal advice. Parliament did not intend that only suspects with no previous criminal history should benefit from legal advice, but that it should be a universal and fundamental right (see *Samuel*[30]). Furthermore, exercise of the right to silence does not mean that the suspect understands the significance of doing so, nor the significance of the accusation. It was held to be relevant that the appellant in *Dunford* had received legal advice in the past, but for a lesser offence. It is unrealistic to expect earlier advice to equip a suspect for all future interrogations when the issues and evidence are likely to be quite different and there is no guarantee as to the standard of advice that was received. Given the complexity of the provisions of the CJPOA 1994 in relation to the suspect's decision to exercise her right to silence, it would be unfortunate if the judiciary were to continue to hold such a cynical view of the (un)importance of custodial legal advice.

However, despite the obvious power imbalance between the police as state agents, and the suspect, the fact of defence access to legal advice is held against the accused at every turn. It is regarded as a *privilege* which places the suspect on an equal, or even stronger, footing than the police, not a *right* which goes some way to redressing the power imbalance. The Court of Appeal's comments in *Alladice*, for example, foreshadowed the government's reasoning in curtailing the right to silence: 'the effect of s. 58 is such that the balance of fairness between prosecution and defence cannot be maintained unless proper comment is permitted on the defendant's silence in such circumstances. It is high time that such comment should be permitted.' (p. 385) This hostility to the position of the suspect is seen in the way in which the court has avoided having to exclude evidence, by invoking adherence to some PACE safeguards (notably access to legal advice) as minimizing the harm caused by the breach of others. In particular, in the case of *Dunn*,[31] there were breaches of COP C which would have led to the exclusion of admissions, but the presence of a legal adviser was held to swing the balance in favour of admitting the evidence. In this way, a due process protection for the suspect was held against the accused in 'negativing' the breach and denying him the remedy of exclusion. In *Findlay*[32] the suspect had been wrongly held incommunicado, but access to legal advice half an hour before he signed the notes of interview justified admitting his confession in evidence. Given the poor quality of legal advice which suspects may receive, the accused may be credited with a benefit which she has never had and be in a weaker position than the suspect who has no legal adviser present. Although the recent scheme of adviser accreditation has improved the provision of custodial legal advice in some ways, it cannot be said to have transformed police station defence practice across the board.

In contrast to *Dunn*, where the court was happy to emphasize the influence of legal advice on suspect behaviour, recent case-law suggests that for the purpose of determining whether it was reasonable for the suspect to remain silent, reliance upon legal advice will not protect the defendant from adverse inferences.[33] Interestingly, the possible exception to this is the vulnerable suspect. When considering drawing inferences under s. 34 CJPOA 1994, the court in *R v. Argent* stated that the jury should have regard to the actual characteristics of the accused and her 'age, experience, mental capacity, state of health, sobriety, tiredness, knowledge and legal advice are all part of the relevant circumstances'. *Condron and Condron* provided an example of when it would be 'perverse' to draw an adverse inference: when a suspect of very low intelligence and understanding had been advised by her lawyer to say nothing.[34] Whilst vulnerable people detained in police custody undoubtedly require additional protection, by focussing upon this (as the RCCJ did in their recommendations on silence) attention is deflected from the vulnerability of all suspects held in the coercive environment of the police station.[35]

Part of the importance of PACE and the Codes of Practice is in ensuring that accurate and reliable records are made which enable the court to reach a proper conclusion in the case. This utility to the wider criminal justice process (as against pure due process value) has been emphasized even in relation to provisions which would appear to be designed primarily for the protection of the accused, such as access to custodial legal advice. In *Walsh*, the main object of s. 58 was described as fairness, not only to the accused, but also to the prosecution in validating police accounts, 'so that ... there might be reduced the incidence or effectiveness of unfounded allegations of malpractice'.[36] The requirement to tape-record interviews with suspects was similarly designed to minimize such allegations, but 'off the record' conversations continue to be admitted in evidence, despite being in clear breach of Code C.[37] This situation is likely to be exacerbated by the right to silence provisions, with disputes over the recording of admissions or silences alleged to have occurred before arriving at the police station[38] and the prospect of 'silent verbals' – where the accused disputes the failure to reply to a question put outside the taped interview. Furthermore, undercover operations,[39] covert questioning by another, or secretly taped conversations, which necessarily take place without the usual safeguards required by Code C, have been admitted. In a classic case of conflating the tests of s. 76 and s. 78, the court in *Bailey*[40] allowed conversations secretly taped in the defendants' cell to be admitted as evidence – even though the men could not properly have been subjected to further questioning. Whilst acknowledging the fact that this covert investigation achieved what would have been impermissible under the regime of Code C, the court held that there was nothing 'unfair' (cf s. 78) about admitting the evidence, as long as there was no suggestion of 'oppresion or unreliability' (cf s. 76). This case was applied in *Roberts*,[41] where the accused was induced to confess by a fellow suspect in a bugged cell. An experienced solicitor-advocate related a similar example to us:

[The police] hid a secret tape recorder in the ceiling of the interview room. After the interview, they switched off the official tape, the solicitor left, and the police then said to this guy, 'Come on, we know you did it.' And he said, 'I'm not doing ten years. If you think you can prove it, do so.' The judge admitted that exchange from the non-official tape in evidence, even though it was flagrantly, flagrantly in breach of the rules. It was obviously very prejudicial to play that to the jury...The reasoning of the judge was 'Well he's guilty anyway, so therefore it doesn't very much matter how the evidence was obtained.'[42]

More intrusive modes of investigation, whilst potentially impinging upon the liberties of citizens, are virtually immune from judicial monitoring. The Interception of Communications Act 1985 makes it an offence to intercept post and public telecommunications unless authorised by the Secretary of State.[43] This is an executive decision and the judicial role is limited to the criminal proceedings rather than the fairness of the investigative methods. Similarly, under the Police Act 1997, the police may enter onto or interfere with property or with wireless telegraphy in order to effect surveillance. Although permission is required from a judicial Commissioner (except in cases of urgency), it is unclear whether the courts will be willing to exclude evidence obtained without proper authority. Given the restrictive approach to the exclusion of evidence, it is unlikely that the judges will be dissuaded from admitting evidence which appears reliable.

The intention here has not been to provide an exhaustive account of the rules and case-law relating to evidence exclusion, but to demonstrate the limited utility of the courts in upholding the importance of compliance with PACE and the Codes of Practice; in protecting suspects' rights; in ensuring that the prosecution do not profit from police malpractice; and in ensuring that accused persons are not wrongfully convicted.

The exclusion of evidence may protect the accused from being convicted on the basis of evidence obtained in breach of PACE or the COP. If no criminal charge is brought, or the complaint does not touch upon evidential issues, this remedy is not available and an official complaint may be lodged, or a civil action brought. A substantiated official complaint may result in an apology and explanation to the complainant and a range of penalties from 'advice' to dismissal for the officer. Civil actions may not result in the officer being disciplined in any way, but the case is aired publicly and the victim may receive compensation. The options available to the individual are not mutually exclusive: thus a civil action may be followed up with a formal complaint. The RCCJ set out the importance of dealing with police malpractice:

> An effective system of police discipline is essential if police officers are to be deterred from malpractice or negligence, either of which may lead to miscarriages of justice, and if local communities are to have the necessary confidence in the integrity of the police. We doubt whether the existing arrangements for police discipline do now command general public confidence. (RCCJ, 1993: 46)

The Police Complaints Authority

Apart from their conduct in investigations, there are many people who have very serious complaints about the way the police operate in relation to those they police. Tens of thousands of complaints are lodged against the police each year, which range from incivility to serious assaults which may lead to death. Depending on the seriousness of the case, complaints may be dealt with by the chief constable of the force concerned or the Police Complaints Authority (PCA). The PCA was set up under PACE, in response to criticisms that its predecessor (the Police Complaints Board) did not have the power or the staff to carry out its own enquiries and was totally dependent upon the police. Under the present system, such complaints are investigated by police officers but the investigation is supervised by a member of the PCA, all of whose members must be independent of the police.

How are cases filtered through to the PCA? First, the complaint must be recorded by the chief constable of the force against whose officer the complaint has been made. No formal action is taken if the complaint is resolved informally by way of an explanation or apology by the police. The complainant must agree to this and it applies only in cases where the conduct complained of, even if proved, would not justify a criminal or disciplinary charge. Around one-third of all recorded complaints are dealt with in this way.

The chief constable of each force is responsible for the investigation of more serious complaints and instances where the complainant is dissatisfied with the informal process. Most forces now have a Complaints and Discipline Department, whose officers will carry out investigations.[44] However, the investigating officer is normally from the same force – unless the complaint is either serious, or a matter of public concern, or if it concerns an officer of the rank of superintendent or above. In these types of cases an officer from another force will be appointed who must be approved by the Police Complaints Authority. The investigation of all complaints that police action has caused death or serious injury must be supervised by the PCA and in other cases it has a discretion whether or not to do so. Where it decides to supervise it must approve the appointment of the investigating officer, and when the investigation is complete it must issue a formal statement indicating whether or not it is satisfied with the result.

The final report is sent to the deputy or assistant chief constable of the force concerned, who must determine whether the report indicates that an officer has committed a criminal offence and, if so, whether she should be charged. If a charge is made, the case goes to the Crown Prosecution Service who must decide whether or not to prosecute. Where the chief constable decides against prosecution the Police Complaints Authority has the power to submit the case to the CPS. In all other cases the chief constable must notify the PCA whether or not disciplinary charges are to be brought and, if not, the reason for that decision. The PCA must then review the entire case and decide whether or not to accept the recommendation of the police force. If it disagrees it is empowered to recommend or require that disciplinary charges be preferred; however, if it wishes to instigate criminal charges, the matter must be passed on to the Director of Public Prosecutions, who alone has the power to make the final decision of whether or not to prosecute.

As noted, all complaints within certain categories (including assault, serious injury and death) must be referred to the PCA, but it also has the power to deal with other categories of complaint. Thus any individual who feels she has suffered at the hands of the police may take her grievance to the PCA which is empowered not only to investigate but to initiate appropriate disciplinary sanctions against police officers where the complaints against them have been substantiated. However, while use of the police complaints system is far more common than taking civil action, its effectiveness is questionable and results in a reluctance on the part of many who feel they have been abused by the police to take action against them.[45] Although the total number of complaints has steadily increased since 1986 by approximately 25 per cent, there has been no corresponding increase in the number of complaints substantiated. On the contrary: while the number of complaints resolved informally has increased by more than 200 per cent, those investigated have fallen by 29 per cent.[46]

A number of factors account for the ineffectiveness of the complaints system. First, the status and authority of the police, and awareness of the wide discretion implicit in their powers, make many people fearful of bringing a complaint against them. Secondly, there is a basic conflict of interest inherent in having the police conduct an investigation involving one of their own members. Loyalty to the force produces a defensive reaction to any external challenge or threat, such as a charge of misconduct lodged by an outsider. The police may be expected to rally round their own as far as possible. Thus in addition to simply not recording certain complaints chief officers often try to dissuade complainants from pursuing action, and this may include veiled threats. Harrison and Cragg (1991), for example, suggest that a suspect under investigation who believes she has been the victim of police misconduct would be advised by her solicitor to delay making

> a complaint until after any criminal matter is over: there is a suspicion among defence lawyers that, if a complaint is made, the police will pursue the criminal case against the complainant as vigorously as possible, so as to vindicate the officers concerned even before the matter [being complained about] is investigated.[47]

This closing of the ranks may be exacerbated if more than one officer is associated with the alleged offending behaviour, or a custody officer or senior officers are privy to what happened.[48] Furthermore, those responsible for receiving complaints and initiating the complaints procedure are the chief officers (the chief constable, or, in London, the Commissioner of Police, or an officer appointed by them) of the police force in which the offending officer is a member. The chief officer is also responsible for the appointment of an officer to investigate the allegation of misconduct. At the conclusion of the investigation, the chief officers, in a private sitting, decide whether the charges have been proved; and if they have, determine what, if any, sanctions will be imposed on the offending officer. Finally, at each stage, including the initial one of deciding whether a complaint should be formally investigated, the senior officers exercise full discretion.

These and other reasons may be expected to discourage the complainant from proceeding with a complaint, and in 1997–8, 38 per cent were not proceeded with;[49] or to have it resolved informally, which happened with 32 per cent of the cases in 1997–8.[50] In all events, the discretion available to senior officers is used wherever possible to limit damage to the force (Harrison and Cragg, 1991: 26–39). Those who do proceed with a formal complaint are critical of the length of time it takes for complaints to be resolved,[51] especially since a long delay reduces the chance for an outcome favourable to the complainant.[52] Moreover, not only is the hearing held in private, but the complainant has no right to know of the outcome. Even the PCA, by its terms of reference, is subject to restrictions on the way in which it may report the results of its own investigations. It has criticized these restrictions in its *1996/97 Annual Report*, arguing that a more open system would increase public confidence in its work. A further problem was that until recently, charges in disciplinary hearings had to be proved 'beyond reasonable doubt', which is difficult to obtain since most incidents occur in places where there are no independent witnesses. From 1 April 1999, the standard of proof will be brought into line with other professional disciplinary bodies and will be 'on the balance of probabilities'.

As a consequence of these factors, very few complaints succeed and the level of withdrawal is high. Thus while 35,820 complaints were made in 1997–8 (having increased from 28,253 in 1985), only 847 (out of 9,832 complaints investigated) were substantiated;[53] and of these disciplinary charges were brought against officers in 172 cases (20 per cent).[54] Criminal proceedings resulted from 23 (3 per cent) substantiated complaints (Home Office, 1998b: 6).

In relation to complaints handled by the PCA, of the 6,191 complaints of assault[55] (which constituted a third of the 19,953 complaints recorded and outstripped the next largest category – incivility – by three to one) less than 1 per cent of cases (53) resulted in formal disciplinary charges having been brought against police officers. An additional 106 were given advice that their conduct or performance fell below the force's standard of acceptability, and five officers were reported as having left the service. For the remaining complaints, the PCA either granted the forces dispensations from the need to investigate (in 3,478 cases), or found evidence for the complaints either insufficient or conflicting (in 2,536 cases).[56]

A comprehensive overview of the outcomes of complaints is provided in the *1997/98 Annual Report of the Police Complaints Authority*. It shows that of the 18,354 complaints recorded, 18 resulted in criminal charges,[57] and 214 resulted in the preferment of disciplinary charges: together they constitute 1.3 per cent of the total.[58] An additional 861 complaints were resolved by 'admonishment or advice' given to the officers concerned 'by a divisional commander or, in more serious cases, by an assistant chief constable', that their conduct or performance fell below acceptable force standards. The remaining 94 per cent of complaints were either dispensed of without an investigation or found to be characterized by conflicting or insufficient evidence.

The data clearly raise questions about how effective the complaints system might be in curbing the unacceptable conduct of police officers. Out of 1,455 complaints of oppressive conduct or harassment on the part of police officers, only 16 officers were subject to disciplinary charges (i.e. 1 per cent of complaints of this nature handled by the PCA). Even if the statistics are not available to them, it may be assumed that the network of information among police would tell them that the chances of being disciplined for malpractice are very few. Of particular concern here is the probable minimal effect of the discipline process upon police behaviour which breaches PACE Codes designed to protect suspects. For example, of 1,240 complaints about breaches of Code C (concerning the detention, treatment and questioning of suspects), a total of only 15 officers (1 per cent) were subject to disciplinary charges; of 258 breaches of Code A (stop and search), none were subject to disciplinary charges. Altogether, there were 2,050 complaints of breaches of codes (A, B, C, D and E) which resulted in a total of only 20 cases in which disciplinary charges were preferred against police officers:

> In sum, it's totally unsatisfactory to have complaints against the police dealt with by the Police Complaints Authority. That has the effect of delaying everything. So instead of PCA speeding things up and ensuring that if there is a case to go to court it will get to court, what it does is take the issue away from the ball park, with the result that you just can't do anything for ages and ages. I mean if there is a death in custody the police themselves report the case to the PCA, and so there is no possibility of any other involvement until the PCA has deliberated. In the police view, this has the effect of taking the heat out of the situation; but in everybody else's view, it has the effect of increasing the frustration.[59]

As noted, prosecutions of police officers arising from complaints are rare (e.g., one-tenth of one per cent in 1997/98), even in the most serious of cases. Indeed, the CPS has rarely prosecuted police officers, even when the result of their misconduct is a miscarriage of justice and the police have been publicly criticised by the judge (RCCJ: 48).[60] Recent examples of the great difficulty in holding police officers accountable for the abusive and unlawful use of their power were reported in July, 1997. The first concerned Richard O'Brien, who was killed within minutes of having been arrested by the police in southeast London in April 1994. Five police officers had knocked him down and knelt on him. His pleas that he could not breathe were ignored and within minutes he suffocated.[61] As required in cases of death involving the police, an investigation was conducted by the PCA and its report submitted to the CPS, which decided against prosecuting any of the officers responsible for O'Brien's death. However, they were obliged to reconsider their decision in light of a 1995 inquest verdict that Mr O'Brien had been 'unlawfully killed'. Despite this, in October 1996 the CPS confirmed their decision not to prosecute on the grounds that there was insufficient evidence to justify criminal charges against any police officer. Subsequently, in February 1997, the Metropolitan Police Service accepted the PCA's recommendation that two officers should be charged with the disciplinary offence of 'neglect of duty' in the handling of Mr O'Brien.[62] Following a successful legal action by the O'Brien family, the CPS again reviewed the case and three officers will be charged with manslaughter.[63]

The second case occurred in December 1994, when Oluwashijibomi Lapite was killed in police custody. Lapite sustained 45 injuries, including the fatal crushing of his neck. Following an investigation by the PCA, the Crown Prosecution Service, in May 1995, announced that there was insufficient evidence on which to prosecute any police officer; but in January 1996 an inquest jury found that Lapite had been 'unlawfully killed'. Despite this, the CPS reaffirmed its decision that a criminal prosecution of the police officers could not be justified. Moreover, after reviewing all the evidence, the PCA announced in December 1996 that no disciplinary action would be taken against any officer. Subsequently, Mr Lapite's widow sought leave to have the decisions of the PCA and the CPS judicially reviewed; finally, in July 1997, in the High Court, the CPS conceded that its decision not to prosecute was 'fundamentally flawed'.[64]

Not infrequently, officers also evade investigation on 'health grounds' or by taking 'early retirement'. In May 1995, Sir Leonard Peach, then chairman of the Police Complaints Authority, stated that 'about one police officer a fortnight is taking medical or early retirement when facing disciplinary action'. He said he was seeking action from the Home Office to close the loophole, 'which means proceedings have to be abandoned once an officer has left'.[65] Despite the serious findings of the enquiry into the investigation of the murder of the black teenager Stephen Lawrence, a number of officers will escape formal investigation, as they have now retired. Under new regulations (to be in force effective September 1999), this will no longer be possible.[66] In addition, police officers accused of offences will no longer be able to claim double jeopardy and there is to be a 'fast-track' procedure for those accused of serious offences.[67]

For the victims of police malpractice, it is not only their wrongful conviction and imprisonment which is a miscarriage of justice, but the fact that those who fabricated and suppressed the evidence which convicted them go unpunished. When convictions do result, which is rare, the penalties are not only inadequate, but generally followed by official police denials of culpability.

Civil actions against police misconduct

While civil suits may be brought against the police on charges of improper or illegal action, the police officers concerned and their superiors often evade confrontation in court by negotiating out-of-court settlements in the form of cash payments to complainants. Information covering the seven years from 1988 to 1994[68] show that hundreds of civil actions were initiated against the police. Although there have been a number of cases alleging trespass, negligence, damaged property, libel, breach of contract and interference with goods, the most common are based on allegations of assault (222), false imprisonment (360),[69] malicious prosecution (148), with many actions involving multiple complaints (that is, a combination of assault, false imprisonment and malicious prosecution).[70]

In more than 80 per cent of these cases, the police succeeded in negotiating cash settlements, thus avoiding the need to defend themselves in court. That this is increasingly the strategy preferred by the police is evident in data on the number of cases involving out-of-court settlements. Over the five-year period from 1988 to 1992 they nearly doubled, rising from 48 to 90; in contrast, the number of court awards declined from a high of 27 in 1989 to an average of ten for the next three years. Unfortunately, figures for 1993 (18 cases) and 1994 (30 cases) are not comparable to those for 1988–92 since reports for the latter years include only cases where the damages paid amounted to £10,000 or more. Moreover, they include only out-of-court settlements and not court awards. However, the annual cost of out-of-court settlements for claims made against Metropolitan Police are known, and they are seen to have increased substantially. According to disclosures by Sir Paul Condon, Commissioner of the Metropolitan Police, the force paid a record of £1.7 million in damages in out-of-court settlements in 1993/94, compared to £1.1 million in 1992/93 and £571,000 in 1991/92. Altogether, £5.5 million were paid out over the six-year period from 1988 to 1994.[71]

Explanations suggested for the police's preference for out-of-court settlements vary. It may be that those advising the police recognise the justness of the complaints and counsel against going to court. Whether culpable or not, Hillyard (1994: 75–6) argues that the police shun the court out of fear of the adverse exposure that accompanies such cases, which may be covered in the media for several days.[72] And while pre-court settlements do not always save the police from adverse media coverage, it does allow them to avoid the possibility of formal censure in the courts. On the other hand, the police themselves claim that settling out of court is simply less costly – both in terms of money and time – than having to contest charges in court. But whatever the facts of a case, the payment of damages may be seen by the police as simply the cost of doing business in the current socio-legal context.

Moreover, this approach tends to alter the perspective that police authorities have of complaints made against police officers, and increases their willingness to pay damages rather than have recourse to administrative procedures that might lead to disciplinary sanctions for alleged misconduct. As Richard Clayton, a barrister who is an authority on legal remedies for police misconduct, points out:

> one of the interesting things about comparing administrative remedies with sanctions resulting from people being sued, is that if you sue people the public authorities regard it, effectively, as simply an insurance claim. It's quite remarkable how even the public authority who loses a case of any kind and has to pay substantial damages, very seldom seems to regard the basic facts giving rise to the incident as something which disciplinary action should be taken in relation to. Somehow when it becomes an insurance claim people sort of stand away from it and don't really tie it together.[73]

In many instances, despite the finding of the court, the police response continues to be a denial of culpability.[74] Assault was included in 75 per cent of the actions brought against the police in 1993 and 1994, with malicious prosecution added in 50 per cent of the cases. All the remaining charges were for false imprisonment.[75] What is particularly unjustifiable, argues Richard Clayton,

> is that many cases brought against the police involve claims of malicious prosecution: and malicious prosecution involves asserting that police officers have been acting dishonestly in fabricating evidence against the person suing them. Now it is simply remarkable that the

police can either lose cases or settle cases for substantial sums of money when that is the basis upon which the case is put; and it is equally remarkable for those policemen to still remain as serving police officers.[76]

Summary

The establishment of the RCCJ provided the ideal opportunity to make root-and-branch reform recommendations, whilst the horror of repeated miscarriages of justice were still fresh in the minds of the public and politicians. Celebrated cases, such as the Birmingham Six, Guildford Four and Cardiff Three, demonstrated the structural flaws in both the investigation and prosecution of crime. However, the Commission's report represented at best a lost opportunity and at worst a damaging and ill thought out set of proposals.

The inadequacies of the appeals process were criticised by those whose convictions it took many years to overturn, and this we will discuss later; but here we consider the other remedies available to those who have been the victims of police misconduct. Firstly, evidence may be excluded at trial. This is mandatory if a confession is found to be unreliable, or obtained by oppression (s. 76 PACE) and discretionary if the court considers that to include evidence would adversely affect the fairness of the proceedings. Potentially, this is a powerful remedy which may bring about the collapse of the prosecution case. In practice, the judges are reluctant to exclude evidence, unwilling to see incriminating material struck out which might then result in the acquittal of the accused. They have expressly rejected the role of monitoring police misconduct. This position is by no means inevitable, as s. 78 specifically requires the court to have regard to the circumstances in which the evidence was obtained.

The second remedy available is making an official complaint. Cases investigated by the Police Complaints Authority may result in disciplinary action against individual officers or even prosecution. However, such outcomes are rare and of the relatively small portion ever reaching the PCA (many are resolved informally), almost none result in any serious action being taken. There are a number of problems associated with the operation of PCA investigations: initial complaints are made to the police themselves; investigations are conducted by police officers; disciplinary hearings are conducted by chief officers of the force concerned, who also decide on the punishment; and the standard of proof has been (until April 1999) beyond a reasonable doubt.

Lodging a formal complaint is a lengthy process and many complainants give up or are persuaded to accept an informal resolution. Others are put off by the prospect of challenging the police so directly and the difficulties in assembling evidence to support their case – often the only other witnesses are other police officers. Of those that persevered with complaints of assault (by far the largest category. 6,191 out of the total of 19,953 in the year 1996/7), less than one per cent resulted in criminal prosecution or disciplinary hearing.

Finally, a civil action may be brought. This allows the complainant the satisfaction of a public hearing and financial compensation, but does not mean that the individual officer will be punished. Increasingly, forces prefer out of court settlements in order to avoid the adverse publicity of a trial.

Each remedy provides a different form of redress. The exclusion of evidence may prevent the accused being convicted as a result of police malpractice; official complaints may result in officers being punished; and civil actions may provide financial compensation and a public airing of the case. However, none of these remedies is automatic and so this has a bearing upon our understanding of the rights of accused persons, for when those 'rights' are infringed, no sanction may be forthcoming. Rights in this sense are not inalienable and guaranteed, but discretionary.

5
The Right to Silence

From debate to reform

The right to silence means that: (i) a person is not compelled to answer questions put to her by the police; (ii) neither is she required to give evidence in court, but may put the prosecution to proof; and (iii) most significantly, no adverse inferences may be drawn from such silence. With several notable exceptions,[1] the accused's right not to incriminate herself has been an integral part of the burden upon the prosecution to prove its case beyond reasonable doubt. The Criminal Justice and Public Order Act 1994 (CJPOA) now permits adverse inferences to be drawn from a suspect's silence where she does not testify at court, or, she raises something for the first time in her defence at trial, which it would have been reasonable to expect her to mention during interrogation.[2]

Provisions similar to those contained in the CJPOA were introduced in Northern Ireland in 1988[3] and reform of the right to silence has never been far from the government agenda.[4] Thus, despite the background of police and prosecution misconduct, the Royal Commission on Criminal Justice was asked to examine the right to silence. In contrast to the general tenor of their report, the Commission rejected the representations of the police and others and recommended retaining the right at the police station.[5] However, this was not expressed as a fundamental principle (such as offending against the right to be presumed innocent and the privilege against self-incrimination), but as something contingent upon other things (Ashworth, 1998: 100). The right to silence should be retained because the risk to innocents outweighs the chance of increasing the number of convictions; because there was no evidence of experienced criminals obtaining especial benefit from silence; and vulnerable suspects required the right for their protection. Leng (1998) has argued that this reasoning undermined the Commission's recommendation: by focusing on these narrow issues, they implied that if these concerns could be met, abolition would be justified. Parliament did indeed consider the existing safeguards for vulnerable suspects to be adequate. And perhaps significantly, an ACPO 'study' which claimed that 47 per cent of suspects with five or more convictions remained silent in police interview was published on the eve of the first reading of the Criminal Justice and Public Order Bill in December 1993.[6]

Arguments for restricting the right to silence,[7] centred on the beliefs that: firstly, silence acts as a shield for the guilty and serves no purpose for the innocent; secondly, silence inhibits the police investigation and therefore allows a significant number of criminals to escape conviction – notably through the presentation of ambush defences at court; and thirdly, that more people would answer police questions, and so disclose their defence, if they were cautioned that failure to do so would make their defence less credible at court and might adversely affect their case (Leng, 1993).

Those (including the Bar Council, the Criminal Bar Association and the Law Society) who rejected claims that the right to silence was no longer necessary and an obstacle to the proper course of justice felt that, despite the protections of PACE, it would be wrong to confront suspects with the threat of adverse inferences should they refuse to answer police questions. There are many legitimate reasons why a suspect may wish to remain silent. She may not understand the nature of the offence of which she is suspected, or the legal definitions upon which it turns. She may wish to protect members of her family, or wait until she has received full legal advice. In addition, the harshness of police detention as experienced by suspects may easily be forgotten in the more public atmosphere of the trial, months or years after the original charge was made. To say that the 'natural' response of an innocent person is to explain herself reflects behavioural expectations in a social context. But it is not clear that such expectations hold good in the threatening and coercive environment of police accusation. As mentioned earlier, additional protections (such as the presence of the appropriate adult) apply to 'vulnerable' suspects, but it does not follow that suspects outside this category are 'non-vulnerable'. Despite the existence of safeguards, at the police station the suspect is isolated from all people and things familiar, and so is likely to feel anxious and disoriented. Even with the benefit of legal advice, the accused is overpowered by the police: they control the physical, legal and information environment in which the suspect is placed (Hodgson, 1994). Even detention periods conducted quite lawfully are likely to be experienced as hostile to the detainee. After all, the primary purpose of arrest is to place the suspect in police custody precisely because it is a context in which a confession is more likely to be forthcoming.[8]

The police, on the other hand, enjoy not only power and control over the suspect, but also the legitimacy of investigating what will become 'the case for the Crown'. Research suggests that this power and authority is directed, not towards a broad-based enquiry which may exculpate the accused, but one which is committed to obtaining a conviction. Through a variety of means, the police case is constructed against the accused (McConville *et al.*, 1991). Thus, although PACE requires that formal police interrogations be tape-recorded, these do not reveal the often significant conversations and 'rehearsals' which take place earlier in police vehicles and cells; and during formal questioning the police frequently resort to strategies which are clearly and even forcefully aimed at obtaining admissions. In addition, some questions seek to foreclose legal issues by asking suspects to agree that they were 'reckless' or 'dishonest', or had other legally significant states of mind. Researchers have argued that far from persuading the suspect to tell the truth, this form of questioning presents a real danger of producing unreliable evidence.[9] And rather then being exceptional, these strategies are used consistently in suspect interrogation.[10] Whilst the police claim to be inhibited in their investigation by silent suspects, research suggests that it is suspects who require protection from inappropriate police interrogation prone to producing unreliable admissions.[11] To require suspects to answer police questions under pain of their silence attracting adverse comment at trial, adds substantially to the pressures under which they will already be responding. The explicit threat that silence may be damaging will increase the likelihood of false or misleading confessions and admissions,[12] and the prospect of a new spate of wrongful convictions.[13]

However, as critics of the right to silence were quick to point out, the suspect need not face the police alone. She may request the presence of a lawyer at any time during her detention period and this legal advice is free to all. Only in exceptional circumstances may access to a lawyer be delayed.[14] The suspect may consult privately with her lawyer beforehand as well as having her present during the interrogation itself. In this way, it was argued, the suspect is on 'even terms' with the police and so no longer requires the protection of the right to silence.[15] However, despite its universal availability, only

25 per cent of suspects received legal advice before the reform (Brown *et al.*, 1992) and even now, only 28 per cent see an adviser at the police station, with a further 6 per cent of suspects receiving advice on the telephone (Bucke and Brown, 1997). Furthermore, research for the RCCJ showed that the power imbalance between suspects and police was not redressed by the provision of legal advice.[16] Those detained were often poorly served, as lawyers too often failed to rise to this adversarial and challenging role. Although custodial duty solicitor schemes were established to provide 24-hour police station advice, individual practices did not make adequate in-house arrangements to meet the demand for 'own solicitors'. In their study for the Royal Commission, McConville and Hodgson (1993) found that solicitors attended suspects at the station in only one-quarter of cases. Clerks – who were typically untrained, inexperienced and lacked legal knowledge or qualification – attended in some 60 per cent of cases.[17] Moreover, work was not delegated directly by a solicitor to a specific authorized representative, but assigned in a routine way to whomever might be available in the firm. The division of labour within most firms was structured such that personal attendance by a solicitor was never even contemplated.

At the police station, adviser–client consultation lasted typically between 10 and 15 minutes and the monitoring of, or intervention in, the interrogation of the suspect that followed was rare. Advisers, whatever their status, tended to be passive and unable to offer 'advice' other than a simple set-piece explanation that the suspect could answer or not as she chose, with no guidance as to the likely consequences of the choice made. Far from protecting them, the passive stance of most defence advisers left suspects vulnerable to police strategies directed at obtaining a confession. Furthermore, it risked condoning police malpractice given the courts' failure to exclude evidence which might otherwise be held to be unfair, when it has been obtained in the presence of a legal adviser.[18]

The Royal Commission expressed concern at the poor standard of custodial legal advice and recommended that 'Steps should therefore be taken to make the suspects' own solicitors and their representatives subject to the same standards as apply to duty solicitors and their representatives' (1993: 38). A scheme was set up in 1995, under the joint initiative of the Law Society and the Legal Aid Board, and only those non-solicitors[19] who have been 'accredited' under the scheme are eligible for payment from the Legal Aid Board. This requires representatives to reach a prescribed standard in criminal law and procedure and to observe and be observed in custodial advice sessions. Bucke and Brown (1997) report that 75 per cent of suspects are now seen by a solicitor and only 10 per cent by an unaccredited adviser. The scheme has improved the quality of advice provided by accredited non-solicitors, who now spend more time with clients, are better prepared for interrogation and are more willing to intervene if necessary (Bridges and Choongh, 1998). However, advisers are still failing to discuss with the custody officer both the case, and her intentions re charge, and clients were not asked about their treatment in custody in more than two-thirds of cases. In addition, the pass rate of clerks has been disappointingly low and there is concern that clerks may avoid the requirement and continue to advise for up to a year, simply by registering on the scheme (Bridges and Choongh, 1998).

Much weight has also attached to the provision of legal advice and the influence of lawyers upon those few suspects who do exercise silence.[20] The police view has been that those receiving legal advice are more likely not to answer questions under interrogation, to confront the prosecution with an 'ambush' defence at court and so, possibly to escape conviction. Lawyers are, of course, perfectly entitled to advise silence and if conviction is avoided in this way, this is quite legitimate. The police view, however, that this is in some way improper (because it frustrates police objectives) has gained currency and the properly adversarial behaviour of the defence lawyer has been demeaned. Ironically, research has shown defence advisers to be insufficiently adversarial. In any event, while some studies suggest that a correlation between silence and the presence of a legal adviser may exist,[21] these conclusions are drawn without the benefit of knowing what takes place during the private lawyer–client consultation prior to interrogation. In some cases it is because the suspect has already decided to remain silent that she requests a solicitor. Many suspects decide on a strategy of silence of their own volition, regardless of, or contrary to, the advice of their lawyer to answer questions. McConville and Hodgson (1993: 178–9) found that only 40 per cent of silent suspects had been advised not to answer questions, and many of these had already decided to remain silent in any event.

Finally, despite the claims of police and politicians, very few suspects refuse to answer police questions and in most cases their silence has little impact on the case: most result in a conviction. The argument that 'ambush defences' have frustrated police investigations and enabled guilty people to go free has also been widely discredited. In assessing the figures collected, what counts as silence (not responding to all or some questions; not responding to improper or abusive questions) is problematic, and in the view of McConville and Hodgson (1993) has more than likely led to overcounting of the exercise of silence in interrogation. Figures derived from studies on the use of the right to silence before the 1994 Act cover a range of percentages depending on the way in which silence is measured, but most record no answers in under 5 per cent of cases.[22] According to Leng (1993), of those suspects that refuse to answer questions, many do respond in later interviews – thus, the suspect is unsuccessful in maintaining silence. Measured in this way, Leng concludes that the true incidence of silence in interview is about three-quarters of the number of suspects who are silent in relation to some, or all, questions. Moreover, in the majority of cases where suspects exercised silence, the prosecution was not disadvantaged.[23] Suspects exercised their right to silence in only 4 per cent of NFAs (no further action cases) and in only 10 per cent of all cases that ended in acquittals. As for silence being used to ambush the prosecution, in the 59 contested trials examined by Leng, there was only one clear case of an ambush defence (p 58).[24] Thus, Leng concludes, the

> picture which emerges suggests that the right to silence is rarely exercised and that about half of those who exercise it are convicted. For cases which fail, there is little evidence to suggest that the prospects for conviction would be enhanced by inducing the suspect to speak or by treating his silence as a evidence against him. (p. 79)

Indeed, the RCCJ itself acknowledged that most suspects who are silent in the police station either plead guilty later, or are subsequently found guilty (RCCJ, 1993: 54).

Given the infrequency with which silence is maintained[25] and the negligible impact this is likely to have upon the rate of conviction,[26] why does the right to silence excite such fierce debate and why was the Conservative government so determined to bring about its downfall? One explanation is the key role played by removal of the right to silence in the Conservative government's law and order reforms. Against a backdrop of rising crime, removing the right formed part of a strategy to turn the tide of public opinion away from dissatisfaction at the number of wrongful convictions, and towards a concern at the number of 'criminals' wrongfully acquitted. Michael Howard told the October 1993 Conservative Party Conference:

As I talk to people up and down the country, there is one part of our law in particular that makes their blood boil ... It's the so-called right to silence ... [It] is ruthlessly exploited by terrorists. What fools they must think we are. It's time to call a halt to this charade. The so-called right to silence will be abolished.[27]

Despite the fact that the Commission, having been requested to consider the issue, rejected arguments for abolition on the basis of commissioned research, these concerns were swept aside and the reform received little opposition in Parliament.

Leng (1998) argues that silence also has a special symbolism, both to civil libertarians committed to due process values, and to the police, who view it as representing public or constitutional distrust of the police investigative role. Silence undercuts the objectives of the police: it frustrates their attempts to gain a confession, and allows the suspect, to some extent, to resist the control which the police exercise over individuals through arrest and detention.[28] Restricting the right to silence, therefore, increases police control over the investigative process. By placing greater pressure on suspects to speak, it also enhances the police's ability to gather information, as well as their legitimacy to act as knowledge workers in a wider role of risk management (Ericson, 1994; Ericson and Haggerty, 1997).

The CJPOA 1994: silence at the police station

The Criminal Justice and Public Order Act 1994 s. 34 now permits adverse inferences to be drawn from a suspect's silence where she raises something in her defence in court which it would have been reasonable to expect her to mention during police interrogation. Although silence may count against the suspect, it cannot be the sole basis of a prima facie case[29] or conviction. It may, however, contribute to the establishment of a prima facie case – though it would be difficult to rely on a fact as part of the defence at this stage.

The caution that the police are obliged to read to those arrested under suspicion of having committed a criminal offence includes a double-edged warning: that is that not only what they *do* say may later be held against them, but also what they *do not* say. In other words, the suspect is warned that failure to provide answers to questions put by the police, and at the time they are put, may somehow harm her.

The wording of the new caution is as follows:

You do not have to say anything. But it may harm your defence if you do not mention when questioned something which you later rely on in court. Anything you do say may be given in evidence.[30]

There has been concern that this wording will not be understood by suspects. JUSTICE notes that research on similar changes to the caution which had already been introduced under the Northern Ireland Order showed that it is little understood and widely misinterpreted, not only by suspects, but by the police themselves.[31] JUSTICE's own report on the Northern Ireland experience, revealed that the solicitors interviewed (that is, the criminal practitioners) were unanimous in their view 'that suspects do not understand the caution when it is read to them by the police, and that only a small minority, estimated at around 5 per cent, actually appreciate its significance'.[32]

These findings are supported by a study of three groups carried out by Gudjonsson and Clare (1994), which found that only 15 per cent of a group of adults with learning difficulties, and 21 per cent of a group of patients,[33] understood all three sentences of the caution. Furthermore, even though a much higher percentage (58 per cent) of the control group of 'A'-level students understood the entire content of the caution, this still left 42 per cent who failed to understand one or another aspect of it.[34] Inasmuch as the majority of detained suspects at police stations are below average intelligence, the researchers believe that many of those affected will not understand the caution.[35] As a result, they concluded, unless the caution is markedly simplified it is likely to result in cases of miscarriages of justice, since some vulnerable suspects could erroneously incriminate themselves.

The suspect's failure to mention facts when questioned by the police or charged will only attract an adverse inference at trial if the accused was under caution and relies in her defence upon a fact which she could reasonably have been expected to mention in the circumstances existing at the time. What does this mean for the suspect? Firstly, although a caution must be administered, this does not necessarily mean that questioning will take place at the police station. The suspect may be questioned at the time of arrest or in a police vehicle. In such circumstances, very few details of the case will be known, the suspect will not have had access to legal advice and there will be no custody officer or tape-recording, though the Codes of Practice do require that a contemporaneous note should be made. If reliance is placed upon silence outside the police station,[36] it may be anticipated that disputes will follow as to what was or was not said.

Secondly, the fact must be relied upon at court in the accused's defence. Typically, this will be done through the accused's own testimony, but the court may hold that the accused has relied on a fact not previously mentioned, and so draw an inference, even without the accused giving evidence at trial. In *Bowers and Others* (1998),[37] the Court of Appeal stated that it would be 'absurd' if an accused 'were able to preclude the drawing of inferences by not giving evidence'. Reliance upon a fact could be established by the defendant giving evidence, or by calling a witness on her behalf, or if defence counsel adopted as part of the defence case some part of the evidence of a prosecution witness.

Thirdly, when is it reasonable not to mention something? What circumstances will be included as relevant in deciding whether to draw an adverse inference? Clearly it would not be reasonable to expect the suspect to mention something about which she was never questioned. However, the extent of the protection offered by these conditions is unclear.

What if at the time of arrest she is asked questions which she is, on the spot, unable to answer because she does not know the answer or is confused or simply does not remember something? Even under non-threatening circumstances, explained one solicitor-advocate, one might not be able to recall where one was or what one was doing at a particular moment in time:

> If I suddenly said to either of you, 'Where were you last Friday or Friday a week ago?' you'd have to think about it; and you would also need to think about it in terms of a specific time. And you may forget that you actually bumped into someone at the station that you knew. That may be totally forgotten.[38]

In *R v. Argent*[39] the Court of Appeal offered some guidance. Account should be taken of circumstances such as the time of day, the defendant's age, experience, mental capacity, state of health, sobriety, tiredness, knowledge, personality and legal advice. References to the accused relate to the actual accused with such qualities, apprehensions, knowledge and advice as she was shown to have had at the time. It would be 'perverse' to draw inferences, for example, where a suspect of low intelligence and understanding has been advised by her lawyer to remain silent.[40] Legal advice may be relevant where, for example, silence was advised because the police had disclosed little or nothing to the solicitor, so that she could not usefully advise the client; or where the nature of the case or evidence is so complex, or relates to matters so long ago, that no sensible immediate response is feasible.[41]

However, in practice, legal advice has offered no protection from inferences. Silence was advised by the defendant's experienced solicitor in *R v. Argent*, on the basis that the police had disclosed little of the case. This was not considered by the court to be a good reason to exclude the drawing of adverse inferences. In *Condron and Condron*, the solicitor advised silence because the suspects were in a state of heroin withdrawal. Although it might be argued that this is likely to adversely affect a person more than her state of 'sobriety or tiredness', the court still thought it quite proper to draw inferences in the case. The police surgeon, in this instance, had declared the accused fit to be interviewed, but does fitness to be subjected to questions imply fitness to provide answers? The police surgeon makes a medical, rather than legal assessment: the decision takes no account of the complexity of the case nor how well the suspect may be able to put across the defence account which will bind her at trial. It is the legal adviser, together with the suspect, who will have to decide whether silence is the best strategy to adopt. The uncertainty arises when the solicitor considers silence 'reasonable in the circumstances' and the client follows this advice (as one would expect that she would) but, later, the court takes a different view. The defendant is then penalized for failing to reject the professional advice of her solicitor, which seems an unrealistic and unreasonable burden to place upon suspects.

Lawyers, it seems, had not anticipated this line of reasoning. Reliance upon legal advice has been argued in the courts as a reasonable exercise of silence and a number of our respondents had anticipated that clients would be protected by the professional advice of their lawyer. For example:

> It's going to be interesting to see how the judges deal with the situation where the lawyer says on tape, 'I advise you not to answer that question.' I mean, I've just dealt with a serious fraud around the corner where the client is very knowledgeable. And he said 'On the advice of my solicitor, I refuse to answer any questions notwithstanding the caution.' Now at a trial, what's the judge going to do? Put the solicitor in the dock? Or is he just going to have to throw his hands in the air and say to the jury, 'Well, I can't criticize

the defendant because he was acting on expert legal advice from Mr X. And while you may think that that advice was wrong, how can that be held against the defendant?'[42]

But the reasoning of the Court of Appeal is not altogether surprising, as it follows the earlier Northern Ireland decisions.[43] The Court of Appeal has held that the question of inferences hinges upon the reasonableness of the defendant's failure to mention certain facts later relied upon, and following legal advice does not make such failure reasonable.[44] In that sense, following legal advice may well disadvantage the defendant, rather than being of assistance to her. The Court of Appeal has also made it clear that if the accused wishes to invite the court not to draw adverse inferences on the ground that silence had been advised, she must state the basis or reason for that advice. This may then require the lawyer to give evidence of what was said, leading to a warning to counsel that privilege may be waived and solicitor–client communication made subject to scrutiny.[45] Technically, this is done with the client's consent, but if waiving professional privilege is the only way to convince the court of what was said at the police station, and so possibly avoid inferences, the client has little real choice. This undermines the nature and confidentiality of the lawyer–client relationship – especially if the judge refuses to hear the evidence in the jury's absence.[46]

The consequence of these decisions is a change in the whole dynamic of custodial legal advice, as defence lawyers must contemplate being called to justify the appropriateness of their advice. This can create practical difficulties for the lawyer advising her client, especially bearing in mind the requirement for defence disclosure. More time is required to take instructions, so that there is an early and accurate record of the client's version of events. Asking for an explanation before the prosecution case has been fully set out may put the defence lawyer in a difficult position, as one experienced criminal lawyer explained:

> The suggestion that we are supposed to be in a situation where we have to consider actually taking a statement from the client to get their case at the police station so we know which way we are going, even if they are going to make 'no comment', again puts us in a difficult position if the prosecution papers subsequently reveal little or no evidence and we have actually got a statement on file which says, 'Yes I did it. This is why I did it. This is how it is.' The

situation may well arise where we end up saying 'You had better go and see other solicitors.'[47]

The defence strategy adopted during police interrogation will now have an even greater impact upon the construction of both the prosecution and defence cases. Advisers must be mindful of the way in which the court might view the suspect's (non–) responses, as well as the legal constituents of the offence and defence.[48] Obtaining case-related information from the police is essential in order to frame proper advice and to consider what it might be 'reasonable' to mention. At the time of McConville and Hodgson's research (1993), the lack of legal knowledge, training, experience and adversarial ideology of most advisers made them ill-suited to play this role and properly to serve the interests of the suspect. Research on the impact of the accreditation scheme shows that advisers are now more likely to consult with investigating officers and obtain details of the police case, and to agree upon an interview strategy with the client (Bridges and Choongh, 1998). However, details of the case were not generally discussed with the custody officer[49] and evidence was not examined, even when the police alleged that the client had made a statement on or after her arrest.[50] A high proportion of advisers are still not taking the initiative in discovering what further enquiries are to be made,[51] and what the police intention re charge and bail is.[52] And whilst most would inform the client of the precise offence of which she is suspected,[53] three quarters of advisers failed to then explain what that meant. Important gaps remain and it is unclear whether the new training arrangements for non-solicitor representatives will raise the standard of advice sufficiently, given the increasing significance of that advice for the defence case.

A recent Court of Appeal case has signalled an even stricter approach to the drawing of inferences. In *R v Daniel (Anthony Junior)*,[54] the court considered it appropriate that the trial judge might direct the jury that if they concluded 'that the accused's reticence could only sensibly be attributed to his unwillingness to be subjected to further questioning, or that he had not then thought out all the facts ... they might then draw an adverse inference'. The appellant had not refused to co-operate, but on the advice of his lawyer, had given a prepared written statement to the police. His explanation that his lawyer had advised silence on the basis that there was no evidence to connect him with the crime, was swept aside. This judgment goes further than earlier decisions in condoning the use of s. 34 inferences as a disciplinary measure against the defendant who is unwilling to cooperate with the police.

The CJPOA 1994: silence at court

Under s. 35 CJPOA, defendants who do not take the stand or, after having done so, refuse to answer any question without good cause, are also liable to have such adverse inferences as appear proper drawn from their silence. Initially, this provision did not apply to defendants under the age of fourteen, but even this small concession has been removed by s. 35 of Labour's Crime and Disorder Act 1998. An exception may still be made if it appears to the court that the defendant's physical or mental condition makes it undesirable for her to give evidence.[55] It is interesting that this exemption relates to evidence at court, where proceedings are supervised by the judge, the prosecution case has been disclosed and the defendant has been advised and is represented. It does not apply to questioning at the police station, where suspects are under far greater pressure and questioning is in the hands of the police. The position of suspects termed 'vulnerable' under PACE and the COP is of especial concern. The RCCJ considered them, above all others, to be in need of the right to silence, demonstrated by the many miscarriage of justice cases which have concerned the unreliable confessions of vulnerable suspects. Yet, their protection is left to judicial discretion in holding that their vulnerability may be a relevant circumstance in determining the reasonableness of their failure to answer police questions.

Only in the most exceptional cases will the court consider it undesirable that the accused give evidence. The first instance decision of *Watts*[56] applied the exemption to a defendant of low IQ. The Court of Appeal case of *R v. Friend*,[57] however, held that the appellant's mental age of nine was insufficient to exempt him on the grounds of his mental condition, even though a defendant who was actually nine would not have been subject to inferences. In relation to an accused's physical, rather than mental condition making it undesirable for her to give evidence, the Home Secretary, during the passage of the Act, gave examples of persons 'unwell', 'confused', or 'not in a position to give a proper account'.[58]

On 12 October 1995, in the case of *R v. Cowan*,[59] the Court of Appeal handed down a judgment which set forth its view of the proper interpretation of s. 35 CJPOA 1994. The appellant had not given evidence at trial and the judge had directed the jury that under s. 35 of the CJPOA 1994 they might draw adverse inferences from the defendant's silence. Defence counsel argued that the new law is at variance with the principle of the defendant's right to remain silent and the requirement that the burden of proof be on the prosecution, and that therefore the discretion to draw inferences from silence should only apply in exceptional cases, and not in the general run of cases.

The defence lawyers' call for a more restrictive reading of the provisions of the new law was vigorously rejected. Lord Taylor said that the provisions of s. 35 were intended by Parliament to alter, and clearly did alter, the law and practice applicable when a defendant in a criminal trial did not give evidence. The court rejected the assertion that the burden of proof had been weakened, as the prosecution was still required to prove its case beyond a reasonable doubt. The court affirmed in the strongest terms that adverse inferences under s. 35 are the norm. Once the jury are satisfied that there is a prima facie case against the accused, only in exceptional cases would an adverse inference from silence not be made:

> We accept that, apart from the mandatory exceptions in s. 35(1),[60] it will be open to a court to decline to draw adverse inferences from silence at trial and for the judge to direct or advise the jury against drawing such inference if the circumstances of the case justify such a course. But in our view there would need to be either some evidential basis for doing so or some exceptional factors in the case making that a fair course to take. (Lord Taylor at 944)

Noteworthy is the Court's view that the trial court judge, in instructing the jury in any case, has the widest possible discretion not only to decide whether inferences may be drawn, but also particulars about their nature and degree of adversity.[61] This aspect of the Court's judgment, argue legal officers at JUSTICE,[62] introduces an inconsistency: in accepting the specimen direction, the Court appears to be endorsing a practice that the trial judge has only to direct the jury in relatively broad terms as to the inference to be drawn from silence; in contrast, it also suggests that the trial judge should be advising the jury in terms as to the 'nature, extent and degree' of inferences.[63] Thus the question as to the kind of directions given to juries by trial judges is left open.[64]

It is also of interest that Lord Taylor had already, nineteen months prior to the judgment of the Appeal Court, signalled his views (attributed also to 'most serving judges') regarding the drawing of inferences from an accused's silence in various circumstances. In January 1994, he stated:

> When a prima facie case has been established by the Crown, and the defendant [at trial] fails to testify, I see nothing unfair in the jury

being told it is open to them to draw a proper inference from the absence of any answer by the defendant ... The burden of proof remains on the prosecution to prove its case, but if they establish a case to go to the jury, that means that a reasonable jury, properly directed, could convict unless there is an answer.[65]

The reasonable drawing of a proper inference also applies where a defendant relies at trial on a fact that she has failed to mention under police questioning and which she could reasonably have mentioned at that stage; or when arrested, she fails to account for the possession of any object or substance or any mark upon her or her clothes giving rise to a reasonable belief that it is attributable to her involvement in a specified offence; or when she is silent when arrested at a place and time reasonably suggesting that she is there because she has committed an offence under investigation. As is clear from the foregoing, almost all of the reasoning of the Court in its judgment of October 1995 was laid out by the Lord Chief Justice not just before he rendered judgment on the subject on behalf of the Court of Appeal in October 1995, but prior even to the final passage of the CJPOA 1994.

The judiciary has interpreted the silence provisions in a way which favours the prosecution, rather than the accused, with two limited exceptions. Firstly, the characteristics of the accused may mean that silence at the police station was reasonable in the circumstances and so, no adverse inferences will be drawn. But, in line with decisions as to the admissibility of evidence,[66] defendants considered to be 'deserving' (notably vulnerable suspects) are the principal benefactors of this approach. Those, such as the heroin addicts in *Condron and Condron*, clearly are not. Secondly, the testimony of the defendant's lawyer may provide evidence of the circumstances in which custodial silence was exercised or rebut an argument of recent fabrication and thereby avoid adverse inferences at court. But this scrutiny of what should be confidential advice, is a high price to pay. In relation to non-testimony at court, the leading judgment in *Cowan* makes clear that the drawing of inferences will be the norm. The discretion to be exercised in these cases is wide, with an appeal to 'common sense'. The Judicial Studies Board specimen direction, for example (approved in *Cowan*), talks of 'the only sensible explanation' for the defendant's decision not to testify. In *Daniel*, too, the court stated that the jury could draw adverse inferences if the accused's refusal to answer questions could only sensibly be attributed to his unwillingness to be subjected to further questions. This reflects the Northern Irish approach, where 'proper' inferences have been 'dictated not by common law but by the circumstances of the particular case applying ordinary common sense'.[67] This confers a wide discretion and, it is argued, takes insufficient account of the presumption of innocence and procedural safeguards (Jackson, 1994a).

Inferences after arrest

Finally, note should be made of s. 36 of the Act, which requires the accused to account for objects, substances or marks which may suggest participation in the commission of an offence; and s. 37, which requires a person to explain her presence at a place, if it may be attributable to her participation in the commission of an offence. In many ways, although only taking effect after arrest, these sections are more draconian. In relation to silence when questioned, under s. 34 the inference can only be drawn if the accused mentions something in her defence at court which she could have, and presumably should have, mentioned at the police station, but failed to do so. But with ss. 36 and 37, the inference can be drawn regardless of whether the accused gives evidence: thus, whatever may be said in the witness box, an adverse inference may already have been drawn during the prosecution stage of the case. That means that the inference can become part of the prosecution case and part of the prima facie evidence.

The Human Rights Act 1998

The HRA is expected to come into force in the year 2000 and it is likely to have an impact upon criminal law and procedure. It requires courts to take into account any relevant judgment of the European Court of Human Rights (s. 2(1)) and to read and give effect to primary legislation in a way which is compatible with the European Convention on Human Rights (s. 3(1)). A number of cases relating to silence have been dealt with by the European Court and the HRA will enable the courts to give full effect to those decisions. Article 6 of the ECHR declares a right to a fair trial and in the case of *Murray v. UK* [68] the Court stated that 'the right to remain silent under police questioning and the privilege against self-incrimination are generally recognised international standards which lie at the heart of the notion of fair procedure under Article 6' (p. 60). In *Murray*, the Court found that drawing inferences from the accused's failure to testify and to account for his presence at the scene did not breach Article 6. However, this does not mean that the provisions of the CJPOA are in all cases in compliance with the Convention. The Court attached much importance to the strength of the evidence against Murray (inferences may not be justified in a weaker case) and the fact that the case was tried by a single judge who was required to give a reasoned decision which was capable of review (p. 62). The inferences drawn by jurors and magistrates are not set out in a written reasoned decision and so are less easily reviewed. In addition, the Court emphasized that a prima facie case must be made out before inferences can be drawn, which casts doubt upon the provisions of ss. 34, 36 and 37 under which inferences are allowed to contribute to the establishment of a case to answer. Pattenden (1998) also questions the use made of multiple inferences – where pre-trial silence may be used in making out a case to answer and then again at trial, as well as inferences from failure to testify and tender a defence statement, as the Court 'disapproved of a conviction based "solely or mainly on the accused's silence or on refusal to answer questions or to give evidence,"' (p. 163, citing *Murray*, p. 60). In *Saunders v. UK*[69] the Court went further and found that compelling a person to answer questions was an infringement of Article 6. It may be that such evidence could now be excluded under s. 78 PACE. Ashworth (1998: 107) comments that as the decision is limited to oral statements, it is unlikely that compulsory powers to take intimate samples can be challenged.

Summary

The reform of the right to silence has far-reaching implications both before and at trial. Suspects must be under caution before any inference will be drawn, but it is not a requirement that questioning take place at the police station, where legal advice and other attendant safeguards will be available. The suspect's silence may be held against her without her properly understanding the implications of her decision whether or not to answer police questions. Adverse inferences may also be drawn from the accused's silence in court. As well as positive evidence such as admissions or fingerprints, the accused's failure to cooperate fully in the police enquiry and the trial process may now be used against her – which has the effect of lessening the burden of proof which rests upon the prosecution.

We argue that the reasons advanced for this reform are ill-founded and flatly contradicted by the research – including much of that carried out for the Royal Commission. Opponents of the right argued that only the guilty would profit from remaining silent. There are, of course, many legitimate reasons why a person may refuse to answer questions and this may in fact be the safest strategy in more cases than the few in which it is exercised, given the overbearing tactics employed by many police. Second, is the myth of the 'ambush' defence, i.e. the defence argument 'sprung' on the prosecution at trial. McConville *et al.* (1994) argue that the reverse is true. Most defence lawyers lack any adversarial ideology and are predisposed towards guilty pleas. Leng (1993) examined a large sample of cases and found the instance of ambush defences to be extremely rare. Third, it was argued that the threat of adverse inferences would induce greater numbers of suspects to speak, thus assisting the police investigation. In fact, only a small percentage of suspects ever exercised their right to silence and many of them made subsequent admissions or pleaded guilty. More people may indeed be induced to speak, but this carries with it the greater risk of pressured and unreliable confessions. Finally, it is argued that suspects are protected adequately by the numerous safeguards under PACE and the Codes of Practice. This is disputed by much of the research carried out post-PACE – the poor (though now improving) standard of defence available and the interrogation techniques employed by police officers being of particular concern.

Reform of the right to silence formed a keystone of the Conservative government's law and order reforms as well as representing a major victory for the police who have long campaigned for the change. Research evidence and the considered opinion of the RCCJ were ignored. More fundamental than the credibility or otherwise of the abolitionist arguments are the principles of the presumption of innocence and the right against self-incrimination. These are trampled on by a requirement to provide an account before the full extent of the accusation has been set out. The passing of the Human Rights Act 1998 may curb some of the excesses of this legislation by requiring a more restrictive interpretation of the CJPOA provisions.

The threat of drawing an adverse inference from silence when questioned by the police can only lead to more, not fewer miscarriages of justice, since it places all suspects (including those identified as the most vulnerable) under greatly increased pressure to respond to police questions, both before and during the formal interrogation process. A wealth of research has demonstrated the dangers of relying upon confession evidence, yet this reform does nothing to shift investigative attention away from admissions: the police interrogation of suspects has become more, not less significant, as what the suspect *does not* say becomes as important as what she *does* say.

The reform has increased both the centrality of interrogation evidence to the prosecution case and the pressures upon suspects (including those recognised as especially vulnerable) to speak – and so to provide the expected answer. This can only increase the risk of false confessions. The suspect at the police station is now expected to provide a specific account of her defence, in anticipation of what might be presented many months later at trial (after the benefit of legal advice as to what might constitute a defence and other case preparation) on the basis of only the bare bones of the prosecution case, or risk adverse inferences. This amounts to a huge and unrealistic pressure upon suspects, given the stressful context of police interrogation. Case-law suggests that the drawing of inferences will be the norm – the pressures upon the detained suspect and the absence of legal advice do not make silence reasonable.

6
Prosecution, Bail and Trial Venue

Introduction

In this chapter we examine the pre-trial decisions concerning prosecution, bail and trial venue. Whilst the police retain the power to charge a suspect, this decision is reviewed by the prosecutor, who bears ultimate responsibility for the decision to prosecute. The legal scrutiny of the police case is an essential safeguard, designed to ensure that weak cases are not proceeded with, thus protecting defendants (such as those who have been the victims of miscarriages of justice) against whom there is insufficient evidence. However, central to our understanding of the role of the CPS in the prosecution process (including decisions as to the disclosure of material) is the police–prosecutor relationship.

The decision to prosecute: the police and the CPS

As the Code for Crown Prosecutors notes, the decision to prosecute an individual is a step with serious implications for all persons involved, not only the defendant but also the victim and any witnesses. However, during the early decades of the nineteenth century there was no public prosecutor and criminal cases could be initiated by anyone. Generally, private citizens who were victims of crimes would lay their complaints, or employ lawyers to do so, against alleged perpetrators before local magistrates, who would decide whether a prosecution was warranted.[1] However, sometime after the establishment of the police service in 1829, officers began to initiate criminal proceedings on behalf of victims. Gradually the magistrates conceded prosecution decisions to the police, and most prosecutions were conducted in their courts by police officers. Eventually the police began to employ solicitors, usually from the same local firms, for their more difficult cases in the magistrates' courts. The vast majority of cases continued to be handled in this way throughout the nineteenth and twentieth centuries.[2]

As a result, the police have a long history of having served as both investigators and prosecutors and they undoubtedly came to view the two sets of activity as steps in a single process. However, this practice was increasingly viewed by critics as inappropriate, lacking as it did the benefit of an independent authority to review the evidence and determine the advisability of proceeding with a prosecution.[3] Although many police forces gradually set up their own in-house departments of prosecuting solicitors and others employed local firms of solicitors to act on their behalf, neither of these arrangements provided the kind of independent review of police decisions to prosecute that might satisfy critics. Police decisions to prosecute were unlikely to be reversed by the solicitors of in-house departments, and local firms might well be reluctant to advise against police decisions to prosecute – even where cases seemed likely to end in acquittal – for fear of losing the valuable business provided by the police.

The Royal Commission on Criminal Procedure (1981) made three central arguments against this dual role of the police. Firstly, in principle, investigation and prosecution should be separate processes. It was wrong for the police who investigated a case to also make the decision to prosecute (para. 6.23). Their central role in the former unduly prejudiced their objectivity in making the decision to prosecute. Secondly, different police forces across the country were applying different guidelines in deciding such matters as whether to caution or prosecute (para. 6.40). And thirdly, police forces, sometimes even against the advice of lawyers, were proceeding with too many weak cases (para. 4.9). This was caused by inadequate case preparation and resulted in a high percentage of judge-ordered and judge-directed acquittals.[4] In 1978, for example, these accounted for 43 per cent of all Crown Court acquittals.[5] In the case of directed acquittals, research done for the Philips Commission by McConville and Baldwin (1981) suggested that about one-fifth of them ought to have been foreseen inasmuch as a proper review of the evidence would have revealed doubt as to whether there was sufficient evidence to justify the initial decision to prosecute; and given an insufficiency of evidence they could have been discontinued.

In seeking to reduce the likelihood of these deficiencies in the system, the Philips Commission recommended the establishment of a Crown Prosecution Service (CPS) independent of the police, which would be charged with the responsibility of taking over all prosecutions initiated by the police, and of deciding whether to proceed with them. This was accomplished with the passage of the Prosecution of Offences Act 1985, which created a national CPS headed by a politically independent Director of Public Prosecutions. The primary task of the CPS is to assess the quality of the cases initiated by the police in order to determine whether or not a prosecution is merited, both on the evidence and in the public interest. Unlike police officers, the CPS are trained lawyers whose job is to scrutinize the evidence of the prosecution case, unaffected by the concerns of those closely involved in the investigation. In this way, it was hoped that they would fulfil a more dispassionate 'Ministry of Justice' role.

The Code for Crown Prosecutors sets out a two-stage test in the decision to prosecute: there must be a realistic prospect of conviction and it must be in the public interest to prosecute. The limited role which committals now play in assessing the strength of the prosecution case[6] has further increased the importance of the CPS in ensuring that weak cases do not proceed to the Crown Court. If such cases are not dropped at an early stage, it is an injustice to the defendant who suffers the stigma and anxiety of being criminally accused, and to the victims and witnesses who suffer the inconvenience and disappointment of a failed prosecution. Resources are also wasted in bringing and defending a charge unnecessarily.

However, the CPS continues to be criticized for the very weaknesses which it was set up to remedy: a lack of objectivity and legal scrutiny in the decision to prosecute; inconsistency in the decision to prosecute and in the choice of offence; and an inability or disinclination to weed out even obviously weak cases at an early stage in the process. At the heart of this decision-making process is the relationship between the police and the CPS, which remains both problematic and ill-defined. The police were historically responsible for the investigation and prosecution of crime in England and Wales, and while the CPS has a sphere of responsibility which is independent, its power remains subordinate to that of the police.[7] The CPS cannot initiate prosecutions, rather, it reacts to the initiatives of police officers; and while it is dependent upon the police for the evidence needed to do its job (including its quality, sufficiency and reliability),[8] it can neither supervise the investigations of police nor direct them to undertake further investigations.[9] The continuing concern about the performance of the CPS is reflected in the terms of reference of the recent review of the CPS, chaired by Sir Iain Glidewell (Home Office, 1998c). The review was specifically asked to examine the role of the CPS in relation to the falling number of convictions for recorded crime and the downgrading of offences, as well as the relationship between the CPS and the police.

The rate of conviction is one measure of the success of the CPS. High numbers of acquittals may suggest that too many weak cases are being prosecuted. There are, of course, many factors which might affect the success of a case at trial – such as the quality of the witnesses, the reliability of statements compiled by the police and relied upon by the CPS, and the decisions of prosecuting counsel. There has been a steady decline in the number of convictions for indictable offences – from 385,000 in 1986 to 302,000 in 1995 and Glidewell examined the contribution of the CPS to this phenomenon. However, this concern may be overstated. Ashworth (1998: 189) argues that the heavy use made of cautioning since the 1980s is a more influential factor. The decline is far less significant if the combined figure of persons convicted or cautioned for indictable offences is considered – falling from 533,000 in 1986 to 504,600 in 1995.

Despite concern at the falling conviction rate (which is suggestive of too many weak cases being sent to trial), implicit in the terms of reference are criticisms that too many cases are being either downgraded by the CPS, or discontinued altogether. Yet, these are the very mechanisms required to weed out weak cases: without them greater numbers of weak cases would proceed. Glidewell's conclusions in relation to downgrading are curious. The report claims to find no evidence of inappropriate downgrading, but, nevertheless, goes on to say that it suspects that inappropriate downgrading does occur. Blame seems to be directed at the CPS, despite the fact that it is the police who make the initial decision to charge. The CPS react to this initiative by accepting, amending or rejecting the charge preferred, and so the disposal of cases by the CPS is conditioned upon the quality of cases sent to it by the police and the appropriateness of the initial charge preferred.[10]

In some instances, there is insufficient evidence to bring even a lesser charge against the accused and the matter is discontinued. Discontinuance rates have risen from 7.7 per cent in 1987 (Crisp and Moxon, 1994: 2) to 12 per cent[11] in 1997–8, but rates vary greatly between different types of offence – the highest being for offences against the person and criminal damage and the lowest being for motoring offences. As with downgrading, these figures may be viewed positively, as an indication that the CPS is actively screening cases and removing the weakest from the system. Others (such as Rose, 1996) have been critical that too many cases are dropped on 'efficiency' grounds: Crisp and Moxon (1994), for example, found that the nominal penalty likely on conviction was the second most common reason for discontinuing a case. Glidewell, too, expresses concern at these figures, but again fails to address the wider context of the quality of cases prepared by the police.

One way of reducing the number of cases discontinued or charges downgraded is through earlier police consultation with the CPS. Advice can be given about the appropriate charge to bring or additional investigations which should be made. The RCCJ favoured this approach and recommended that the police make greater use of the CPS at the investigative stage, but this occurs in only a minority of cases. The CPS report that their advice was sought in only 5 per cent of cases between 1993 and 1995[12] and a Home Office study found that rates of advice varied regionally between one per cent and 14 per cent.[13] Both Glidewell and the RCCJ have noted the tensions that exist between the police and the CPS, and the former's reluctance to involve the CPS before charge. Police representatives told the Commission, for example, that it was rare for the police to refuse (what they considered to be) reasonable requests by the CPS for further investigation; in contrast, the CPS reported that in some force areas it was not uncommon for their requests to be ignored or refused (RCCJ, 1993: 74). Having conceded their power to prosecute, the police are unwilling to lose any ground on the matter of investigation.[14] Yet, given that insufficient evidence from investigators accounts for nearly half of all cases discontinued, it would seem that some early input from the CPS is required in many more instances than under current practice.[15]

In 1996, a pilot scheme was initiated at 12 sites whereby Crown prosecutors were available at the police station to provide early face-to-face advice to officers. Unsurprisingly, officers did not embrace the opportunity to consult with and be advised by the CPS. Reviewing this initiative, Baldwin and Hunt (1998) are pessimistic about its success. They found that with the limited evidence available at this early stage, prosecutors (like the police) were operating on intuition and 'hunches' rather than making a clear legal review of the case. Furthermore, such schemes 'cater only for those officers perceptive enough to recognise a legal problem when they see one. This means that those officers in greatest need of advice are the ones least likely to benefit from what is on offer' (p. 536).

If cases are to be discontinued, it is imperative that this be done as soon as possible to prevent anxiety, inconvenience and unnecessary cost. The Crown Court study (Zander and Henderson, 1993) reported that the prosecution case was weak in about a fifth of Crown Court contested cases,[16] and that over 80 per cent of these ended in acquittal. A study by Moxon and Crisp found that only 12 per cent of cases were discontinued on or before the first hearing.[17] The most recent figures, although an improvement, show that only 27 per cent are now terminated before the second hearing.[18] The reduction of both cost and delay in the criminal process has become a government priority and it is likely that the CPS will be encouraged to improve further in this respect.

The number of non-jury acquittals was of especial concern prior to the establishment of the CPS, demonstrating the high numbers of evidentially weak cases which were being prosecuted. The situation was expected to improve with the independent scrutiny of cases by the CPS, but it has declined to the point where more defendants are now acquitted in the Crown Court on the order or direction of the judge, than on the decision of the jury. Prior to the establishment of the CPS, judge-ordered and judge-directed acquittals accounted for between 43 per cent (1978) and 48 per cent (1985) of all Crown Court acquittals, and they now stand at 54 per cent,[19] having peaked at 58 per cent in 1990. The increase has been in the category of judge-ordered acquittals, which has risen from 26 per cent to 38 per cent of all non-jury acquittals. The number of cases dismissed by the judge in this way is one measure of weak cases which are not filtered out of the system, although there are other, unforseeable reasons which may result in cases being dropped at court – the non-appearance of a key witness, for example, or witnesses whose evidence at court proves unreliable. According to Block *et al.* (1993), the dismissal of cases at court tends to be initiated by the CPS as a result of a weakness in their case seen as likely to preclude conviction, and represents cases which have been identified between committal and trial. However, despite its weakness having been recognised, the case must go to court: the CPS cannot formally discontinue it once it has been committed for trial, but must ask the judge to order an acquittal before the trial begins.

The question remains, however, as to why the CPS fail to discover the case's weakness before allowing it to go as far as committal. A Crown Court study of 100 cases of non-jury acquittals carried out for the Royal Commission found that in 55 per cent of them evidential deficiencies were sufficient to make acquittal either clearly foreseeable (27 per cent) or possibly foreseeable (28 per cent). Moreover, it also found that in 15 per cent of the cases the evidential weakness was apparent prior to committal, and that unless the evidence deficiency was rectified they should have been discontinued (Block *et al.*, 1993: 12).[20] More recent research by Baldwin (1997) found that 80 per cent of non-jury acquittals were foreseeable. Weaknesses were generally known to the CPS before trial and were often recorded on the file itself. Yet, prosecutors failed to discontinue cases despite the lack of evidence, in the hope that the accused may plead guilty in any event. The lack of defence scrutiny of the prosecution case suggests that this hope is a reality in many instances (McConville *et al.*, 1994). In addition, Baldwin found that many prosecutors lacked confidence and so tended simply to endorse the initial police decision. This was especially so in serious cases (where, arguably, the potential for injustice and resource wasting is greatest) where they preferred to leave the decision to the jury. The organizational pressures made case review a 'hurried, even perfunctory, exercise' and shortage of time militated towards a decision to 'play safe and allow the case to continue to the next stage' (1997: 554). The picture which emerges is not one of the careful evidential scrutiny of cases, but of CPS lawyers wading through large numbers of poorly organized files, making hurried and inconsistent decisions which fail to test out the initial police view.

One of the principal reasons for the establishment of an independent prosecution service was to provide a system of independent review of the police case before a prosecution is brought. The police decision to charge is taken by the custody officer, who is independent of the case. However, as we saw in Chapter 3, she is unlikely to make a decision in conflict with that of the investigating officers, on whose information she depends. Although the CPS is independent of the police in the sense that prosecutors are no longer in its employ, in making the decision whether or not to prosecute they remain dependent upon the information assembled by officers. Research by McConville *et al.* (1991) found that prosecutors tended to endorse the initial police view, constrained by the police-generated information on which they based their decisions. This resulted in a prosecution process dominated by the police, where evidence selectively assembled by officers was not probed for weaknesses. The lack of adversarial defence work and the guilty plea orientation of most criminal defence lawyers compounds this problem, as they too are unlikely to challenge the basis of the prosecution case (McConville *et al.*, 1994).

It seems that very little has changed. Baldwin's research demonstrates a continuing CPS dependence upon and acceptance of police assembled evidence, as well as a shared value system between CPS and officers. Prosecutors seek to maximize the number of prosecutions, continuing even with weak cases in the hope that the defendant will plead guilty. Ironically, the defence often fail to spot, or they ignore, these weaknesses and shepherd defendants towards a guilty plea. And as the Glidewell terms of reference demonstrate, the success of the CPS is measured not by the number of weak cases actively screened out of the process (this is regarded as too high), but by the number of convictions (regarded as too low). Given what we know of the operation of police powers of stop, search, arrest and interrogation, and the non-adversarial nature of much defence lawyering, the failure of the CPS to go beyond the police case represents a greater danger than the waste of resources through judge-instigated acquittals. The most obviously weak cases may be dismissed by the judge, but in other instances, the CPS are content that defendants are convicted despite weak and unreliable evidence. Prosecutions brought after an apparently independent legal review of the evidence remain, essentially, police-constructed cases.

Prosecution practice has not altered dramatically, because the structural relationship between police and prosecutors remains the same. In an adversarial system, the goal of the CPS is to assist the police in achieving a maximum conviction rate, rather than the more neutrally defined 'Ministry of Justice' role (Sanders, 1992). But prosecutors, like others in the process, will respond to the practices of other criminal justice actors. If the courts admit improperly obtained evidence at trial, it is unlikely that the CPS will discontinue cases because of it. And if the defence fail to challenge deficiencies in the prosecution case, there is little incentive to discontinue a case (even though weak) which may well result in a conviction. Two particular factors point to the need for a different police–CPS working relationship: the majority of cases discontinued are because of insufficient evidence collected in the police investigation; and more weak cases are proceeding to the Crown Court, as evidenced by the levels of judge-ordered and judge-directed acquittals.

The setting up of Criminal Justice Units (CJUs) for 'fast track' cases (summary offences where a guilty plea is anticipated) is recommended by Glidewell as having a number of advantages, and is worthy of closer examination. It is hoped that it will bridge the gulf between the police and CPS and eliminate the 'blame culture' that exists between the two. The CPS and police can work together in assembling evidence and requesting further investigation if required. It will reduce delay by streamlining the procedure of case management, having input from both police and prosecution and dealing with matters from preparation through to advocacy. Costs can be minimized through increased use of non-qualified caseworkers, notably in presenting cases in the magistrates' court, as provided for in s. 53 of the CDA 1998. Finally, the initiative will contribute to the proposed shift in emphasis towards greater involvement of the CPS in Crown Court work. Whilst these aspirations are commendable, their realization comes at a cost. The move towards a more Crown Court-centred service risks downgrading and routinizing summary cases, which account for the bulk of cases tried. Much will depend on the nature of what comes to be defined as 'fast track', but at a time when the CPS is being criticized for failing to challenge weak police cases, there is a danger in delegating work to non-legally qualified staff, based in or near a police station, who may themselves then become institutionalized within police culture.[21]

Although the CPS needs to be more closely involved in the investigation and collection of evidence, paradoxically, greater distance between the two is needed to enable the CPS to develop and sustain an approach which does not reflect policing objectives. The historical and structural dependence of the CPS upon the police has prevented the evolution of a legal culture which would allow prosecutors to work closely with officers, without being dominated by them. Moves such as placing prosecutors in the police station, or the introduction of CJUs to assemble and manage case files for 'fast track' cases, represent a half-hearted attempt at creating closer working relationships. On the one hand, they do not go far enough, since consultation is not systematic (Baldwin 1998). On the other hand, an initiative such as the CJU risks both compromising the independence of the CPS by moving it into police territory and, ironically, moving the functions of investigation and prosecution closer together.

Liberty before trial – the granting of bail

The potential for injustice to defendants remanded in custody was made clear by Lord Donaldson of Lymington (the Master of the Rolls from 1982 to 1992). Reacting to proposed changes to restrict the granting of bail he called to attention the fact that '... until the alleged criminal has been tried, we do not know whether he is a criminal. If he is innocent, there can be no greater injustice than to have denied him bail.'[22] To deprive a person of her liberty, or the benefits that flow from it, requires strong justification (Ashworth, 1998: 208–9).

The principle that innocent persons should not be imprisoned is implicitly acknowledged in s. 4 of the Bail Act 1976, which, in the absence of important public interest considerations to the contrary,[23] sets out an individual's presumed right to bail. However, a number of exceptions to this have been introduced in CJPOA 1994. The presumption in favour of granting bail does not apply to defendants charged with an indictable offence committed whilst already on bail (s. 26); and s. 25 singles out a category of defendants to whom the right to bail does not apply at any stage of the criminal process. These include persons charged with murder, attempted murder, manslaughter, rape or attempted rape, if the accused has previously been convicted in the UK of one of these offences. The Human Rights Act 1998, which requires judges to read and give effect to UK legislation in a way which is compatible with the ECHR, may make the operation of s. 25 problematic. Although it is unlikely that bail would be granted in any event in many of these most serious cases, Article 5 of the Convention requires the court to actively consider whether there are 'relevant and sufficient' reasons to justify continued detention in each case.[24] Furthermore, the Law Society argue that recent changes in committal procedure have reduced the defendant's opportunities to apply for bail. A defendant who has been refused bail by the magistrates is usually allowed a second application without having to show a change in circumstances. However, the new procedure under s. 51 CDA 1998 denies defendants this second opportunity, as the case is sent directly to the Crown Court after the preliminary hearing before the magistrates, where bail and legal aid are decided.

The granting of bail is guided by three principles: (i) that unconvicted persons charged with criminal offences must be presumed to be innocent until proven otherwise, and should suffer no greater loss of liberty than is necessary to secure the course of justice; (ii) that the public has the right to be protected against persons believed, with good reason, to constitute a threat to persons and property; and (iii) that justice delayed is justice denied. The granting of bail is subject to wide local variations,[25] but there is a strong tendency for the court to confirm the decision of the police, seemingly with the agreement of the CPS and defence, who contested only 9 per cent of remand hearings (Hucklesby, 1997b).

Apart from the injustice of being deprived of liberty without any criminal charge having been proven, other harmful consequences flow from a remand in custody. Firstly, the accused is deprived of a normal life, relations with family and friends are strained, and she may suffer the loss of a job and its income; secondly, incarceration hampers the accused's ability to prepare a defence against the charges made; and thirdly, even though untried, the condition of the accused's incarceration is worse than that of those who have been imprisoned following conviction.[26] In 1990 the Council of Europe Committee for the Prevention of Torture pronounced that the conditions in English custodial institutions, in which many remand prisoners were being held, were 'inhuman and degrading'.[27]

Yet a growing proportion of those held in custodial institutions are on remand awaiting trial – currently, some 20 per cent.[28] Of these, one-quarter are subsequently acquitted or the case against them is discontinued, and around one-quarter of males and nearly half of all females remanded in custody receive a non-custodial sentence. Bail is about ensuring the attendance of the defendant and the prevention of further offences, whether or not a custodial sentence is likely, and so these figures are not necessarily indicative of injustice. However, the figures are high and, in particular, it is of concern that one-quarter of those incarcerated before trial are either acquitted or not proceeded against. This is an unacceptable price to pay for what is, in many instances, the tardy discontinuance of weak cases.

The refusal of bail impinges upon the liberty of the unconvicted individual and although the police were able to release defendants on unconditional bail following charge, an application to attach conditions to bail or for a remand in custody had to be made before the magistrates. Under s. 27 CJPOA, the police are now empowered to impose conditions on bail granted at the police station after charge. The RCCJ proposed this change as an efficiency measure, enabling more defendants to be released directly from police custody, and so avoiding the necessity of bringing defendants to court simply to attach conditions to bail.[29] This represents an important shift of judicial power into the hands of the police, but it has failed to result in the anticipated efficiency savings. Further paperwork is generated for the custody officer, staffing levels for the transport of prisoners are unaffected and court time is not saved when courts feel it necessary (which many do) to subject the decisions of the police to rigorous scrutiny (Raine and Willson, 1997).[30]

There is also evidence that the police use their power to bail accused persons in targetted and discriminatory ways. Phillips and Brown (1998), for example, found that suspects from ethnic minorities are consistently refused bail more often than white suspects, irrespective of the charge or the individual's previous convictions. The danger in this new power is that, in certain circumstances, the police may choose to use (or abuse) it as a means of further controlling or regulating the behaviour of members of suspect groups.[31] Indeed, preliminary research (Raine and Willson, 1997) shows that the new power has not been directed (as intended) simply at those who would otherwise have been held overnight (detention rates fell by 2.5 per cent in 1994–5) but more significantly, to impose conditions on those who would have been bailed unconditionally (unconditional bail fell by nearly 10 per cent). Although a person may only be remanded in custody by the decision of the court, this new power allows the police a significant discretion to restrict the rights and liberty of citizens and to effect further surveillance.

Trial venue – restricting the defendant's right to jury trial

Whilst indictable offences must be tried by the Crown Court, either-way offences may be tried either by the magistrates or the Crown Court and the decision is made at a mode of trial hearing. Prior to the Criminal Procedure and Investigations Act 1996, determination of the mode of trial for either-way cases required that the court ask the accused where she wanted to be tried, and she had the right to decide to elect trial either by jury or by magistrates.[32] Twice as many either-way cases were sent to the Crown Court by the magistrates than through the election of the defendant,[33] and in 96 per cent of cases, the magistrates' decision was in line with the recommendation of the prosecution (Riley and Vennard, 1988). Whether resulting from committal or election, either-way offences being tried in the Crown Court continue to constitute about three-quarters of its total.[34]

During the 1980s the number of either-way cases committed to the Crown Court rose sharply,[35] resulting in an overall caseload which was viewed as burdensome for the Court and unnecessarily costly for the criminal justice system. Each contested case heard in Crown Court costs roughly £12,000 more than it would have done if tried by magistrates; furthermore, the Crown Court lacks sufficient court rooms and judges to handle the backlog of cases, and this has led to an overcrowding of the prisons that must house defendants in custody awaiting trial, to longer waits for those on remand, and to rising legal aid bills.[36]

Since the main criterion for determining where a case is to be heard is the classification of the offence concerned, efforts to deal with the Crown Court's overload have focused on restricting the types of cases that may be committed for jury trial. Thus in 1988, four either-way offences were reclassified as 'summary only';[37] and in 1990, 'national guidelines' were issued which suggest that magistrates adopt a presumption in favour of trying cases summarily rather than committing them to the Crown Court.[38] Reclassification of offences reduced the Crown Court's caseload by 6 per cent, but this was hardly sufficient to solve the problems noted above: hence, the matter was brought to the attention of the 1993 Royal Commission on Criminal Justice. Following the suggestion of the Director of Public Prosecutions, Barbara Mills, the Commission's Report proposed to further reduce the number of cases going to the Crown Court by eliminating the accused's automatic right to elect trial by jury (RCCJ, 1993: 85, 87–8). The scheme provided that where the prosecution and defence agreed on the venue for an either-way offence, it should be binding; but where they disagreed, the magistrates, after having heard the views of both prosecution and defence, would decide on the mode of trial.

This proposal was widely condemned and opposed by academics and criminal defence lawyers as a further attempt to eliminate a defendant's basic right to a trial by jury.[39] In the eyes of Helena Kennedy, QC, it was seen as an expression of 'contempt for ordinary people and a failure to recognize that the jury system is one of the ingredients of democracy. Juries do what judges should at times also be doing: calling the authorities, especially the police, to account' (1992: 10). Richard Ferguson, former chair of the Criminal Bar, noted that the proposal 'was opposed very vociferously by the Bar';[40] and even the Lord Chief Justice expressed his opposition, stating that the recommendation violated the perception shared by many that under existing law 'trial by jury is a fundamental right'.[41] Although the RCCJ's recommendation was implemented in an amended form, we will examine the reasoning behind the proposal as it has recently been put forward again in a Home Office consultation paper.[42] Reportedly, it has the support of the current Lord Chief Justice, although it has been sharply criticized by Lord Steyn as 'bad practice' whose purpose is 'to cut costs'.[43]

Most defendants elect Crown Court trial because they believe that the magistrates are on the side of the police, and that they stand a better chance of acquittal before a jury.[44] This view is held even more strongly by defence advisers, who, as 'repeat players' in the process, have wider experience of trials;[45] and it is also borne out by the statistics. The CPS record an acquittal rate of 25 per cent in the magistrates' court and 40 per cent in the Crown Court.[46] The Judicial Statistics put the latter figure even higher, at 60 per cent. Hedderman and Moxon (1992) found that although 27 per cent of defendants interviewed intended to plead not guilty from the outset, 83 per cent of these pleaded guilty to some or all offences by the day of trial. This study was limited to defendants who were ultimately convicted, and therefore excluded those who did not change their plea and were acquitted. The Commission, however, used these figures to dismiss the claim of defendants that they elect jury trial in the belief that they will stand a better chance of acquittal, on the grounds that most plead guilty in any event. Furthermore, whilst some defendants may enter a tactical plea of not guilty, the Commission's cynicism ignores the pressures which defendants are placed under by their own counsel, often on the day of trial itself,[47] to plead guilty (McConville *et al.*, 1994: ch. 10).

For the Commission, efficiency was the overriding objective. In 62 per cent of cases sent to the Crown Court, the sentence imposed was within the power of the magistrates and savings could be made if these were tried summarily.[48] However, there may be reasons other than sentencing which influence the decision of the magistrates to commit cases to the Crown Court. Apart from the local and idiosyncratic nature of benches, magistrates may feel, for example, that the gravity of the case merits trial before a judge and jury.[49]

The Commission's recommendation to eliminate the defendant's right to elect jury trial discounted the views and wishes of defendants in favour of a more 'rational division of either way cases'(p. 87). They did not consider it desirable that 'defendants should be able to choose their court of trial solely on the basis that they think that they will get a fairer hearing' (p. 88). The perception that justice has been done was not a relevant consideration for the Commission. The 35,000 cases where defendants may insist on jury trial contrary to the wishes of the magistrates would be eliminated at a stroke – avoiding the 'controversial' exercise of reclassifying offences.[50] This represented a naked and contemptuous denial of the defendant's right to choose where her case is heard, based upon pure assertion – that magistrates should be trusted to try defendants fairly, simply because they already deal with the great majority of criminal cases (p. 88).

The recommendation was all the more astounding given the absence of research commissioned into any aspect of summary justice, where, after all, 93 per cent of all criminal cases begin and end. The RCCJ did consider existing research, which demonstrated the very negative views of summary justice held by defendants and defence lawyers. Anecdotal support is offered in the following comment by a solicitor-advocate:

> Proceedings in the Crown Court tend to be conducted at a somewhat slower pace and tend to be more thorough than in the magistrates' courts. This is principally because you're more likely to get a good

result from a well-prepared presentation before a jury than you are before magistrates, who tend to become blasé. To say they are prosecution-minded is, I suppose, perhaps unfair to them, but it is close to the mark. (Interview, May 1995)

The relative rates of acquittal suggest that an increase in summary trials will result in an increase in conviction and with it, an increase in low visibility miscarriages of justice. To take one example only, the provision that prosecution disclosure is required in summary cases only where the offences charged are triable either way[51] suggests a considerable potential for the prosecution to withhold material from the defence which might strengthen their chances of acquittal.[52] Summary trials are less visible because of the sheer volume of cases processed by these courts, the lack of focus on their proceedings, the perception that less serious offences are tried in them, and the (generally) more lenient punishment meted out to those convicted. Also, the seriousness of the miscarriages in the magistrates' courts, as measured in terms of sentences, may not be as great as those that flow from wrongful conviction in Crown Court, but, as Ashworth (1993) has argued, the fact of conviction itself, and the loss of reputation that accompanies it, may be the most damaging event for the defendant, irrespective of the sentence (p. 833). Bridges and McConville (1994: 13) argue that the move to reduce jury trials serves another, unstated purpose: 'to minimise even further the number of criminal cases reaching the uncertain, fully adversarial stage of jury trial, where serious miscarriages of justice are deemed – and are seen – to occur'. The number of serious and more visible miscarriages is reduced by redefining cases as less serious and moving them to a venue where they will be sheltered from the public gaze.

The reform enacted in the CPIA 1996[53] takes a different form from the RCCJ's proposal, restricting the defendant's choice, but in a less draconian manner. Defendants who indicate that they will be pleading not guilty in either-way cases continue to have the right to elect jury trial, but those intending to plead guilty do not: they will be treated as though charged with a summary offence. The case will be heard by the magistrates but may be committed to the Crown Court for sentence. The result is that the accused may have the case against her tested by the jury, but may not elect the Crown Court as her preferred sentencing forum if an early guilty plea is indicated.[54]

There is nothing to prevent a defendant who intends to plead guilty from indicating a plea of not guilty when first asked, in the hope that the charges against her will be withdrawn or reduced and also giving her the opportunity to elect jury trial.[55] On the other hand, in pleading not guilty the accused will not benefit from the maximum sentence discount available for an early guilty plea. An alternative tactical reason for pleading not guilty is the hope that the disclosure of prosecution material may provide a viable line of defence.[56] In fact, under the CPIA's disclosure provisions, the only way for the defence to obtain unused material from the prosecution is for the accused to plead not guilty.

However, the reform has not brought about the anticipated savings in time and resources. The magistrates continue to commit some 53 per cent of either-way cases for Crown Court trial and whilst many more cases which would have been tried on indictment are now being heard by the magistrates, increasing numbers are also being committed to the Crown Court for sentence – the numbers have risen more than threefold since the new provisions came into force.[57] The new procedure has restricted the choice of defendants, but it has not transformed the sentencing practice of magistrates, who continue to ensure that the more serious cases are sentenced by the Crown Court. The Home Office consultation paper (1998a) published in Autumn 1998, however, advances the same arguments for restricting the defendant's right to jury trial as were made in 1993 by the RCCJ. It is perhaps ironic that the same party who so vociferously opposed the proposals when in opposition now advances them in government.

As Brownlee and Furniss (1997) conclude, the whole approach to pre-trial procedures reflects an essentially bureaucratized, rationalized approach to law enforcement which openly promotes cost-efficient crime control at the expense of due process, fairness and justice. In this framework, any consideration of the defendant is simply pushed out of sight in favour of reducing court caseloads and streamlining the process. The diminished role of committal proceedings (discussed in Chapter 3) eliminates another avenue of filtering out weak cases and further tilts the balance in the criminal justice process towards crime control and away from due process by emphasizing the version of events constructed by the police investigation (for instance, by precluding 'any evidence at all on behalf of the accused'), and shielding it from the scrutiny of the magistrates. And the reform potentially contributes to an immediate injustice by potentially exacerbating the loss of liberty of an accused who is held in custody awaiting trial which may or may not find her guilty of a criminal offence.

Summary

The influence of the police in constructing the prosecution case is felt throughout the pre-trial process. The large degree of autonomy enjoyed by officers during the initial investigation period ensures them a key role in shaping the information which is gathered and recorded and upon which those with subsequent responsibility for the prosecution case depend.

Although the decision to prosecute a case rests with the Crown Prosecution Service, its roots lie within the police. Until recently, the police, or solicitors acting on their behalf, prosecuted crimes in the criminal courts. The Philips Commission identified the problem of weak cases going ahead for trial and the Prosecution of Offences Act 1985 established a new national, independent prosecution service, the CPS. The specific problem of failing to weed out weak cases, however, has not been remedied by the appearance of the CPS, with the percentage of judge-ordered or judge-directed acquittals in the Crown Court remaining high.

There are a number of procedural and structural features which compromise the role of the CPS as an effective and independent decision-making body. In the first place, they are unable to discontinue proceedings after committal: only the judge can do this. In this way, a case will still be booked to go ahead for trial, despite known weaknesses in the prosecution case. Secondly, at a more general level, although the decision to prosecute rests with the CPS, this cannot be separated from their highly dependent relationship with the police. The CPS cannot initiate prosecutions; it can only respond to the initiatives of the police. If they consider that further investigations should be made, they can request this, but have no power to require it. They have no control over the information gathered by the police, nor the means by which it is acquired. Thus, given that they are unable to go beyond reconsidering the police-constructed case, it is unlikely that they will adopt a radically different view from that taken by the investigating officers. The CPS dependency upon the police for case-related information is significant in other pre-trial procedures, including recent reforms. For example, in the instance of secondary disclosure by the prosecution (see Chapter 7), it will be the CPS who decide what is relevant and appropriate to disclose – but this will be on the basis of lists and information provided by the police disclosure officer.

The CPS exists as an available resource for the police, but their advice is sought only in a small minority of cases. As yet, operational dependency is only in one direction. Given that nearly half of cases discontinued are because of insufficient evidence provided by the investigators, it would seem that further consultation would be beneficial. The RCCJ, however, roundly rejected proposals for the CPS to enjoy supervisory powers over the police, or to make consultation mandatory. They describe the French and German systems, where the prosecutor does enjoy such power, as failing to work in practice[58] and giving rise to tensions between police and prosecutors. Yet some degree of tension in such a relationship is inevitable and even desirable.

There are a number of other pre-trial procedures which impact upon likely miscarriages of justice. The RCCJ proposal to limit the defendant's right to elect jury trial was made without commissioning further research into magistrates' court justice and ignoring the findings of existing studies which suggest that defendants are much more likely to be convicted by magistrates than by a jury. This is not simply a consequence of the nature of cases tried summarily, but a host of other factors which the Commission chose to ignore. The new provisions in the CPIA 1996 do not mirror the RCCJ proposals, but they do set out to achieve the same objective of diverting cases from the Crown Court. Defendants contesting either-way charges against them may elect jury trial, but those indicating a plea of guilty have no choice as to the sentence venue – they will be convicted and sentenced by the magistrates.[59]

Denial of the defendant's right to bail represents a serious infringement of her liberty, as she remains innocent until proven guilty. Yet, one-quarter of defendants incarcerated before trial are acquitted or have the case against them discontinued, and a further quarter of males and nearly half of females receive only a non-custodial sentence. Despite a growing remand prison population, the accused's right to bail has been withdrawn in certain cases and the police have been empowered to attach conditions to those bailed after charge. This new power has been used by the police against those who would have received unconditional bail, rather than as a means of avoiding court hearings simply to attach bail conditions.

A further area of pre-trial reform is the vexing question of committal procedure (discussed in Chapter 3). Committals were to be abolished under the CJPOA 1994, but a modified form of the existing procedure was introduced under the CPIA 1996, before the earlier reform came into effect. The new procedure does nothing to remedy the essentially passive role of magistrates and the heavy reliance placed upon the defence to challenge weaknesses in the prosecution case. The prosecution is not encouraged to scrutinize cases more carefully and suffers no disadvantage from not assessing properly the sufficiency of evidence against the accused – especially since the poor quality of defence work results in guilty pleas even where the prosecution case is weak.

7
Disclosure and Sentence Discounts

Introduction

In this chapter, we examine a number of pre-trial procedures which have been introduced to promote the efficient handling of cases tried in the Crown Court. They are designed to shift the resolution of issues away from the trial to the pre-trial stage, where they can be dealt with more efficiently and at less expense. The procedures seek to settle issues of plea, evidence admissibility, law, and the disclosure of information from both the prosecution and the defence. They represent a move away from the due process protections of the public courtroom, towards a process which maximizes the opportunities for the production of knowledge helpful to the prosecution. The absence of full disclosure of the prosecution evidence has led to a number of miscarriages of justice. Yet the new provisions place an onus upon the defence to disclose the outline of their case, in order that they may have access to prosecution material which is relevant to the defence. Together with the curtailment of the accused's right to silence at the police station and in court (discussed in Chapter 5), this represents a significant attack upon the principle that it is for the prosecution to prove its case against the accused.

Pre-trial hearings

The pre-trial review (PTR) is an informal meeting of the defence and prosecution lawyers, presided over by a court clerk or judge, which discusses matters likely to arise at trial. These include questions of plea, the simplification of factual and evidential matters (such as admissibility), and the resolution of issues of law. Introduced at some Crown

Courts, various forms of PTR had long been in use as a means of streamlining trials or (where possible) of settling cases before trial. The Royal Commission (1993: 101–8) reviewed the operation of PTRs, and concluded that their use in Crown Court cases would result in shorter, fairer and more efficient trials and enable juries to reach their verdicts with the clearest appreciation of the facts. They proposed formalizing PTRs in the more complex cases (either the prosecution or defence could demand a PTR as of right or the court could order one), and recommended that the decisions made at them would bind the trial judge. They claimed that the Bar Council, the Criminal Bar Association, the Law Society, the CPS and the police service all agreed that PTRs could improve the administration of justice. The proposal was opposed by Professor Zander (RCCJ, 1993: 223–33). While accepting that there are serious defects in the preparation of defence cases, he argued that implementation of PTRs would seriously complicate the pre-trial stage, greatly increase costs and delays, and would not work in the way intended. The Legal Action Group (1994) concurred; in their view, PTRs were essentially plea-bargaining mechanisms, and they opposed them in any form. As with many other Commission proposals (such as those concerning defence disclosure), LAG believed that in practice PTRs would commit the accused to cooperatively participate in her own prosecution, thus making PTRs just one more aspect of a general legal culture of cooperation that is increasingly displacing the demands of an adversarial system.

Evidence in support of LAG's fear is found in a study of PTRs in two busy city-centre magistrates' courts (Brownlee *et al.*, 1994). While the data show that PTRs can produce efficiency gains for the courts as a result of speedy case settlements (representing, on average, only five minutes of a clerk's time) and early warning of collapsing trials, their success clearly rests upon the maintenance of an essentially non-adversarial spirit. Thus, although it was not the focus of their inquiry, the researchers 'were indeed struck by the importance of informal co-operation' in both of the PTR systems they observed:

> During the PTR hearings ... relations between the parties were cordial, even jocular, with the participants addressing each other on a first-name basis ... Defence and prosecution advocates were usually keen to engage in negotiations with a view to achieving some form of case settlement, and they were often encouraged in this by the court clerk who administered the hearing. We found many examples ... where the language employed by the lawyers

betrayed a common view of the merits (or, more usually, demerits), of the defendant's position and evidenced a common desire for a speedy resolution *based upon the prosecution's assessment of the case.*[1]

Moreover, defendants are excluded from PTRs on the grounds that PTRs are more effective when conducted in their absence.[2] Acknowledging that their study did not address the impact of PTRs on 'substantive justice' outcomes, these researchers none the less expressed agreement with the Bredar warning (1992: 159) that in pretrial discussions defendants need to be protected from the danger of entering guilty pleas based on overly optimistic *prosecution* predictions about their evidence and the consequent probability of conviction.[3] Thus, as Walker and Starmer (1993) noted, defendants may also need protection from their own lawyers.[4] In considering PTRs from the perspective of possible unfairness and injustice to the accused, they observe that 'the non-controversial atmosphere of the PTR may encourage defence solicitors to weaken their guard and to feel a greater antipathy towards their defendant-clients than towards the prosecution representatives, who are their social peers' (ibid.: 158). The Law Society has, in fact, issued stern warnings about precisely this danger.[5]

When the government turned its attention to this matter it introduced a Practice Direction in 1994 which provided a uniform system of plea and direction hearings (PDHs) in the Crown Court.[6] At the PDH, the court first determined the defendant's plea, and where the plea was guilty, it moved directly to the sentence. Where a not guilty plea was entered, the hearing attempted to identify the issues in the case, and resolve any legal questions (for example, concerning the admissibility of evidence). Depending on the complexity of the case, the judge could order a further hearing to consider issues in more detail.[7]

In practice, this system proved unsatisfactory as a means of clarifying issues prior to the trial for two reasons: firstly, the defendant was not obliged to disclose her defence in advance; and secondly, the PDHs were handicapped where the parties involved declined to participate in them, and by the lack of the judge's power to make binding rulings. In response to these factors, on application by a party to the case or on the judge's own motion, the judge is now empowered to make binding rulings on questions of law and the admissibility of evidence (s. 40 CPIA 1996). The government also took the drastic step of requiring the defendant, in all contested cases, to disclose her defence in advance of the trial; and to ensure compliance the court has been given the power to invite the jury to draw adverse inferences of guilt with respect to the accused.

Non-disclosure and miscarriages of justice

The requirement of advance defence disclosure (together with the curtailment of the right to silence at the police station and in court) represents a significant infringement of the principle that the prosecution must prove its case against the accused. The primary purpose of prosecution disclosure is to ensure that the failure to disclose relevant material, as well as 'unused material',[8] does not lead to a wrongful conviction. The requirement that the prosecution disclose its case against the accused is inherent in the burden of proof falling upon the prosecution. It is a partial recognition of the basic inequality that characterizes the status of the prosecution and defence in an adversarial system and is seen as a step toward diminishing that inequality. Thus, in the final judgment in the Birmingham Six case,[9] the Court observed that:

> A disadvantage of the adversarial system may be that the parties are not evenly matched in resources ... But the inequality of resources is ameliorated by the obligation on the part of the prosecution to make available all material which may prove helpful to the defence. (At p. 312)

Even assuming full disclosure by the prosecution, the gross inequality of the contest between the state and the accused remains, given the central and dominant role played by police in early stages of the criminal justice process.

> The police are involved at the very outset of a case; whereas the defence does not become involved until very late in the process, and this puts the defence at a serious disadvantage. It's the police who usually arrive at the scene of the crime and are there to find exhibits, and are there to record the crime scene; and they have the resources to conduct investigations and discover evidence. The police construct the case and are then followed by the prosecution. It's only late in the day – it may be weeks and maybe months later – that the defence arrive on the scene. (Interview, May 1995)

Thus, the prosecution side of the case has the initiative: it conducts the initial investigation, fixes on a suspect, arrests, detains, charges and prosecutes. In sum, it sets the parameters of the case.

The history of miscarriages of justice offers many examples of cases where there were failures to disclose relevant material. In the Birmingham Six case, about 2,000 statements, judged by the West Midlands Police to be 'non-material', had, without explanation, disappeared from police possession;[10] and in the 1987 appeal proceedings, forensic evidence in possession of the Crown that would have had a significant impact on its case was not disclosed to the defence.[11]

The original conviction of the six men was based in part on testimony by the prosecution's forensic expert, Dr Skuse, that his Greiss test on the hands of the accused proved with 'ninety-nine per cent' certainty that two of them had handled nitroglycerine (Mullin, 1990: 237).[12] Yet on the same night, Dr Bamford, a colleague in the same laboratory where the Birmingham Six had been tested, had obtained positive results with the same test from the hands of two salesmen on the Belfast ferry, which were dismissed as having arisen from the salesmen's use of adhesive tape for wrapping their samples. In addition, Dr Skuse had conducted three negative tests using TLC (thin layer chromotography, touted to be at least as sensitive as Greiss) and other tests which indicated the possibility that the scientist himself might have contaminated the hands of Walker (one of the Six). This information was not disclosed at trial, for if it had been, it would have destroyed Dr Skuse's credibility and the prosecution's case. Forensic evidence was also withheld in the case of the Maguire Seven and eventually led to the concession by the Director of Public Prosecutions that the convictions of the Maguires were unsafe and unsatisfactory (Rozenberg, 1992: 101).

Non-disclosure by the prosecution in the Guildford Four case was equally grievous and damaging for the defence. In October 1975, the Guildford Four (three men and a woman) were convicted of five murders resulting from the October 1974 bombing of a pub in Guildford.[13] The convictions rested entirely upon alleged confessions by each of the accused. However, an additional set of interview notes were found which undermined the authenticity of the confession evidence presented at trial:

> The interview notes had never been disclosed and their contents bore no resemblance to the evidence given by the officers as to how Hill [one of the Four] agreed to make his fifth statement. The inescapable conclusion was that the true interview was suppressed and a false version given by the officers to the court ... [Moreover] it was the Crown's view that the *prima facie* evidence that five of the twelve officers responsible for the interviewing of the Guildford

Four had seriously misled the trial court in relation to the interviews of Hill and Armstrong. (Sir John May, 1994: 294)

The Crown concluded that had this material been available at the trial it would have contaminated the case for the prosecution as a whole, for the 'case depended entirely upon the confessions and in turn upon the integrity of the officers taking them'. Given that the Crown at trial had pointed to Armstrong's confession as the one that was closest to the truth, it is 'inevitable that anything which affects the reliability of [his] confession must affect the case as a whole'. With serious doubt having been cast on the alleged confession of Armstrong, and given its centrality to the prosecution's evidence, 'it would not be right for the Crown to contend that the conviction of any appellant was either safe or satisfactory'. The appellate judges agreed that the disclosure of this evidence, not made available to the original court, might have made a grave difference to the outcome of the 1975 trial.[14] Thus the Court found that the case against all four defendants was undermined and, in 1989, quashed the convictions (ibid.: 295–6). More recently, Stefan Kiszko's conviction for murder was quashed, when it was discovered that the semen found on the schoolgirl victim's body could not have been his as he was infertile. This evidence was available at the time of trial, but was not disclosed. Within two years of his release, Kiszko died, aged 41.

Towards full prosecution disclosure

These cases make it clear that evidence gathered in police investigations must not be treated as the exclusive property of the police and the prosecution, and for the sole use of securing convictions. In the absence of judicial control over investigations, and given the inequality of resources between prosecution and defence, the defence must be allowed access to evidence in the possession of the prosecution which may point to an accused's innocence. The Attorney-General's Guidelines, issued in 1982, aimed at establishing a clear presumption in favour of advance prosecution disclosure to the defence, not only of the prosecution evidence but of all the unused material gathered in the course of investigation.[15] According to para. 2: 'In all cases which are due to be committed for trial, all unused material should normally [subject to discretionary exceptions] be made available to the defence solicitor if it has some bearing on the offence(s) charged and the surrounding circumstances of the case.'[16] Moreover, the Guidelines instruct that 'disclosure should be made as soon as possible before the date fixed' for committal proceedings; however, a delay in the proceedings might be justified 'if the material [to be disclosed] might have some influence upon the course of the committal proceedings or the charges upon which the justices might decide to commit' (para. 3).

The Guidelines were extended beyond the CPS and prosecuting counsel, to the police, forensic scientists and others with some prosecution responsibility for criminal proceedings in the case of *R v. Saunders and Others*. This was followed, in 1992, by advice to the police from the DPP.[17] The 'Guinness Advice' (1992), as it came to be known, reminded police officers 'that the prosecution in criminal proceedings has a duty to disclose to the defence all 'unused material' ... unless it is incapable of having any impact upon the case in question or there are good reasons for withholding the material'; however, whether it was 'relevant' was not a matter for the prosecution.[18] The duty was made specific to police officers, who were advised to preserve any possible relevant material that came into their possession (para. 10).

The consequences of non-disclosure in the celebrated bombing cases of the 1970s have already been discussed. However, the incidence of non-disclosure by the prosecution and its potentially harmful effects for the defence did not cease with the issuance of the Attorney-General's Guidelines of 1982. In *Phillipson*, where the prosecution had held back incriminating documents until cross-examination of the accused, the Court explicitly rejected the Crown's excuse for non-disclosure, asserting that 'an accused needs to know in advance the case which will be made against him, if he is to have a proper opportunity of giving his answer to that case to the best of his ability. The accused is also entitled, when he decides whether or not to go into the witness box ... to know what the case is which he has to meet.'[19] The Court also quashed a conviction in *Sanson*,[20] on the basis of a very similar non-disclosure irregularity.

More recently, in *Taylor and another*,[21] where two sisters were convicted for the murder of Alison Shaughnessy, the Court quashed the convictions because the prosecution had not disclosed to the defence that an identification witness called at the trial had made an earlier statement (for which he claimed a reward) that one of the girls might have been black: neither defendant was. The Court determined that the police detective in charge of the case knew this but did not disclose it to the CPS nor to the prosecuting counsel for fear that they would disclose it to the defence. This became known to the defence only in the post-conviction period when the CPS, pressed by the defence as to whether there was still any material which had not been disclosed, permitted a junior defence counsel to go to the police station to read a large quantity of documents, including those which contaminated the witness evidence, which was central to the appeal.[22]

Shortly after the Guiness Advice the Court was called upon to review a number of serious cases, many of them stemming from the prosecu- tion of terrorist activity, where it was alleged that the defendants had been deprived of a fair trial due to serious failures by the prosecution to disclose relevant material. The landmark case was that of *Judith Ward* (1993), who had been convicted of murder many years before. Her conviction was quashed by the Court on the grounds of material non- disclosure of prosecution material, to which the Court said the accused would have been entitled in the interests of securing a fair trial. Moreover, the Court further widened the prosecution's duty of dis- closure by ruling that it was for the court (and not the prosecution) to decide whether material could be properly withheld from the defence on the grounds of public interest immunity.[23]

In subsequent cases the Court proceeded to establish the precise nature of the prosecution's duty to disclose. These culminated in *Keane* (1994), in which Lord Taylor set out the stringent test of *materiality* that the prosecution, in the realm of disclosure, must satisfy, to wit

> that which can be seen on a sensible appraisal by the prosecution: (1) to be relevant or possibly relevant to an issue in the case; (2) to raise or possibly to raise a new issue whose existence is not apparent from the evidence the prosecution proposes to use; (3) to hold out a real (as opposed to a fanciful) prospect of providing a lead on evi- dence which goes to (1) or (2) (Lord Taylor, p. 1289).

Effecting a retreat: from prosecution to defence disclosure

The stringent rulings on prosecution disclosure laid down by Lord Taylor were a recognition by the Court of Appeal (per Steyn LJ in *R v. Winston Brown*, 1994) that in 'our adversarial system in which the police and the prosecution control the investigatory process, an accused's right to disclosure is an inseparable part of his right to a fair trial'. However, the police and prosecution bitterly resented the Court's rules on prosecution disclosure of 'unused material', including matters against prosecution witnesses.[24] In their view, these rules obliged them either to disclose sensitive and confidential material (of only marginal relevance) or to discontinue prosecution. In addition, the prosecution complained of the administrative burden and cost of supervising the inspection and copying of material, and of the fact that some defendants would tailor their instructions to take advantage of the material disclosed.[25]

The complaints of the police and CPS clearly had the ear of the Royal Commission which, despite the danger of future miscarriages of justice, recommended that the prosecution should no longer be required to disclose 'non-relevant' information to the defence about (i) a police officer who had been disbelieved by a jury in a previous case, or, (ii) disciplinary proceedings against such an officer.[26] This was clearly a step backwards from the status quo established by *Edwards* (1991),[27] which obliged the prosecution to disclose to the defence any known adverse information (such as disciplinary hearings against a police officer or witness of the prosecution). Thus, under the Commission's proposals in this area it would still be possible for a conviction to be based on the allegation of a single police officer where neither the defence nor the jury are made aware that the police officer has been disbelieved in a previous case (Bridges and McConville 1994: 18).

However, the Commission was less concerned with how proposed changes might affect the accused than with the prospective dangers of disclosing confidential and sensitive information (such as the identity of informants or undercover police involved in investigations);[28] and with the practical problems that could arise in disclosure where a large volume of material is involved; and finally with the issue of cost and efficiency. Thus, after primary disclosure by the prosecution,[29] they provided for *secondary* disclosure by the prosecution[30] *only if and when* the defence has disclosed the substance of its own defence, and then only if the latter is able to establish the relevance of the prosecution documents requested (RCCJ,1993: 95–6). Where the parties disagree on the relevance of the material sought, the court could weigh the potential importance of the material to the defence and make a ruling. This would introduce a disclosure obligation on the defence where none had existed – other than for alibis (s. 11, CJA 1967), expert evidence (s. 81, PACE 1984) and preparatory hearings in serious fraud cases (s. 9, CJA 1987).

In a strongly worded dissent, Professor Zander opposed the Commission's recommendation on secondary disclosure, the heart of which was *defence* disclosure. He argued that it would be wrong in principle since the effect would be to shift the burden of proof on to the defendant:

> Defence disclosure is designed to be helpful to the prosecution and, more generally, to the system. But it is not the job of the defendant

to be helpful either to the prosecution or to the system. His task, if he chooses to put the prosecution to the proof, is simply to defend himself. (RCCJ, 1993: 221)

The Legal Action Group agreed with Zander's position and added that on practical grounds such a provision could be manipulated by the prosecution to its own advantage and at the expense of the defence. While police routinely suppress inconvenient evidence, there is less expectation of similar behaviour by the prosecution: but it still occurs. Many wrongful convictions, including some of the most infamous, have been the result of the misleading effect of partial disclosure of evidence by the police or the prosecution or both. Moreover, evidence subsequently considered critical to the outcome of certain cases has been kept from the court as well as the defence, thus contributing to miscarriages of justice.

Despite this, and ignoring the greater resources of the prosecution in building its case, as well as its ability to control evidence, the Commission's recommendations on disclosure focused attention instead on defence disclosure. They proposed that the defence be obliged to disclose, *in advance*, the substance of their case or risk suffering a penalty at trial. Once the prosecution case has been fully disclosed, they explained, 'defendants should be required to offer an answer to the charges made against them at the risk of adverse comment at trial on any new defence they then disclose or on any departure from the defence which they previously disclosed' (RCCJ 1993: 55).[31] Refusal to provide disclosure would subject the accused to possible adverse comment at trial. Although the judge must continue to stress to the jury that they must not treat silence as guilt, it would be proper under the Commission's proposal for the judge to point out to the jury that such silence denies them the benefit of any account the defendant might be able to provide: 'it means that there is no evidence from the defendant to undermine, contradict, or explain the evidence put before [them] by the prosecution' (1993: 56). Moreover, any defence departure at trial from its pre-trial disclosure would allow the judge, at her discretion, to invite the jury to draw such adverse inferences from such changes as they think appropriate. This, according to the Commission, would not only discourage last-minute 'ambush' defences by defendants, but encourage better pre-trial preparation of the defence's case, which could lead to early prosecution discontinuances, as well as facilitate better estimates of trial length and thus more efficient use of court resources.

The ability of defendants to resort to an 'ambush' defence to avoid conviction has been the single most powerful and persistent argument used by the police in relation to both disclosure and in their effort to secure the abolition of the right to silence. Yet research (including investigations conducted for the RCCJ by Zander and Henderson) has shown that last minute defences are raised in less than 10 per cent of Crown Court cases where an ambush defence was said to have been used;[32] and that half of even these ended in convictions. The end-result is very close to the findings of Leng (1993) that ambush defences were raised in no more than between 2 and 5 per cent of trials, although in Leng's sample *all* ended in conviction. Finally, in their study of 100 cases of non-jury acquittals, Block *et al.* (1993) did not identify any that involved ambush defences. Despite its empirical weakness, the claim of the police that ambush defences were allowing the guilty to escape conviction was one of the factors cited by the Royal Commission in recommending advance defence disclosure.[33] Even more emphasis would be placed on this issue by the government in its passage of the Criminal Procedures and Investigation Act 1996, which provides for defence disclosure.

The disclosure provisions must be viewed in the context of the CJPOA 1994, which curtailed the right to silence in fundamental ways. In addition to being seriously compromised by a *caution* (intro-duced in 1995), which warns the suspect that the failure to provide police with any information that may subsequently be relied upon in the accused's defence may invite an adverse inference, the require-ment of *advance defence disclosure* introduced in the CPIA 1996 emas-culates the right of silence by requiring the accused in the pre-trial period, to provide the prosecution with a defence statement, and by providing, further, that failure to do so will invite possible adverse inferences of guilt to be drawn at trial. Thus, rather than be allowed to remain silent the accused must lay out her defence against the charges brought by the police and prosecution – under the threat of having adverse inferences being drawn if she refuses. In short, the new rules on defence disclosure appear to be the final step in the effective abolition of the right of silence. Moreover, they overturn the principle that the *prosecution* must prove its case without the assistance of the accused. The accused is now obliged to cooperate with the prosecution in the state's effort to convict her. As one expe-rienced criminal lawyer commented, 'I think we've actually lost the situation now where we can actually say to the prosecution, "Plead your case"'' (Interview, August 1997).

The CPIA 1996 and compulsory defence disclosure

The changes in disclosure included in the CPIA 1996 reflected the concern of Conservative government officials, prompted by growing complaints from the police, that the balance of advantages in the realm of disclosure which had evolved from Court of Appeal decisions, had tilted too far in favour of the defence, thus allowing criminals to escape punishment. The 1996 Act[34] was meant to correct this imbalance. In introducing the bill at second reading, the Home Secretary, Michael Howard, explained that 'it is designed to restore the balance in our criminal justice system – to make life tougher for the criminal'[35] by simultaneously lessening the obligations upon the prosecution imposed by the common law to disclose unused material, and by requiring the defence to disclose its case at a pre-trial stage (Corker, 1997: 885–6).

Primary prosecution disclosure

Under s. 3(1)(a) CPIA 1996, the prosecution must disclose to the accused unused material previously undisclosed, which they do not intend to use at trial, but which, in the prosecution's opinion, might undermine its case against the accused.[36] To satisfy the disclosure requirement the prosecution must also serve the non-sensitive and sensitive schedule of unused material. According to the Home Office, 'primary disclosure is designed to ensure that the prosecutor discloses at the first stage material that, generally speaking, has an adverse effect on the strength of the prosecution case' (Sprack, 1997: 309–10). But the prosecution is reliant upon the police to compile the schedules of material and to determine what should be reported to the prosecution. It is on the basis of this information that the prosecutor must decide precisely what should be disclosed to the accused at this stage of the process.

To regulate the gathering, documenting, recording and revelation of material and information gathered by the police responsible for investigating an offence, the CPIA's disclosure scheme is complemented by a Code of Practice. Its objective is to ensure that the police and prosecution fulfill their responsibility of disclosing all unused material that is relevant to the defence. Under the Code, the investigator has three major obligations related to disclosure: (i) to record relevant material obtained in the investigation;[37] (ii) to retain relevant material on an ongoing basis; and (iii) to prepare schedules of *unused* relevant material, including a short but adequate description of the items, for the benefit of the prosecutor.[38] The purpose of the foregoing is to enable the prosecution to have available all material and information gathered by the investigation in order to exercise judgment regarding its relevance to the defence.

Para. 3.4 of the COP states that 'the investigator is obliged to pursue all reasonable lines of inquiry, whether these point towards or away from the suspect'. The government included this provision in response to those who, being aware of the police practice of focusing exclusive attention on one suspect, had argued that investigators should be under a duty to consider alternative suspects and to pursue inquiries which exculpate as well as incriminate. Thus this provision obliges police to investigate all case-theories fairly, not just the one pointing to the presumed guilt of the accused; and failure to do so opens the prosecution to criticism at the trial (Corker, 1997a: 886); however, Leng and Taylor (1996: 35) argue that in a context of scarce resources it would be easy for the police to conclude that it would not be reasonable to pursue other lines of inquiry.

Moreover, unlike PACE Codes, with their built-in mechanisms to scrutinize whether the police are compliant (e.g. the presence of a solicitor at the relevant time, the tape-recording of interviews), the task of determining whether police comply with their duties under the CPIA's COP on disclosure is more difficult and less certain of success. In addition, no formal sanctions for breaches of the code are provided in the 1996 Act or its COP.[39] Thus while developments in the common law duty of disclosure by the prosecution have been a major factor in uncovering procedural breaches and omissions by the police, and have led to a number of acquittals, the 1996 Act 'will make it very difficult for the defence to learn of breaches of the code which the prosecution side does not wish to reveal' (Leng and Taylor, 1996: 42).

Defence disclosure

But the most radical change introduced by the CPIA is the requirement that in all cases to be tried on indictment the accused must send to the prosecution in advance of the trial, a written defence statement (s. 5(1)). This must be done within 14 days from the time the prosecution has complied with its primary disclosure duty.[40] The defence statement must set out in general terms the nature of the accused's defence; indicate the matters in which she takes issue with the prosecution; and in the case of each such matter set out her reason(s) for doing so.[41] The compulsory nature of defence disclosure derives from a number of provisions which may trigger the risk of inferences of guilt (see below).

Apart from undermining the principle that the prosecution itself should have to prove its case, the new rules not only oblige the accused to assist in the effort but also place hurdles in her path, and pose threats to her claim of innocence if she is unable to overcome them. For example, because the accused cannot know what inferences and conclusions the prosecution may draw in making its case, it may not be possible, as required in the written defence statement, for her to say in what way she takes issue with the prosecution case, or what her reasons are for doing so.[42] Yet it is necessary that this be done within 14 days. In one major step, then, the defendant has moved from having *no* obligation of disclosure to being obliged to reveal, within a strict time-frame, everything of substance about her defence. As one experienced criminal lawyer explained:

> There's no doubt in my mind, the intention of the Act is that you reveal your entire defence case and then say, 'This is our case ... That, to me, is totally against ... the idea of the defendant being innocent until proven guilty. And my concern is that it also provides the prosecution [with the opportunity] to bolster up their case when they see what the issues are going to be ... [T]hat has always happened. Alibi is a prime example: you can serve the alibi notice and [be certain] that within a month they will be out to see the alibi witnesses and crack it. This [provision] provides them with the opportunity of doing it to the entire defence case. (Interview, August 1997)

While there is no sanction against the prosecution for an incomplete disclosure, the accused is faced with the threat of adverse inference if full disclosure of her defence is not made. Moreover, if she fails to provide a defence statement the prosecution is not obliged to provide secondary disclosure (see below).

A further problem is that in preparing a defence statement in advance of trial, it is in practice the solicitor, not the accused, who will be responsible for negotiation over disclosure and the drafting of the written statement. While it is to be hoped that defence statements will be prepared by experienced solicitors or other legally qualified personnel, McConville *et al.*'s (1994) study of defence lawyers found that most Crown Court work was carried out by non-legally qualified staff, an arrangement encouraged by the fee structure of Legal Aid.[43] Even if we assume the support of well-qualified defence lawyers, compliance with the new disclosure regime is likely to move the prosecution of an accused person a further step away from a public adversarial trial and closer to a semi-closed pre-trial forum in which the prosecution and defence mutually disclose their cases and assess the case against the accused, perhaps even reaching agreement on how it will be settled.

Secondary disclosure

Following defence disclosure, and only then, the prosecution (under s. 7) must disclose to the defence any previously undisclosed material which, in light of the defence statement, might reasonably be expected to support the accused's defence.[44] Related to this, para. 8.2 of the Code obliges the investigator to re-examine all unused material and to draw to the prosecutor's attention any which might assist the defence as disclosed in the defence statement. Thus the material the prosecution may disclose in the second round is intended to be in direct response to what is contained in the defence statement. As Corker (1997: 962) points out, 'The Act presumes that with the aid of the defence statement the prosecutor and investigator can act as adequate judges of what unused material can assist the defence.' Corker also notes that if the prosecution is in possession of material which would support a defence but that defence is not included in the defence statement, such material is not disclosable.[45]

The problem of securing compliance is even greater with respect to secondary disclosure. As with primary disclosure, the defence must rely not only on the good faith and insightfulness of the prosecutor but also on the police investigator charged with bringing to the prosecutor's attention the material which is to form the basis of secondary disclosure. At this stage of the process there will be little incentive to the police to ferret out relevant material. Apart from the fact that they will have concluded that the accused is guilty, in most instances the investigation will have been closed, and the case material handed over to the CPS. In any event, the police investigator is likely to lack both the legal insights and skills to determine whether any material might assist the defence. However, even assuming good faith on the part of the police and prosecution, it is unclear whether the defence statement alone will suffice to prompt disclosure of all relevant information. It may depend upon the skill and experience of the defence lawyer in second-guessing the type of evidence which the police may have.

Section 8 provides that at any time the defence has reasonable cause to believe that there is undisclosed prosecution material which might reasonably be expected to help the defence case, as disclosed in the defence statement, they may apply to the court for an order requiring the prosecution to disclose.[46] If the court is satisfied with the defence application, it can order disclosure. However, even with the benefit of the prosecution schedule of unused material it may be difficult for the defence to identify the relevance of unused material that has not been disclosed, much less succeed in persuading the court that it has 'reasonable cause' to believe that such undisclosed material exists which might assist the defence.[47] Moreover, the prosecution has a continuing duty from the event of primary prosecution disclosure until the end of the trial to review whether there is material which in her general opinion might undermine the case of the prosecution against the accused; and which might be reasonably expected to assist the defence as disclosed; and which has not been disclosed to the defence.[48] However, as noted, the defence is largely reliant on the good faith and diligence of the prosecutor and investigator who cannot be expected to have the defence's interest uppermost in their minds. As a result, concludes Corker (1997: 962), 'this duty is likely to be honoured more in the breach than in the observance'.

Public Interest Immunity

Public interest immunity (PII) claims provide a further opportunity for the prosecution to withhold evidence from the defence. These are claims made on public interest grounds to withhold documents or information from being given in evidence in court proceedings. PII was brought sharply to the public's attention in the Matrix Churchill case, where three men were charged with exporting machine tools to Iraq whilst concealing from the government licensing authorities that they were intended for use in the manufacture of munitions. Part of their defence was that government authorities had known this but had in any event granted the export license. In order to demonstrate this to the court, the defendants required government documents to show that the intended use of their machines was known, or that would provide a basis from which that knowledge might be inferred, and which could be used to cross-examine government witnesses. The government responded to the application with PII claims. 'Ministers signed certificates stating that if the various documents covered by the certificates were disclosed, grave and unquantifiable damage might be done to the public interest' (Scott, 1996). The judge, having read the documents, refused the PII claim. The material disclosed provided the basis for cross-examination which subsequently led to the discontinuance of the prosecution, following a statement by Alan Clark (who had been the Minister for Trade at the relevant time) stating that he did not regard the possible use of the machine tools to manufacture weapons as a matter of concern (ibid.).

The possibility for the Crown to make a PII claim continues under the CPIA 1996, and the same common law rules are to be applied in deciding the issues, including ensuring that the defence should be made aware of the application, unless the material is too sensitive even for this.[49] Under sections 14 and 15 of the CPIA, the defence may at any time, in both summary and Crown Court trials, apply for a review of the order and the judge must keep the issue constantly under review. If it becomes in the public interest that the material should be disclosed, the prosecutor is informed, and may choose either to comply with the disclosure requirement, or to discontinue the case. A recent example concerns Samar Alami and Jawad Botmeh, accused of bombing the Israeli Embassy (see Paul Foot, *The Guardian*, 16 March 1999).[50]

The principle is that the names of informants, or the channels through which information about the offence has been obtained, will not be revealed to the defence, unless to do so would prevent a miscarriage of justice. This was stated clearly by Lord Esher MR in *Marks v. Befus* (1890) 25 QBD 494 at 498, as follows:

> if the judge should be of the opinion that the disclosure of the name of the informant is necessary or right in order to show the prisoner's innocence then one public policy is in conflict with another public policy, and that which says that an innocent man is not to be condemned when his innocence can be proved is the policy which must prevail. (Cited in Scott, 1996)

Clearly this was not operative on the minds of government ministers in the Matrix Churchill case.

The issue of PII is a sensitive one since it is yet another way in which material can be withheld from the defence who are reliant upon the judge to decide its relevance to the defence case. The issue is again being debated in the case of Alami and Botmeh.

Although the position on PII appears to remain unchanged, the COP accompanying the CPIA 1996 contains important changes which may undermine that procedure. Under the COP, the *police* may determine information to be sensitive and so not in the public interest to disclose. Such material should be listed in a separate schedule. Paragraph 6.8 of the Code lists examples which may fall into this category. These are many and varied and, in practice, may avoid the need to make PII claims, resolution of the issue being made by the police and checked only by the prosecutor on her own initiative.[51]

Defence disclosure and inferences of guilt

If the accused fails to provide a defence statement, or it is late or incomplete, she risks having adverse inferences drawn at trial.[52] As stipulated in s. 11(3), in the event of defence failures, the court or, with the court's leave, any other person (i.e. the prosecution and/or any co-defendant) may make such comment as appears appropriate; and the court or jury may draw such inference as appear proper in deciding whether the accused is guilty.[53] It may be argued that this infringes Article 6 of the ECHR and related case-law on the freedom from self-incrimination – especially as other fair trial guarantees, such as the duty of disclosure, have been rendered conditional upon the provision of a defence statement. Under the HRA 1998, the courts will be obliged to give effect to the European Convention.

Sprack (1997b) raises another potential weakness in the procedure: whether sanctions may be applied to the accused which arise from inconsistencies within a defence statement, or between it and the defence submitted at trial, in light of the fact that the statement is prepared by the defendant's solicitors. 'The position at common law ... is that in criminal cases a client is not bound by statements written by his or her solicitor in the absence of proof of specific instructions' (p. 128). He also observes that the CPIA 1996 contains nothing that could be used to establish that the defence statement made pursuant to s. 5 was issued with the accused's authority (p. 128). There is also the danger that the prosecution may seek to use the defence statement (and any admission it contains) as part of its case. 'If this is allowed, the Crown will be heavily weighting the scales in its favour by relying on an admission made out of court, by a person on the defendant's behalf, not under caution, and contained in a document required by law to be served.' (Thompson, 1998: 805)

Moreover, apart from providing for adverse inferences where 'appropriate', Sprack (1997a) draws attention to the fact that s. 11(3) of the CPIA 1996 contains no equivalent to s. 34(2) of the CJPOA 1994, which specifically envisages the use of inferences from silence in interview to establish a prima facie case. It may be possible to infer from this omission that the inferences relating to defence disclosure cannot be used to help the prosecution raise a prima facie case (p. 313).

On the other hand, Murray (1996) suggests that the cumulative effect of the defence disclosure requirements, following upon previous changes which provide for inferences to be drawn from the exercise of the right of silence, puts the accused at ever more risk of being convicted where silence is consistently exercised. The danger, he believes, is 'that the accused who relies on her right of silence at the police station, during the disclosure process, and in court, will be convicted on the cumulative weight of adverse inferences' (p. 1289). Sprack (1997a) also warns that to the extent that the CPIA 1996 changes seek to limit prosecution disclosure and lead to conceal-ment of material, they are likely to produce more miscarriages of justice.[54]

Charge bargaining, sentence discount for guilty pleas and early pleading

The final issue for consideration in this chapter is sentence discounts. This is where the defendant receives a reduction in sentence in recog-nition of her admission of the offence. In response to the problem of 'cracked trials', where defendants change their pleas to guilty at a very late stage in the process, the Commission called for the establishment of a system of graduated discounts on sentences that are tied to the stage in the criminal process when a guilty plea is entered (1993: 110–14). It suggested, 'the earlier the plea the higher the discount' (p. 111) and suggested that the defence lawyer be allowed to query the judge at any stage in the prosecution (a so-called 'sentence canvass') to obtain information on what would be the maximum possible sentence if her client were to plead guilty at a given point (p. 110).

The Commission attributed the late pleas of defendants to 'their reluctance to face the facts until they are at the door of the court' (1993: 112) and urged counsel to discourage the accused from waiting until the last minute to change her plea. However, defendants often have no intention of pleading guilty on the day of the trial: it is the barrister who seeks to persuade her client to abandon a contested trial and to plead guilty in exchange for a charge reduction.[55] This provision stands to benefit the prosecution, rather than the defence, as many 'cracked trials' are weak cases and would not likely stand the test of trial (Zander and Henderson, 1993).

The Commission acknowledged that 'it would be naive to suppose that innocent persons never plead guilty because of the prospect of the sentence discount' (p. 110); and that to confront defendants 'with a choice between what they might get on an immediate plea of guilty and what they might get if found guilty by jury ... amount[s] to unacceptable pressure' (p. 113). Nevertheless, the Commission was quite prepared to accept the risk involved in imposing such 'unacceptable pressure', for against this risk it weighed the resources saved by avoiding the full prosecution of 'defendants who know themselves to be guilty' (p. 110), as well as the various costs in time and energy for thousands of police, forensic experts and ordinary citizen witnesses (p. 111).

Some prominent defence lawyers agree with the Commission's suggestion that the criminal justice system should be willing to trade off sentence discounts for early guilty pleas. According to Roger Ede, Secretary of the Criminal Law Committee of the Law Society:

> It's a necessary part of a system that where you are satisfied there is evidence of a person's guilt and that they are truly guilty, they should get some credit for an early indication of a plea of guilty ... Without sentence discounts there will be more time spent in court on cases that could be dealt ... by way of a guilty plea, and less time and resources available – and resources are limited – to deal with cases where people are not guilty, and where there should be proper trials.

When queried about the risk that some innocent people will plead guilty when given options that make it favourable to plead early and get a reduction in the charge or a lesser sentence, Ede echoed the view of the RCCJ that there would be that danger, but added:

> that is something that you have to live with and try and minimise ... by limiting the amount of discount that people get. Typically the discount will be between a quarter and a third: no more than that. As long as it is no more than that then I don't think that the risk is unacceptable.

The Commission's recommendations on sentencing discounts were incorporated into the CJPOA 1994. Section 48(1) provides that when determining the sentence of a defendant who has pleaded guilty, the court should take into account the stage in the proceedings at which the offender indicated her intention to plead guilty, as well as the circumstances in which this indication was given. In assessing this provision, Wasik and Taylor (1995) note that the practice of giving a reduced sentence for an early plea is far from new in the British system, and that s. 48(1) does no more than provide legislative authority to a well-established judicial principle of sentencing: that an accused who pleads guilty very early in the process attracts a lower sentence than would be imposed following a trial and conviction (pp. 16–17). The rationale is that the guilty plea is indicative of remorse on the part of the accused, and should be treated as a mitigating factor; however, the court also recognises that in pleading guilty the accused has made a full trial unnecessary and thereby saved a great deal of time, inconvenience and public expense, as well as sparing witnesses the distress of court appearances.

However, sentence discounts are frequently coupled with plea bargains – the offer of a reduced charge in exchange for a guilty plea – and this places increased pressure upon the defendant to capitulate to the advice of the legal expert – her own lawyer – and to plead guilty. Despite the assurances of Roger Ede, clients are likely to be ill-served by these arrangements: it is entirely possible that the defendant may be 'ambushed' into entering a plea of guilty when she may in fact be innocent.[56]

It is evident that the discount provisions are attractive to those, including the Law Society, who seek to reduce costs to the criminal justice system of 'processing' accused persons. Illustrations of such considerations are found in the following commentary by the Law Society's Roger Ede:

> One has to recognise that there is only a set amount of money available to pay for the criminal justice system. We are concerned that court time, court facilities, and lawyers' time are not wasted ... and if you have a client, firstly, who is truly guilty, that is, there is sufficient prosecution evidence to convict; and secondly that your client instructs that he or she is guilty, then there are advantages to everybody to give that person some credit for pleading guilty. (Interview, May 1995)

Several points should be noted. First, it seems clear that for Ede the charge against the accused of having committed a criminal offence is not something that has to be proven beyond a reasonable doubt. Although sufficient evidence should be given to satisfy the court that the accused is guilty, this determination can be made in the privacy of the judge's chambers, the result having been negotiated by the legal professionals (the judge and counsel for the prosecution and defence). Secondly, there is an apparent willingness to override due process values and a 'just' outcome in favour of the efficient use of the resources of the criminal justice system and the lawyers. Thus the Law Society seems perfectly willing to have the innocence or guilt of an accused person decided basically *by* the lawyers – and with the minimum expenditure of their own and the court's time; for if 'evidence has to be given and the court has to be satisfied that the person is guilty ... the whole system would become clogged up ... ' (ibid.). Accordingly, to resolve the matter of the accused's guilt it should only be necessary for the defence lawyer to be satisfied on the papers that there is sufficient prosecution evidence to convict; and that the accused be willing to plead guilty, having been persuaded by her counsel of the presumed advantages of doing so – as against the costs of pleading not guilty.

Summary

Reform relating to the disclosure of material is perhaps one of the most significant in terms of its impact upon miscarriages of justice (it has been at the root of many) and its fundamental shifting of the burden of proof. Although considered separately here as a pre-trial issue, it should be assessed in the light of other changes to the accused's right to silence discussed in Chapter 5. The requirement that the accused reveal her case before, and in order that, the prosecution provide further information, some of which may be relevant to her defence, infringes the accused's right to silence. As such, the RCCJ's recommendations on disclosure prompted a strongly worded dissent from one of its members, Michael Zander.

The police are at a great advantage in terms of their powers and resources for gathering evidence, as well as being first on the scene. The defendant is left to react to the accusations made against her some time later, and in preparing her defence she may inadvertently be denied information discovered by the police, but discounted as unhelpful to the prosecution case, which may be relevant for her defence. It is the suppression of such information which led to many of the more notorious miscarriage cases. Guidelines in the 1980s sought to clarify the prosecution duty to disclose all relevant material to the defence, but their effectiveness was limited by the adversarial context of the criminal justice process, where the police (as controllers and producers of case-related information) are seeking a conviction and have no incentive to assist the defence.

Despite this, the RCCJ appear to have ignored the plight of the under-resourced defendant and went much further in recommending secondary prosecution disclosure only after the defence have disclosed the substance of their case. This has been implemented in the

CPIA 1996 and its Code of Practice. In addition, although retaining the common law position on PII claims, it confers a controversial power upon the police to classify as sensitive, information whose disclosure they consider to be against the public interest. The legislation replicates many of the weaknesses uncovered in PACE, such as the prosecutor's dependence upon police-constructed information (here, in making decisions about the disclosure of information) and the absence of proper sanctions for breaches of the Code of Practice. The process of disclosure no longer reflects the burden of proof which the prosecution must discharge. It has become a complex 'cat and mouse' game where the partisan prosecutor (for she has not suddenly become an impartial investigator) controls the slow release of information. This is wrong in principle, but combined with what we know of the poor quality of defence preparation for Crown Court cases it creates a real danger that relevant information will not be revealed, leading to further miscarriages of justice. The prosecution must disclose material which may assist the defence case – but only to the extent that this is set out in the defence statement. There is no obligation to disclose something which would support a defence not made out in the statement. Thus, the degree of prosecution disclosure is *directly related* to the ability of the defence lawyer to prepare a defence statement that will trigger the disclosure of relevant information. The fate of the accused is determined increasingly by the conduct rather than the content of her defence.

Defence lawyers are also encouraged to become increasingly complicit in the pressures upon the accused to plead guilty. Sentence discounts have been formalized and they represent another disincentive to the defendant (together with the possibility of adverse inferences from silence and the difficulties in obtaining access to the whole of the prosecution evidence) to contest the charges brought against her. The accused who wishes to avail herself of the system's basic protections – consulting with her defence solicitor, her barrister, or even testing out the evidence at trial – will suffer a graduated system of punishment in the form of an increased sentence if convicted. The place of the trial seems to have been forgotten. The burden of proof must rest squarely upon the state, as it is the state which seeks to limit the freedom of individuals.

The new rules on disclosure infringe the accused's right to silence and the right to expect the prosecution to prove its case, moving towards the out-of-court resolution of issues which is more typical of civil, rather than criminal, procedure. Much will depend upon the skill and commitment of lawyers, with the court acting as an administrative arbiter. This more limited judicial role may be acceptable in a full adversarial trial system, where evidence is publicly aired, but as we move more and more to the pre-trial resolution of issues, the role of the judge must also adapt.

8
The Trial

Trials and miscarriages of justice: the role of lawyers, magistrates and judges

The goal of the trial is to determine whether the accused person is guilty as charged. This requires a decision on the basis of evidence put before the court by the prosecution, and on the countervailing arguments of the defence. In the Crown Court, which tries indictable offences,[1] the presiding judge is educated in the law and has acquired considerable trial experience before being appointed to the bench. She regulates the proceedings, determines the admissibility of evidence, and ensures that the trial is conducted fairly. Following presentation of evidence by the prosecution and the response of the defendant, the judge sums up the case and charges a jury (whose members are randomly selected[2]) with the task of determining, on the facts of the case, whether the accused has been proven guilty beyond a reasonable doubt.

Proceedings in the magistrates' courts, where more than 93 per cent of all cases are processed, differ from those in the Crown Court.[3] First, whereas the accused in Crown Court trials must be present to plead to the indictment, and should normally be in court throughout her trial, summary trials may take place in the absence of the accused.[4] Secondly, some safeguards for accused which apply to Crown Court trials do not apply to summary trials. For example, prosecution disclosure is required in Crown Court, but in the magistrates' courts the accused have no legal right to have the prosecution case disclosed prior to trial;[5] and while Code E, PACE requires that all police station interviews with persons suspected of indictable offences must be tape-recorded, this does not apply to summary offences. Thirdly, summary

147

court trials are less formal and more hurried, and the magistrates who process them generally lack formal legal training.[6] Thus they are less schooled in due process rights than judges. 'Such training as the magistrates get', observed a solicitor-advocate,

> is organised by either the courts or the prosecution [who] are predominantly telling them about how to convict ... [and] the courts have a liaison judge ... who comes down to tell them about sentencing. They aren't telling them about the importance of seeing that the rights of the accused are protected, and there is no equal balancing act with a defence lawyer telling them about their problems. So all the training is biased towards the prosecution, and that's a problem.[7]

As a result, trials in magistrates' courts are likely to be less attentive to procedural safeguards aimed at protecting accused persons against wrongful conviction.[8] Finally, in contrast to Crown Court, where verdicts are decided by juries,[9] in summary court the issue of guilt is resolved by the magistrates, who are seen as pro-police and prosecution-oriented.[10] This perception is widely shared by both defendants and solicitors.[11]

A number of factors shape the magistrates' perspective. In addition to the historical tie between magistrates and the police, a close and positive relationship exists between them as a result of their frequent and mutually respectful interaction in the courts. Magistrates identify the police as trusted allies in the task of processing persons accused of criminal offences. In contested cases, for example, police testimony was found to account for 53 per cent of those which depended upon direct evidence, and 70 per cent of those involving circumstantial evidence.[12] Given the determining role of police testimony in most summary court trials, the magistrates' acceptance of the credibility of police evidence, as against that of the accused, is essential. As Wundersitz *et al.* (1991: 201) argue, 'In ... direct contests between the defendant and the police, the magistracy itself, as a representative of the state, has a vested interest in upholding the reputation of the police, who also represent the state, by accepting their side of the story. In addition to the legitimacy accorded to the police per se, their testimony is assumed to be credible because its presentation is practiced, assertive and depersonalized (supported by the "objective" testimony of other police witnesses)' McConville *et al.* (1994: 237).

Conversely, given the hiatus in socioeconomic status between the magistrates (who are appointed by the Lord Chancellor) and those whom they must judge, together with the tilt in the political profile of most lay justices,[13] it is difficult for magistrates to identify or empathize with those accused of criminal offences. Rather, they are inclined to disbelieve defendants and to be predisposed to assume their guilt.[14] Thus while the underlying perception that the accused are guilty may begin with the police, it is carried forward to those on the bench and reflected in their decisions. And while the magistrates are said to be less inclined than previously to accept without question what the police do, officers' testimony against the defendant (explained a solicitor with 30 years of summary court experience) still weighs heavily with the magistrates. The latter remain 'predisposed to convict the accused. There is still a 'no smoke without fire' syndrome of thought: 'The guy wouldn't be in the dock unless he'd done this.' And this contributes to the very high rate of conviction in summary court'.[15] The effect of the foregoing is that the burden of proof is reversed in the magistrates' courts: it is now up to the defendant to establish her innocence (McConville *et al.*, 1994: 227).

The perception held by lawyers that the magistrates believe most defendants are guilty, and that this may affect their ability to make judgments based on the facts of a case, is confirmed in other interviews. In reference to the high conviction rate of accused persons in summary court (98.2 per cent), another solicitor stated frankly: 'Well, in the last analysis 90 per cent of them are guilty. We know that, they know that.'[16] Thus the notion that 'this person wouldn't be here if they weren't guilty',[17] continues to be shared in varying degrees by those of like mind – the police, magistrates and some solicitors.

The overarching objective of cutting costs, which is ceaselessly pursued by those who manage the criminal justice system, also influences proceedings in summary court. The constraints now imposed on magistrates by the Treasury create pressures to process cases as quickly as possible – whatever the consequences for the defence. The magistrates, explained a defence solicitor,

> [have] got to get through so many cases per day in order to qualify for funding. The magistrates' clerks have to make sure that their lists are moving quickly, not delayed by adjournments, even when there is good cause – as when a witness may be needed. No one wants proper preparation. The defence may have a very difficult time in the face of all that. He's put under pressure

because he knows that he is going to be [seen as] irritating if he holds things up in any way. (Interview with John Davis, solicitor-advocate, June 1995).

Financial considerations also influence case preparation in summary court. The introduction of fixed fees has contributed to a diminished defence, and to an increased number of convictions, by discouraging lawyers from doing more than the minimum required.

> One of the factors accounting for the ever higher conviction rate in the magistrates' court is that the Lord Chancellor introduced fixed fees for contested trials. In the past you were paid by the hour, but now there are fixed fees for a trial. And while the fee for a plea of guilty, which takes very little time, is about £200, the fee for a fully contested defence in a summary trial is only about £500 – no matter how many hours you work. So the incentive to prepare cases is gone. Many of my colleagues ... have adapted by developing practices which just pile it high and sell it cheap. They just take their fee and run. They do one interview with the client and then defend him. There is no incentive to do anything more. No one wants proper preparation. The courts don't want it, the Lord Chancellor doesn't want it.[18]

The attitude of magistrates toward the accused is shared by some defence lawyers who represent defendants in the magistrates' courts and in the Crown Court. The findings of McConville *et al.* (1994), that defence lawyers are predisposed to a belief in the guilt of their clients, are confirmed by a number of our own interviews. They suggest that a number of lawyers have a negative, or at least equivocal, attitude toward their role as defender of the accused. Among solicitors, this is reinforced as a consequence of very high conviction rates in summary court. Like the magistrates, they become increasingly inclined to assume the guilt of those who are charged by the police, and to empathize with the latter's desire and effort to convict them. This is illustrated in the remarks of a Birmingham duty solicitor, who is intended to serve as the frontline defender of a person suspected of a criminal offence:

> My personal view is that a lot of those people, perhaps most of them, have in fact committed the offence for which they are brought to the police station. Now my job should not be to allow people who've committed offences to get off. I say this *shouldn't* be

my job, but in a sense it *is* my job ... [B]ut looking at it from the viewpoint of the population as a whole, that's not right, is it?[19]

An attempt to explain why some solicitors harbour a cynical attitude toward their clients, as well as a high degree of ambivalence about their own role in the criminal process, was made by a former Assistant Secretary General of the Law Society.

> People do get case-hardened. Most people ... are charged with a standard set of offences: thefts, shop-lifting, burglaries, etcetera. Therefore, solicitors see the same kind of case happening time and time again; and you can't exactly blame them for thinking: 'I have seen many of these cases before and it will surprise me greatly that this person is going to be somebody who didn't actually do it.' So the fact that defence lawyers can jump to that sort of conclusion fairly early on in a case is hardly surprising.[20]

The guilty-plea orientation of most defence lawyers is reflected in the way solicitors' firms are structured and in the approach adopted in preparing cases (McConville *et al.*, 1994). Widespread delegation of responsibilities to non-solicitors is common. It is clear also that they do very little proactive defence work for their clients. They do not seek to find evidence to support their client's case, nor do they attempt an independent investigation of the evidence of the prosecution.[21] In fact, observed Roger Ede,

> it strikes me as odd here that in preparing cases for the magistrates' court, you don't actually go out and try to find out whether what the prosecution witness is saying is true, or ... whether they can shed any other light on matters [which might] point you to other witnesses or to other inquiries you can make. (Interview, May 1995)

Instead, what is done by way of case preparation reflects a strategy largely limited to trying to shoot down the prosecution case: typically taking a proof of evidence to affirm or rebut the prosecution case.

The inadequacy of trial preparation is not limited to solicitors in summary court cases; it applies equally to barristers and to the Crown Court, where the pre-trial preparation of solicitors may be aggravated by the poor advocacy of counsel. In 1989, Marcel Berlins described the standard of performance of barristers as 'competently mediocre'; and this assessment was endorsed in 1996 by Helga Drummand. Having observed the performances of 60 advocates in court, both prosecuting and defending, she concluded that while roughly one-third of the presentations were good, the remainder were shot through with faults of one kind or another. Thus, 'for every confident presentation, there are at least two advocates floundering' (1996: 656). In her view, advocacy involves telling a story in a systematic fashion,[22] and she noted that those who performed best were armed with well-filled, hand-written notebooks. She suggested that many of the faults observed were due to inadequate preparation followed up by attempts to disguise such inadequacy. However, neither inadequate pre-trial preparation by defence solicitors nor the poor advocacy of counsel at the trial are considered grounds for appealing against conviction.[23]

Part of the weakness of the defence in court is traceable to the last-minute receipt of briefs: the less time a barrister has to prepare a case, the longer it takes to present it in court and the poorer the performance. But it is equally clear that barristers are not helped by the inadequate pre-trial preparation of solicitors. Moreover, the division of labour that exists in the legal profession introduces a 'moving part' to the criminal justice system; and moving parts increase the need for liaison and coordination – which is notable largely for its absence. The result too often is a lack of critical information at trial, which cripples the process. Drummand (1996) cites one court session concerned with bail applications in which half the cases were adjourned, as counsel were unable to produce vital evidence because communication with the solicitors had broken down. Each party had assumed that the other would take the initiative. The judge was quite displeased, especially as this was the second time in one week that the system had failed to work.

Overall, the failures of defence lawyers may contribute to the wrongful conviction of innocent persons. Yet the harmful consequences to defendants of poor advocacy have been especially difficult to correct because of the clear reluctance of judges to question the performance of defence lawyers, particularly that of barristers. Although defence lawyers may inadequately prepare or otherwise perform poorly in either the pre-trial or trial stages, the Court of Appeal has been strongly averse to consider this matter as grounds for overturning a conviction.[24] This was unambiguously stipulated in the remarks of Taylor J in the case of *R v. Gautam*:[25] 'It should be clearly understood that if defending counsel in the course of his conduct of a case makes a decision, or takes a course which later appears to have been mistaken or unwise, that generally speaking has never been regarded as a proper ground for appeal.'

Nor has the Court indicated much flexibility on the issue in more recent cases: incompetency of counsel as the grounds for a criminal appeal still remains very limited.[26] In *R v. Swain*,[27] the Court held that if it had a lurking doubt that the defendant might have suffered some injustice as the result of 'flagrantly incompetent advocacy' by his counsel, then it would quash the conviction. This was reiterated in *R v. Ensor*,[28] where the Court held that counsel's errors may constitute valid grounds for appeal *only* in the case of 'flagrantly incompetent advocacy' and affirmed in *R v. Wellings*.[29] Again the Court was unsympathetic to an appeal grounded only on a mistaken decision by counsel at a trial. It is only when counsel's conduct could be described as flagrantly incompetent advocacy, observed Lord Lang CJ, that the court would be minded to intervene.

However, exceptional conditions may be taken into account. Thus, in *R v. Clinton*,[30] Rougier J. said that where counsel had made decisions in good faith after proper consideration, and where appropriate after due discussion with the client, her decisions could not possibly be said to render a subsequent verdict unsafe or unsatisfactory. But where it was shown that the decision was taken either in defiance, or without proper instructions, or when all the prompting of reason and good sense pointed the other way, it might be open to an appellate court to set aside the verdict. These *exceptional* conditions were found in *Clinton*: the Court held that a positive defence had never been presented to the jury; and that the nature of the case, and of the prosecution evidence, made it essential for the appellant to be advised to give evidence, and the failure of his counsel to call him as a witness had been a grave error. The verdict was found unsafe and unsatisfactory, and the conviction was quashed.

In contrast to the equivocal posture of the appellate court, JUSTICE has long been concerned about miscarriages that flow from errors in defence strategy leading up to and during the trial. In Anne Owers' view, this is a major problem:

> You're talking about a solicitor who has not been sufficiently robust in protecting his client at the police station; or a solicitor or a barrister who, under pressure at trial has just made the wrong decision, or has decided not to call evidence that should be called or not to challenge some evidence when it should have been challenged. [I]t's our view that if those decisions go to the safety of the conviction then they should be arguable grounds for quashing. But the Court of Appeal is particularly suspect in the way in which it deals with defence errors at

trial. Some courts will accept it, some won't. You can feel the profession kind of clamming up together, particularly if it's a barrister that you're talking about. The courts are now readier to criticize solicitors, but where barristers are involved the judges are more closed.[31]

The RCCJ joined JUSTICE in criticizing the Court for ignoring the harmful consequences for the defendant that may flow from the incompetency of defence lawyers, and for the perpetuation of the harm resulting from the unwillingness of the appellate court to take corrective action. Its Report pointedly noted that:

> wrong jury verdicts of guilty may be the result of errors by the lawyers – whether of judgement or of performance – which do not amount to 'flagrantly incompetent advocacy'. It cannot possibly be right that there should be defendants serving prison sentences for no other reason than that their lawyers made a decision which later turns out to have been mistaken. (1993: 174)[32]

In expressing disapproval of the Court's routine dismissal of appeals made on the grounds of incompetent advocacy, the Commission signalled their awareness that the quality of defence provided in the Crown Court often falls far short of what is necessary to ensure adequate protection for the accused. However, as already indicated, the problem begins with the split in the legal profession between solicitors and barristers, and with the division of functions assigned to the two types of lawyers. Solicitors may represent defendants in the magistrates' court, but most must instruct barristers to represent their clients in the Crown Court.[33] This discontinuity of representation ill-serves the interests of clients of the legal profession, especially in criminal cases. Under the prevailing regime, responsibility for the preparation of the defence's case is assigned to a solicitor; but once the preparation is complete, the brief (containing copies of documents relevant to the case) must be passed to an advocate who has the task of representing the defendant in court. As a result, in cases involving indictable offences most solicitors are prevented from representing their client in court.[34] Thus, the brief is passed to counsel, and the accused suddenly finds her fate is in the hands of a barrister with whom she has had no prior contact. Nevertheless, from that moment the determination of whether the accused is acquitted or found guilty will depend in part upon counsel's knowledge of the case, her skills, and her posture toward possible outcomes for the case.

This truncated role encourages the solicitor to disengage from a case as quickly as possible, and with the least amount of involvement. Thus less time and care is spent on case preparation than might be were she to bear an ongoing responsibility for the fate of her client. The resulting harm to the interests of the accused is considerable. According to an experienced solicitor:

> The most serious indictment of the system in many ways is the disincentives it gives to lawyers on both sides of the fence to prepare cases properly ... [T]here is no incentive for the solicitor to prepare it. He's not going to be facing the judge in court. The judge is not going to tear him up for having failed to produce this or that witness; it's the barrister who is going to get it in the neck ... So the solicitor says to himself, 'Well I don't know what some barrister is going to advise so I'll just prepare the papers in some sort of bog standard way: that is, put in a client's statement, witness statement, wrap it up and send it off to the barrister.' Consequently, briefs are all inadequately prepared.
>
> Nor is there any incentive to take any major decisions, because once counsel gets the case he's going to assert his authority about how it should be run. So the solicitor will say, 'Well, what's the point in me doing any more work on this case – like trying to make some deal with the prosecution by pointing out that they don't have any evidence on this or that charge? What's the point in my doing all that if the barrister might take a different view? So I'll leave all that.'[35]

These factors contribute to the disinclination of solicitors to commit effort to the preparation of cases for Crown Court. However, other factors are at work. McConville *et al.* (1994) argue that financial considerations strongly influence the attitude of solicitors in other respects. In looking at the operation of the majority of firms, they found that much of the preparation associated with Crown Court cases – such as investigations, conferences with counsel, pre-trial discussions and court appearances – is delegated to staff who are non-qualified, have little experience or both. The reason: their services cost less. Thus, it is the primacy of profit which underpins the operations of many firms, including their willingness to devolve all important decisions to counsel (McConville *et al.*, 1994). However, they found exceptions: operating within the same financial limits, some firms are able to provide substantial solicitor input into the preparation of Crown Court cases, whilst others employ non-legally qualified but experienced staff. These exceptions (as in police station work) demonstrate that it is not only financial constraints, but the ideological commitment of lawyers which in part governs their practice (McConville *et al.*, 1994: 239–43).

Despite the solicitor's early disengagement from a Crown Court case she is none the less deeply implicated in the result, for the quality and thoroughness of the brief she passes to counsel very likely influences the latter's view and reaction to the case. Thus, faced with a poorly prepared brief, counsel may seek to avoid trial by persuading the defendant to plead guilty to the charge or to some (negotiated) lesser offence, with the promise of a lesser sentence. Under the worst scenario, an innocent person may be convicted for want of adequate defence. Meanwhile, the barrister can move on to a new brief.[36]

Case preparation by the solicitor should not, although it often does, stop with the handing over of the brief. After discussion of the case with counsel, or on receiving additional information from the prosecution, further investigation may be required, such as following up on witnesses, taking statements or instructing forensic experts. In some firms, in fact, experienced and legally qualified staff handle Crown Court work, carrying out detailed investigation and legal research as well as liaising closely with counsel.[37] However, in many practices Crown Court work is considered routine, requiring only the 'attendance' of someone to 'sit behind counsel' who will take notes and report back on the case outcome; thus, inexperienced staff with little or no knowledge of the case are employed; typically this may be a clerk or secretary, and in some instances even friends or family. Moreover, having transmitted the brief to a barrister, the solicitor relinquishes responsibility.

Apart from relieving the solicitor of a sense of responsibility, the introduction of counsel as the defendant's new representative serves other purposes. The barrister is presented as 'the expert' who has been 'specially chosen' for the client, and as someone who can provide a further independent and dispassionate opinion on the case. However, rather than having the benefit of a second legal adviser in the construction of their defence, defendants may find themselves ambushed into pleading guilty. Most do not meet their barrister until the day of trial, and conferences held prior to the trial date may often form a part of that 'ambush' strategy. Thus, despite expressing personal commitment to the client, doubts are raised by counsel about the way in which the court would view the evidence and the credibility of the witnesses, as well as how the defendant's story might look to the jury.

This paves the way for further pressure to be applied on the day of trial, when the defendant is at her most vulnerable.

In instances where this ambush strategy runs counter to the instructions in the brief, the presence of a solicitor's clerk is often ineffectual. She may have little or no prior involvement and be in possession of insufficient information about the case to raise any objections, as well as being generally overawed by the whole process and so unable to resist counsel's actions. Lesser charges are negotiated by defence counsel with the prosecution on the day of the trial and then sold to the client and clerk as a good deal which the barrister has fought hard to secure.[38] Defendants are in no position to contradict the 'professional' (who claims access to the personal views of the judge, together with insider knowledge of the daily workings of the court), least of all in the emotionally charged setting at the door of the court.

One reason counsel might encourage the defendant to plead guilty is the pressure felt by the barrister herself. Because of the unpredictability of the 'list system' used in Crown Court, barristers may confront conflicting case responsibilities on a given court day which necessitate the hurried passing of a brief to another barrister. This is reportedly a very common occurrence and it means that the barrister to whom the brief is passed must prepare herself to represent the case on the shortest possible notice – perhaps on the afternoon before the case is to be heard, if not on the trial date itself. Zander and Henderson (1993) found that there were barrister changes before trial in 48 per cent of cases, and 25 per cent of barristers received their brief only in the afternoon before trial. Thus on scant notice and without ever having met the client, the barrister must review the evidence and somehow be prepared to defend 'her' client in court. Not surprisingly, some barristers might look for an easy way out by persuading the client to plead guilty, accept a negotiated sentence, and thus avoid the trial. The results of counsel having received a late brief in terms of the consequences for her client were explained by a solicitor as follows:

> Most of the barristers I see will come straight into court to see a client they've never met before. They will arrive at the courtroom, three-quarters of an hour before the case starts, and meet the client for the first time with a bundle of papers that they would have read the night before. And the barrister will almost immediately start saying to the client 'Look, I've read all your papers; your solicitor is

a wonderful man, but I can tell you that you really haven't got a chance ... I know you thought you might be pleading not guilty, but having looked at everything there's no way that you are going to get acquitted ... If you plead not guilty and you contest this sort of thing, you will almost certainly go to jail. And I can see exactly why you don't want to plead guilty, but this is what you are going to do. But don't worry old fellow, because we're going to stop you going to jail.'[39]

The RCCJ acknowledged that last-minute changes of counsel lead to hurried reviews of evidence, and to efforts to encourage defendants to plead guilty to avoid severe sentence and/or to secure a lesser negotiated sentence. Their response was to propose changes to limit the number of late or 'returned' briefs, backed up by judicially imposed sanctions in the form of costs, or referral to the Professional Conduct Committee of the Bar, who should make and enforce the appropriate rules to ensure effective pre-trial preparatory work (1993: 108–9). However, failing a drastic change in the courts' list system, it is unlikely that anything will be done about returned briefs.

The RCCJ acknowledged that things go wrong in court as a result of incompetent and poorly prepared barristers, and that 'action is seldom taken to put them right or to prevent a recurrence' (1993: 139). Accordingly, they proposed (i) measures to ensure that barristers are adequately trained and fully competent; (ii) the creation of a code of practice for the conduct of advocates in court; (iii) compulsory training in forensic science and psychiatry for lawyers involved in criminal work; and (iv) the enforcement of professional standards and sanctions for incompetent performance of lawyers.

However, despite the Commission's stated commitment to increasing the fairness of trials, they appeared to be far more preoccupied with their cost and efficiency. Thus, in addition to proposals for preparatory hearings, plea bargaining and sentence discounts, they also recommended (pp. 120–2) that: indictments be drafted more precisely (no more than a listing of offences and the briefest of facts to support the allegations); the prosecution's opening speech be shortened to 15 minutes; judges be allowed to cut the presentation of irrelevant or repetitive evidence and to punish 'time-wasting counsel' by ordering a cut in their fees; and, wherever possible, the reduction of evidence to written statements. All of these proposals, whatever the RCCJ claims to the contrary, may be seen as designed more to streamline and cut the cost of trials than to make trials fairer.

Trials: evidence, convictions and wrongful convictions

The Commission were not willing to concern themselves with the more fundamental aspects of trials that have contributed to miscarriages of justice. Firstly, there is the matter of evidence: very little is required to convict.[40] With few exceptions, a single type of evidence will suffice to convict, provided only that the jury believes it and is satisfied that the guilt of the accused has been established beyond a reasonable doubt. Thus in their study of 45 contested cases in magistrates' courts, McConville *et al.* (1991) found that in 77.7 per cent of them witness testimony was the principal piece of evidence relied upon by the prosecution; and these findings parallel those in Vennard (1982).

Unfortunately, reliance upon a single type of evidence may lead to wrongful convictions, as occurred in the cases of the Birmingham Six and Tottenham Three. Uncorroborated confessions have been found to be unreliable in many cases,[41] yet courts do not find them to be. The Commission, despite alarming evidence of oppressive police behaviour used to extract confessions, rejected all significant proposals to deal with the problem.[42] Instead, they accepted the 'general rule' of the courts that 'the evidence of a single witness (except for cases of perjury, sexual offences and treason) is sufficient to prove any issue' (1993: 63). To prevent wrongful convictions the Commission relies on the 'safeguards' of the PACE Code of Practice (pp. 57–9), police professionalism, and suspect access to defence lawyers, together with the judicial warning to juries of the dangers of convicting on a single piece of evidence (pp. 66–8). Unfortunately, a vast body of research – and recent cases – have shown that the 'safeguards' cited are inadequate protection against the conviction of innocents; and juries are free to ignore judicial warnings.

The requirement that confessions be corroborated by other supporting evidence has been advanced as one way of improving the standard of evidence in criminal prosecutions and avoiding miscarriages of justice. Although the trend has been to move away from corroboration requirements, this has been related to the evidence of particular categories of witness.[43] There are cogent reasons for treating confession evidence differently from other forms of evidence. Whilst it is now acknowledged that the evidence of children or rape victims is not inherently unreliable, the reverse is true of confession evidence (Greer 1994: 113). A wealth of empirical research, as well as numerous miscarriages of justice, have demonstrated the unreliability of confessions.

Indeed the Royal Commission itself notes that the reliability of the accused's own admissions can no longer be assumed;[44] and in the light of this, it considered a requirement that a confession should be admissible only if there is other independent supporting evidence or, alternatively, that the trial judge be required to issue a warning to the jury.

It began by recognising that the belief that individuals will not make statements against their own interests can no longer be sustained. Accused persons may confess to crimes which they have not committed for a number of reasons, and this is more likely under the pressures of police–suspect interrogation, even where safeguards are applied.[45] The Commission marks out four distinct categories of false confessions (1993: 57). People may confess out of a desire for notoriety or because they cannot distinguish between reality and fantasy. Secondly, suspects may confess in order to protect someone else. Thirdly, there are coerced-compliant confessions: the suspect may see an immediate advantage in confessing, such as the end to questioning and release from custody. Finally, some individuals may be persuaded temporarily by the interrogating officers that they have in fact committed the crime, a phenomenon known as the coerced-internalized confession.

The Commission went on to note that confession evidence takes on too central a role in police investigations, and improper pressure leading to inaccurate statements may be applied in order to achieve this objective. Once admissions have been obtained, further enquiries are unlikely: this signals the close of the investigation. A requirement to obtain further supporting evidence may encourage a wider investigation and act as a check upon the validity of the confession. However, the Commission rejected the proposal, arguing that a corroboration requirement 'would not by itself prevent miscarriages of justice resulting from fabricated confessions and the production of supporting evidence obtained by improper means' (1993: 65).

No rules or procedures can guarantee against human error or deliberate falsification and so this is not a good reason for their rejection. Indeed, as Greer (1994: 113) points out, there is no evidence to suggest that the risk of supporting evidence being falsified is higher than that of convicting innocents on the basis of uncorroborated confessions. Leng (1994: 181) criticizes the Commission's reasoning as 'ludicrous': while a corroboration rule could never protect suspects against 'determined and sophisticated efforts to frame them', it would protect defendants against being convicted solely on the basis of evidence which is intrinsically unreliable.

The Commission further argued that the small percentage of cases whose outcomes might be affected by corroborative evidence[46] did not justify the additional resources that would be required to produce it (p. 65); however, it had already undermined its own argument by acknowledging that the absolute numbers of cases impacted by a corroboration rule would be quite high: over 100,000 cases are tried annually in the Crown Court, and as many as 1.5 million in the magistrates' courts. Yet the RCCJ persisted in its view of corroborative evidence as not only unnecessary, but even counter-productive.[47] Overriding concerns about the unreliability of confessions is the Commission's inability to countenance the loss of any convictions along the way. It is assumed that the trial process itself will rectify and deal with any errors, and that magistrates and jurors will assess properly the weight to be given to evidence produced. This, of course, ignores the fact that few cases go to trial and many defendants will plead guilty as a result of there being no corroboration requirement, since they effectively have no choice. There will not be an opportunity to evaluate the evidence. These recommendations also fail to distinguish between recorded and unrecorded confessions. As Leng notes, 'Stated baldly, the Commission proposes that a criminal conviction can be based on a police officer's assertion that the defendant confessed, where the defendant denies this and there is not a shred of further evidence' (1994: 182).

Based on the willingness of judges to admit police evidence secured in breach of PACE Codes, to tolerate poor preparation by defence lawyers and to allow juries to convict solely on the strength of confessions (which often turn out to be unreliable: for example, fabricated by police or made by innocent persons under pressure of police interrogation), it would not be unreasonable to infer that some judges, along with the police, magistrates and lawyers (perhaps the judges' colleagues before they were appointed to the bench), may also view the accused as guilty.[48] At minimum, the conduct of some judges in summing-up a trial has displayed an unwarranted tilt toward the prosecution rather than adhering to the role of a neutral umpire in a trial to determine innocence or guilt. A judge may influence the view of the jury by means of pointed interventions during the presentation and cross-examination of evidence, but their potential influence is greater during summing-up, when they are given free rein to comment as they wish upon the evidence, provided only that it is made clear that the jury must make their own judgment about the facts. But however clearly the judge may assert that the jury is free to ignore her views, it does not exclude influence; and in a number of miscarriage of justice cases judges have made summations to the jury which were prejudicial to the defence.[49] Thus, in order to enhance the fairness of trials, the Commission proposed eliminating the judge's summing-up of facts where this is not necessary, and that judges be completely neutral where it was (p. 124). They also proposed more attention to monitoring the overall performance of judges (pp. 140–1).[50]

Forensic science, other expert evidence and wrongful conviction

Forensic science evidence and the testimony of scientific experts play an increasingly important role in criminal proceedings. However, flawed forensic evidence, the misuse of forensic data by prosecution and the withholding of critical forensic evidence from the defence were either the main or contributing factors in a number of well-known cases of wrongful conviction.[51] In the *Guildford Four*,[52] for example, two Defence Ministry forensic scientists allegedly colluded with police investigators in altering their statements (Mullin, 1991: para. 27). The *Birmingham Six*[53] convictions were based on the 'Greiss test', which Home Office scientists claimed was an indicator of the handling of certain explosive substances. Subsequently, other scientists at the same Home Office laboratory found the test to be unreliable, yet none acknowledged this finding. The convictions were upheld in the Court of Appeal on the strength of further evidence from a Home Office scientist at Aldermaston. However, three years later she acknowledged that the Lord Chief Justice had misrepresented her evidence in his 1987 judgment, although she said nothing at the time of the appeal (Mullin, 1991: paras. 28–30). Such behaviour, explains Mullin, lies in the influence of relationships that develop between police officers in charge of criminal investigations and Home Office forensic scientists.[54] 'The moral of all this seems to be: 'put not thy faith in experts'- particularly forensic scientists in the employ of the Home Office or the Ministry of Defence (ibid.: paras. 32–3).'

These cases, along with other miscarriages of justice, provided the impetus for creating the RCCJ. However, its *Report* was particularly inadequate in dealing with problems highlighted by wrongful convictions resulting from mistaken or fabricated forensic science evidence in criminal trials. However, as a growing body of research has demonstrated the unreliability of confession evidence, so the police and prosecution have come to rely increasingly on forensic science evidence as

a new and almost unchallengeable substitute. DNA evidence, in particular, seems destined to play an ever greater role in the investigation
and prosecution of criminal offences, at least in serious crime cases.
With the help of scene of crime officers (SOCOs), DNA samples may be
obtained which may then be sent to a Forensic Science Service (FSS) lab
which has the capability to search for a match either by conducting a
mass DNA screening of potential suspects,[55] or by using the FSS database. If found, a match provides evidence likely to be seen as nearly
irrefutable. DNA regulations issued by the Home Office in 1995 stipulated that the police cannot force a suspect to submit to DNA testing;
but if a person suspected of involvement in a recordable offence[56]
refuses without good cause to give consent, a court or jury is allowed to
draw such inferences from the refusal as appear appropriate.[57]
However, any sample taken from a volunteer[58] can be used only in
relation to that incident; assuming it does not match the sample taken
from the scene of the crime, it should be kept only until the end of
court proceedings and then destroyed.

While critics of DNA and the databank see these less as a tool of
investigation for offences already committed than as the latest instru-
ment available to the police in their surveillance of suspect populations,[59] some criminal lawyers are prepared to view the development as
a means of reducing police reliance on confessions to secure convictions. As Roger Ede explained:

> [We said] that the police rely too much upon interviews to obtain evi-
> dence ... that they should not rely upon confessions to the extent that
> they do – they should try and obtain independent evidence. Now if
> you say that then you've got to allow them the opportunities to do so.
> And so ... we are not against the increase in their powers to take
> samples ... to conduct DNA analysis, providing that there is ... an
> increase in the availability of legal aid so that defence lawyers can ...
> test the accuracy of the analysis which is used in a particular case.
> (Interview, May 1995)

Despite cases which demonstrate that the alleged certainty of forensic
science is a fallacy, lawyers ignorant of scientific evidence, especially
DNA evidence, tend to view it as objective and unambiguous
(Redmayne, 1997). Confronted with it, they may abandon hopes of
securing an acquittal for their client.[60] Yet 'there are nearly always
alternative explanations for apparently incriminating evidence, and
if these are put to a FSS scientist in the witness box they have to be

conceded' (Roberts and Willmore, 1993: 128). Moreover, defence experts in Crown Court cases (in which advance disclosure of prosecution evidence is required[61]) may conduct tests which may oblige prosecution forensic experts to modify their scientific opinion by calling attention to the significance of some factor they have overlooked. However, this assumes that the defence lawyer decides that it is worthwhile to have forensic tests conducted, that she secures Legal Aid Board authorization for payment and that she succeeds in locating a forensic expert who is willing and has time to conduct tests and make a report prior to the trial date.

The task of merely locating an appropriate defence expert can be a problem for the defence. FSS scientists have been able to undertake work on behalf of the defence ever since the FSS became independent in 1991. Thus, theoretically, defence lawyers have access to the same forensic science expertise that is available to the police and prosecution. However, several factors make defence lawyers reluctant to use the FSS: its historic and ongoing connection with police authorities, for whom 90 per cent of FSS services are still performed;[62] its relative lack of accessibility to defence; and client and lawyer distrust of the FSS's ability to keep defence matters confidential.[63] The alternative is the independent expert: however, there are far fewer experts in the private sector to serve criminal defence lawyers than in the state's FSS, who serve the police and prosecution. Moreover, many independent experts view criminal legal work as non-lucrative and fraught with payment problems, i.e. often characterized by long delays sometimes coupled with reductions based on Legal Aid Board decisions that cases merit lower levels of expertise (Roberts and Willmore, 1993: 74). Dependence on Legal Aid also discourages defence lawyers from seeking forensic expertise: getting authorization from the Legal Aid Board is cumbersome and takes time, little of which may be available to the defence lawyer.

Finally, the dependence of the defence on prosecution disclosure creates disadvantages for defence lawyers: they cannot know whether forensic evidence forms part of the prosecution case until this is served on them, at which point they must scramble to secure forensic expertise to assess it.[64] Frequently this is less than one week before the date of trial or plea hearing.[65] Assuming the defence lawyer succeeds on short notice in securing a forensic expert, two factors make it difficult for the latter to prepare the case properly. Firstly, physical evidence at the crime scene may be depleted, degraded or contaminated, thus handicapping her ability to conduct scientific analyses; secondly, the time to conduct tests and prepare a report is sharply limited. And while

defence lawyers may request an adjournment, there is a growing reluctance of courts to grant them.[66] Faced with these constraints, the
defence tends to be limited to either criticizing the scientific evidence
of the prosecution or conceding guilt (ibid.: 67). Remarking that this
was not unusual, a CPS solicitor sympathized with the defence's plight:
'That's why so many cases go guilty at the last minute, because the
defence are being pushed into things. They probably only had full
instructions the day before ... The [magistrates'] court doesn't give
anyone much chance here' (ibid.: 70–1).

However, another (unrelated) factor also contributes to guilty pleas:
that is, the paucity of pre-trial meetings between prosecution experts
and lawyers.[67] Once the FSS have completed their scientific report the
prosecution seldom asks them to elaborate, hence there is little opportunity for the prosecution expert to explain potentially *misleading* parts
of the report or to correct any misinterpretation the lawyers may have.
This situation, conclude Roberts and Willmore (1993: 63), 'affords considerable scope for misunderstanding between lawyers and scientists,
in which case a fair and accurate account of the strengths and limitations of forensic science evidence may not be presented to the court'.
The results are, obviously, harmful to the accused: 'In the great majority of cases these reports will either induce the defendant to plead
guilty, or be agreed by the defence and read to the court according to
the s. 9 procedure' (ibid.: 57).

Even when defence lawyers secure their own forensic evidence, their
ability to challenge the prosecution is often limited by their lack of
familiarity with forensic science. According to FSS experts, 'defence
counsel and defence solicitor-advocates frequently [appear] to lack
sufficient understanding of scientific evidence to enable them to
subject expert prosecution evidence to adequate scrutiny or to high-
light its limitations' (ibid.: 126).[68] This raises serious questions about
whether scientific evidence can be adequately tested in the trial
process, especially given that, in most cases, it is presented in written
form, without the benefit of explanatory testimony in court by the
scientific expert (ibid.: 121).[69] Finally, and significantly, if defence
lawyers are unable to assess and point to potential flaws or limitations
of scientific evidence, the jury – whose members are not likely to be
familiar with scientific evidence – may feel obliged to accept its validity. This could, as the RCCJ acknowledged, lead to miscarriages of
justice (1993: 159).

A number of the RCCJ's recommendations to deal with problems
associated with the use of forensic science by the prosecution were

unfavourable to the accused. For instance, they recommended that where a suspect does not supply an intimate or non-intimate sample in non-serious arrestable offences, the court may draw inferences from the refusal capable of corroborating any other evidence; and that certain minor offences (assault and small-scale burglary) be reclassified as serious arrestable offences for the purpose of allowing the police to take non-intimate samples without consent.[70] On the other hand, their proposals for addressing the handicaps of defence lawyers in dealing with scientific evidence were hardly adequate. It was suggested that lawyers should become familiar with forensic scientific issues by continuing education, vocational training and interdisciplinary exchanges with scientific experts (1993: 161); however, if lawyers are disinclined to meet with scientific experts or cannot find the time to do so in the process of defending their clients, it seems unlikely that they would be agreeable or find the time to do the things recommended by the Commission. In any event, the RCCJ's recommendations fail to address the prospect that forensic evidence in the possession of the prosecution might not be forthcoming despite the operation of the disclosure regime, unless the defence statement indicates its potential relevance.

Other Commission recommendations were sensitive to the plight of the accused. Thus to prevent repetitions of injustice resulting from prosecution misuse of forensic evidence, the RCCJ recommended full prosecution disclosure to the defence of forensic science evidence and other scientific material in its possession, as well as sufficient Legal Aid to enable the defence to secure forensic expertise (1993: 155–6). However, as noted earlier, while full disclosure is now required in Crown Court cases, it does not extend to summary court, where the vast majority of offences are processed. Moreover, even where disclosure is required it can only benefit the accused if defence lawyers have sufficient access to forensic expertise to enable them adequately to assess the strengths and limitations of the prosecution's scientific evidence, and here problems remain.

Mindful that wrongful convictions that resulted from the misuse of forensic science might never have occurred were it not for the virtual monopoly of this resource by the prosecution, critics see only limited change in this respect. Prosecution forces not only have primary and ongoing control over forensic data; they also enjoy a preponderance of forensic expertise as compared to the defence. In the investigation of criminal offences the cost of forensic analysis is met by the police during investigation; when the case comes to trial, the cost is borne by the CPS and, notably, in more than one-third of all contested Crown

Court cases forensic evidence is used; yet defence funding for forensic expertise remains dependent on the Legal Aid Board, and it may therefore be restricted or denied on cost grounds. This tips the balance strongly against the defence, for its ability to challenge the forensic evidence of prosecution is very limited.[71] In 1997–8, for example, police expenditures for forensic analysis from the FSS were ten-fold greater than forensic expenditures by defence.[72]

The RCCJ also recommended the establishment of a Forensic Science Advisory Council to monitor the performance of forensic experts, encourage research and the development of expertise, and formulate codes of practice for forensic scientists (1993: 151). The Advisory Council never materialized, but the FSS did adopt a Code of Practice, and certain other proposals made by the RCCJ were realized by means of legislation. Thus the findings and reports of the FSS, when used in prosecutions, must now be made available to the defence under the prosecution disclosure provisions of the CPIA 1996, as well as to the Criminal Cases Review Commission (CCRC; see Chapter 9) under provisions of the CAA 1995.[73] The expertise of the FSS is also at the disposal of defence lawyers and the CCRC, who may request the FSS to conduct forensic investigations, with the costs to be paid by Legal Aid funds.

Meanwhile the role of the FSS in crime solving has grown greatly. Established in 1991 as a nondepartmental executive agency of the Home Office, the FSS set up a National DNA Database on behalf of the police in April 1995, and in 1996 it merged with the Metropolitan Police Forensic Science Laboratory to create a national service. In addition to the Laboratory at its Birmingham headquarters, the FSS has several regional laboratories, and by January 1997 it was the principal provider of forensics to the 43 police forces in England and Wales, as well as to the Home Office and other law enforcement agencies.[74]

The RCCJ suggested that by enabling the FSS to support itself entirely from payments for services rendered (which it now does) it may be expected to acquire a sense of independence from its customers (1993: 146). However, this seems unrealistic for two reasons. Firstly, the sheer volume of FSS commitments to the prosecution – its DNA Database in Birmingham alone receives an average of 4,000 submissions a week from the police[75] – structures its relationship with them. Secondly, since FSS reports are conditioned by daily requests for tests which will support or refute the investigative hypotheses of the police, the scientist is constantly oriented to the perspectives and concerns of the prosecution. This may cause her, inadvertently perhaps, to exclude or overlook things which might be material to the defence case; and in this way the forensic expert becomes part of the prosecution team. The result, as Roberts and Willmore (1993) argue, is a FSS scientist cannot help but operate in a subordinate and reactive position relative to the prosecution agencies.

Summary

The pre-trial processes of arrest, interrogation, prosecution and defence preparation are all crucial in shaping the case that comes before the court. But the trial itself is the forum where the evidence can be presented orally, tested through cross-examination and the issue of guilt or innocence decided by an impartial tribunal. Yet, the conduct of trials in both the magistrates' and the Crown Court fails to achieve this objective in several respects.

The vast majority of cases are heard in the magistrates' court by lay justices with no legal training. They are widely perceived by defendants and their lawyers as being favourably disposed towards the police, whose evidence makes up the prosecution case in the majority of instances, and whom they view as defenders of decent society. The high number of guilty pleas, together with the magistrates' negative view of defendants, has a tendency to make lay benches case-hardened and unsympathetic to the accused.

In an adversarial system, it is the job of the defence to test out the prosecution evidence, and to present the defendant's case in the best possible light. This involves thorough pre-trial case preparation as well as skillful advocacy. Once a guilty plea has been entered, the court will not seek to 'look behind' it in any way. It is assumed that the plea is entered on the basis of legal advice, after consideration of the prosecution evidence: the judgment of the defence lawyer, therefore, is crucial. Most defendants, however, are poorly served by their own defence lawyers who lack an adversarial ideology in which to ground their practice. Delegation to non-legally qualified and inexperienced staff is widespread, and this trend is further reinforced by the Legal Aid fee structure. Solicitors and clerks alike are guilty-plea oriented and engage in little proactive defence work.

The employment of a barrister in Crown Court cases also presents problems. Briefs are inadequate and conferences rarely take place before the day of trial. The solicitor's representative is often unfamiliar with the case, and so unable to resist counsel's pressure upon the defendant to plead guilty. Whilst the most flagrant breaches of professional duty attract comment from the court, as in the Cardiff Three case, or that of Ivan Fergus, and exceptionally, they may constitute grounds for appeal, in general, the courts are reluctant to interfere in the professional lawyer–client relationship and the decisions which flow from it.

The nature of the evidence presented at trial, and the weight attached to it, may also contribute to wrongful convictions. Despite the unreliability of confession evidence, the RCCJ failed to recommend safeguards which might diminish the centrality of admissions to the prosecution case. Forensic evidence is becoming an increasingly significant factor in many trials and both prosecution and defence lawyers are reluctant to challenge the view of the experts whose evidence they view as objective and therefore unassailable. However, such evidence is not objective: consciously or unconsciously, forensic scientists working for the police have tailored their evidence to the prosecution case and alternative explanations which might benefit the defence have been neglected. Increased police power to take DNA samples and the creation of a DNA database bank will continue this trend. But whilst DNA evidence can reliably demonstrate that a person could not be the offender, the reverse is not necessarily true. Lawyers need to be more knowledgeable and more confident in dealing with these types of evidence, if they are to be able to test and challenge them at trial. The establishment of the FSS offers some hope of a more independent service, but given that only a minority of its work is conducted for the defence, the close ties with the police are likely to continue.

9
The Appellate System and Miscarriages of Justice

The appellate system and miscarriages of justice

Since all systems are fallible, the existence of mechanisms to review and rectify errors made is of central importance. Within the criminal justice process errors of the trial court may result in either a wrongful conviction or sentence. Access to an effective appeal process is required both to remedy errors and injustices and (it is hoped) to deter practices which lead to them. Beyond the injustice which may be suffered by individuals, wider damage to the integrity of the system may result from wrongful convictions; therefore, miscarriages must be rooted out and put right as quickly as possible. As Zander noted in his Dissent to the RCCJ report: 'Where the integrity of the process is fatally flawed, the conviction should be quashed as an expression of the system's repugnance at the methods used by those acting for the prosecution' (RCCJ, 1993: 234).

This chapter examines the operation of the appeal process with particular reference to its adequacy in dealing with alleged miscarriages of justice. As a result of the recommendations of the Runciman Commission, the Criminal Cases Review Commission (CCRC) was established under the 1995 Criminal Appeals Act (CAA). This body replaces the much criticized system of Home Office referrals to the Court of Appeal, and we evaluate its first year of operation in order to assess the extent to which it has been successful.

Appeals from the trial court

Appeals against summary convictions are mainly dealt with by the Crown Court,[1] but decisions by the magistrates may also be challenged in the High Court by way of case stated. Any person convicted by a magistrates' court following a plea of not guilty has an automatic right of appeal to the Crown Court against conviction and sentence. A guilty plea normally debars an accused from appealing against summary conviction, unless the plea is found to be in some way 'equivocal' (MCA, s. 108(1)). This may be where it is entered under duress or oppression, or the accused raises a legal defence – for example, admitting assault but stating that it was in self-defence.

An appeal against conviction is heard by a circuit judge or recorder who normally sits with two lay magistrates;[2] and the appeal takes the form of a re-hearing of the summary trial, with the possibility of calling fresh evidence. When the hearing has concluded the Crown Court's decision is announced by the judge, who identifies the issues in the case and how each was resolved. The Crown Court may dispose of an appeal by confirming, reversing or varying any part of the decision which is the subject of the appeal; or it may remit the matter, together with its opinion, to the magistrates (s. 48, CJA 1988).

Table 9.1   Magistrates' courts: caseload and types of case, 1997–98

	Number	*Per cent*
Summary	794,441	56.0
Indictable/either way	559,749	39.5
Advice	52,233	3.8
Other	11,362	0.8

Source: CPS (1998) *Annual Report, 1997–98*: 38.

Table 9.2   Disposition of cases by magistrates' courts, 1997–98

	Number	*Per cent*
Heard by magistrates	967,539	71.5[1]
Committed to Crown Court	104,784	8.0
Discontinued	—	12.0
Other dispositions	—	9.0

Source: CPS (1998).
Note: 1. About 60 per cent of the cases heard by the magistrate's court are motoring offences. See Home Office (1997: 135).

Figures for the trial venue of all cases show in Table 9. 2 that only 8 per cent are committed to the Crown Court and an overwhelming proportion of all criminal offences are processed by summary trial. Given the emphasis placed upon disposing of cases in the most efficient manner possible, there is considerable potential for errors in procedure and judgment. Yet the Royal Commission appeared quite sanguine about the outcomes of cases handled by the magistrates and gave scant attention to them. Based on the very small percentage of appeals against conviction relative to the total number of cases processed, it concluded that most people tried in summary court are satisfied with the quality of justice received. However, given the negative attitude of both defence lawyers and defendants towards the magistrates, the widespread view that magistrates are pro-police and pro-conviction,[3] and reports of poor quality defence case preparation by untrained personnel in solicitors' firms,[4] the Commission's assumptions about the quality of summary justice appear misplaced. Moreover, the number of appeals as a percentage of the total of all cases processed by the magistrates is not a good gauge of either the relative magnitude of appeals, or of the degree of 'customer' satisfaction with the quality of summary justice. A more realistic measure is the number of defendants tried and convicted who are likely to appeal against them. Therefore, the first step is to exclude traffic offences, which account for roughly 60 per cent of summary court convictions,[5] and which (with exceptions) are unlikely to be challenged. Secondly, four-fifths of all convictions follow guilty pleas (see table), and thus are excluded from appealing. When these factors are taken into account, both the proportion of cases involving appeals against conviction and their significance increase. In addition, a not insignificant number of defendants who believe themselves wrongfully convicted are discouraged from appealing either by

Table 9.3 Disposition of cases heard by magistrates, 1997–98

	Number	Per cent
Total convicted	953,753	98.1[1]
of which:		
Guilty pleas	788,364	81.1
Found guilty in absence	111,687	11.5
Convictions after trial	53,702	5.5
Dismissals/acquitted	18,407	1.0

Source: CPS (1998).
Notes: 1. This figure is almost identical to that recorded in 1996–97.

their legal advisers or because of their pessimism about the prospects of success: with almost three-quarters having lost the first round in the trial court,[6] they may well expect to lose again.

Nevertheless, in 1997, 16,269 defendants, or more than one-quarter[7] of the 53,702 defendants convicted after a contested trial,[8] appealed to the Crown Court against their conviction and/or sentence. In 1997, 42 per cent of the appellants had their appeals allowed or their sentence varied.[9] These data provide at least one indicator of dissatisfaction with the quality of justice in the magistrates' courts. Secondly, in 1996–7 the number of appeals to the Crown Court to correct summary-court decisions was reported as 26.1 per cent lower than the number for 1995–6, due to the extended power granted to magistrates themselves to 're-open cases and rectify mistakes';[10] however, while being told that mistakes are made, and that their number has been reduced by a quarter, no absolute numbers are provided (ibid.).

Furthermore, while there is no leave requirement for appeal to the Crown Court, there are problems associated with challenges to summary conviction. Firstly, to be effective it is essential that, immediately following conviction, the convicted prisoner be provided with at least provisional legal advice as to whether there are grounds of appeal. Yet following convictions in the Crown Court, where custodial sentences are more common and onerous, the provision of post-conviction advice is uneven and of variable quality (Plotnikoff and Woolfson, 1993a).[11] One can well imagine that the provision of advice following summary court judgment where prison sentences are shorter and less frequent, is even more random and of poorer quality. Secondly, the 21-day period allowed to prepare a case for appeal is often too short, especially given the limited recording of evidence and decisions that characterize summary court judgments. Thirdly, the possibility of having a custodial sentence imposed by the Crown Court if an appeal is unsuccessful discourages challenges to summary convictions, where a non-custodial sentence was imposed by the magistrates. Finally, Legal Aid is not always available for advice or representation at Crown Court for re-hearing a case on appeal. The cumulative effect of these impediments is sufficient to reduce considerably the number of appeals initiated.

Where a person has been unsuccessful in appealing to the Crown Court, she may apply for review to the Criminal Cases Review Commission (CCRC).[12] Prior to 1997, this review was undertaken by the Home Office's C3 division, which received around 100 summary cases each year. This represented approximately 17 per cent of their total caseload, but JUSTICE suggest that this percentage would have been higher save for the fact that this avenue of review was little known by either lawyers or the general public.

Despite the impediments and disincentives related to appeal against summary judgment, and limiting attention to the number of convictions actually quashed on appeal, it seems highly questionable to assume, as did the Royal Commission, that the 'great majority of criminal trials [in magistrates' courts] are conducted in a manner which all the participants regard as fair' (RCCJ, 1993: 6).[13] Overall, the number of errors that occur in summary court convictions that result in wrongful convictions is undoubtedly much greater than the Commission suggested.

The Court of Appeal, Criminal Division (hereafter, the Court),[14] which is the next layer in the appellate system, hears appeals from cases tried on indictment. Subject to obtaining leave of the Court of Appeal or a certificate of fitness for appeal from the trial judge in a Crown Court case[15] (rarely granted), any person convicted on indictment (whether she pleaded guilty or not)[16] or sentenced in the Crown Court following committal from the magistrates' court, may appeal against that conviction and/or the sentence to the Court of Appeal. Evaluation of applications is assigned to individual High Court judges who read the application and, without hearing oral argument, decide whether or not to grant leave.[17] The judges conducting the reviews have no special training, and while some have criminal trial experience to draw upon others may not. This makes for unevenness in the knowledge and expertise applied to applications. Moreover a judge may screen a large number of applications after a day in court, and in competition with a preparation for a hearing or judgment on the following day. As a result, applications are not likely to receive similar attention by all judges, or be evaluated according to consistent criteria by even the same judge. Inconsistencies in decisions about appellants are inescapable, and rather than offering detailed reasons, comments attending refusals are often confined to stating that the conviction was 'safe and satisfactory'. Together, these factors lead to unevenness in the overall appeal process.

If leave is refused, as happens in about 60 per cent of the cases, the appellant may have the application decided by a full Court of the Criminal Division; and about half of those refused appeal by a single judge do so. However, the appellate system is more inadequate at this stage: Legal Aid is not available, there are long delays before a hearing takes place and when it does the applicant has no right to be present. Applications are heard without representation since most appellants lack funds to pay for a barrister; and renewals of applications to the

Table 9.4   Data on appeals against conviction: Court of Appeal, 1997

Total number of applications for leave to appeal considered by single judge	2,318
Granted leave to appeal by single judge[1]	537
Granted leave to appeal by Full Court after having been refused by single judge[2]	87
Total number of applicants granted leave to have convictions reviewed by Full Court	624
Appeals against conviction allowed by the Court	186[3]

Source: Lord Chancellor's Department (1998b: Table 1.7).
Notes: 1. 1,457 of the 2,318 were refused leave to appeal; no indication was given of disposition of remaining 324 applications: ibid.
2. These were among the 643 applicants, out of the 1,457 rejected by a single judge, who renewed their applications to the Full Court: ibid.
3. Representing 35 per cent of the 624 granted leave to appeal: ibid.

full Court 'are distinctly less likely to succeed where the appellant is unrepresented' (RCCJ, 1993: 164). Finally, the Court is not obliged to provide reasons for its decision: an appellant is only informed that leave has been allowed or refused. For those granted leave, appeal against conviction is heard before three judges who consider only whether errors of law or procedure characterized the original trial, and whether there is 'fresh evidence' or other considerations that raise doubts about the safety of the verdict. Two-thirds of the appeals that the Court hears are dismissed, convictions are quashed in about a third, and in a very small number of cases retrials are ordered.

Overall, the percentage of appeals allowed by the Court is fairly small, although the 8 per cent figure for 1997 is lower than the 13 per cent average for the ten years from 1988 to 1997.[18] The Court also ordered 30 re-trials in 1997 – equivalent to 1.5 per cent of total applications.[19]

The Court of Appeal is essentially the final review body for appeals against conviction, although its decisions may be appealed to the Judicial Committee of the House of Lords in the very few cases each year which involve a point of law of general public importance. The number in any given year is small. Judgment was rendered on 18 appeals (which included carry-overs from the previous year) during 1997, ten of which were allowed.[20] Finally, those alleging a miscarriage of justice who have exhausted the normal appeal process could (prior to 1997) petition the Home Secretary to refer a case back to the Court, or to grant a pardon.[21] However, this procedure was widely criticised, and has now been replaced by the CCRC.

Despite multiple layers of appeal, critics have charged that the post-conviction process has failed to root out miscarriages of justice in a timely fashion. Some argue that the appeal system itself could be regarded as the ultimate miscarriage of justice (Mansfield and Taylor, 1993). For those tried in the Crown Court, problems begin with the failure of lawyers in advising those who are convicted. About half of the latter are advised not to appeal and many others receive inadequate advice. Legal Aid is available for counsel to draft grounds for those who decide to appeal, but ceases where counsel considers there are 'insufficient' grounds, even though, as the RCCJ observed, it would 'be unwise to assume that...where counsel advise would-be appellants that they do not have good grounds for appeal, the case is therefore bound to be without merit' (1993: 164). Those who do appeal when advised to the contrary, are likely to do so without legal representation; thus their grounds of appeal are apt to be badly drafted; and lacking legal representation their petitions will have little chance of success. To correct this situation, JUSTICE (1994c) recommended that Legal Aid should be available for advice from a different barrister in all cases where serious allegations of defence error are made leading to an unsafe conviction.

Most criticism of the process for dealing with alleged wrongful convictions was directed at the roles of the Court and the Home Secretary. Complaints against the latter included its historically restrictive attitude to petitions for referral of cases back to the Court; its lack of independence relative to the Court; and the tardy, insensitive and secretive manner in which the Home Secretary, and the C3 Division, dealt with petitions claiming wrongful conviction. Criticisms of the Court centred on its restrictive interpretation of its powers to quash convictions – specifically, its aversion to overturning the verdict of a jury in the original trial; its largely unreserved acceptance of convictions based on confessions; its highly sceptical approach to appeals alleging that police misconduct led to a wrongful conviction; its reluctance to consider errors by lawyers as grounds for quashing convictions; and its strong resistance to appeals referred back to it by the Home Secretary.

Yet the Court had considerable discretionary power to deal with miscarriage of justice cases. The CAA 1968 permitted the Court to allow an appeal against an alleged wrongful conviction if under all the circumstances of the case the conviction was unsafe and unsatisfactory; if the trial judge made a wrong decision on a question of law; or if there was a material irregularity in the course of the trial: otherwise, the appeal was to be dismissed. But the Court has been averse to overturning jury verdicts, mindful that cases commonly look different to those who have directly seen the witnesses and heard their evidence than to those who only read about them. Reinforcing this is a commonly held judicial belief that juries too often acquit the guilty and rarely convict the innocent. Thus where any discrepancies and weaknesses of evidence have been laid before the jury, and where the judge has summed up fairly and correctly, the Court has been reluctant to interfere with the verdict.[22]

The Court's reluctance to overturn jury convictions was singled out for criticism by the RCCJ (1993: 2).[23] To make it easier for the Court to quash convictions in cases alleging a miscarriage of justice, the Commission made two recommendations which were incorporated into the CAA 1995. Firstly, the ground on which the Court may allow an appeal has been simplified. Prior to the 1995 Act, in order for the Court to allow an appeal a conviction had to be viewed as 'unsafe and unsatisfactory'; the only criterion now is that they think that the conviction 'is unsafe'. However, at the Second Reading of the Bill, the Home Secretary argued that its language simply restates the existing practice of the Court of Appeal. In addition, the Home Office Minister stated that 'The Lord Chief Justice and members of the senior judiciary have given the test a great deal of thought and they believe that the new test re-states the existing practice of the Court of Appeal.' Thus, Parliament passed the clause on being assured that it restated existing practice, thereby expressing its intention that the practice should continue (Smith, 1995). As a result, this provision does nothing to achieve the RCCJ's aim of having the Court be more receptive to overturning verdicts on the grounds of pre-trial malpractice, jury mistakes or other errors at trial.

The RCCJ's second recommendation focused on the criteria for receiving fresh evidence. Whereas the CAA 1968 required that the Court receive evidence if it was 'likely to be credible', under the 1995 Act this is changed to 'capable of belief'. The Commission viewed the latter as a looser standard which would give the Court 'greater scope for doing justice' by encouraging the admission of evidence which might be excluded under the superseded test (1993: 174). But, as Smith (1995) notes, 'credible' means 'believable', which is the same as 'capable of belief'. Thus this clause, like the foregoing, has to be viewed as a non-starter. The problem with both changes is that the meaning assigned to them will depend, in the end, upon the interpretation of the judges. Thus everything comes back to the Court.

The most common ground of appeal against conviction is an error or irregularity occurring during the trial.[24] The specific complaint advanced in 60 per cent of successful appeals has been an error by the trial judge, involving such matters as an incorrect legal ruling to allow or exclude evidence, a misdirection to the jury, or some failure in observing the rules that govern a judge's summing up (ibid.). This is so despite s. 2(1) in the 1968 Act, which permitted the Court to dismiss an appeal even where there has been a wrong decision on the law or a material irregularity at trial if, in its opinion, 'no miscarriage of justice actually occurred'. Thus in *Cooper*, the Court said that they have the power to allow an appeal against conviction if there is a 'lurking doubt' about whether an injustice had been done (L. J. Widgery at 167).[25] But apparently the Court has had few doubts, for between 1969 and 1989 the test had been applied to quash convictions in only six cases (JUSTICE, 1989).

Whatever the grounds for an appeal, the consensus among critics is that the Court has not been sufficiently responsive to cases of alleged wrongful convictions. Several reasons have been cited. First, as noted, appellate judges are loath to second-guess jury decisions. Moreover, they have limited time to work through a large number of appeals, the bulk of which concern legal and procedural technicalities, with comparatively few containing merit as regards innocence. Secondly, there are specific grounds that have been advanced in support of appeals which the Court generally has been unwilling to accept. Of particular concern to critics is its reluctance to quash convictions which rely heavily on admissions made to police officers, or where it is alleged that police misconduct has contributed to a conviction (JUSTICE, 1989: 48–50). Yet in several high-profile cases – for example, those concerning the Guildford Four, Judith Ward, the Darvell brothers and the Cardiff Three – the confessions on which convictions rested were proven false, and the Court ultimately was obliged to overturn them.

Yet despite reversals such as these it is still possible to convict solely on the basis of an allegation of a single police officer that the defendant made an informal and unrecorded confession which the Court may be expected to uphold (Leng, 1994: 184). The reasons have to do with the judges' almost unshakable belief that people do not confess to guilt unless they are guilty – along with the generally unflagging support of police that has characterized all levels of the judiciary.[26] However, apart from confessions that may result from oppressive questioning, the vulnerability or suggestibility of the suspect may lead people under police questioning to make false and misleading admissions harmful to their interest (Gudjonsson *et al.*,

1993). These findings led the Commission to recommend that a general judicial warning, tailored to the facts of the case, be given to juries about the dangers of convicting mainly on confession evidence (1993: 6–68), and that judges be allowed to prevent cases going to a jury if confession evidence appears unsafe (p. 59). However, in the absence of legislative change, the judges are free to accept or ignore these recommendations.

The effectiveness of the Court in correcting alleged miscarriages of justice has been limited also by its unwillingness to quash a conviction because of the alleged failings of defence lawyers which are said to have rendered a conviction unsafe. While evidence submitted to the Royal Commission by JUSTICE (1993), showed that serious errors of defence lawyers contributed significantly to wrongful convictions, these have rarely been rectified on appeal. In the 1,300 cases of alleged miscarriage of justice that JUSTICE researched over three years (January 1990 to December 1992), complaints relating to counsel arose in 47 per cent of them; in 28 per cent there was also dissatisfaction with case preparation by solicitors. Complaints against counsel include short, last-minute encounters with defendants (often on the trial date) and pressure upon defendants to plead guilty.

There is no doubt that the Court is aware of shortcomings in the provision of criminal defence services. The lack of preparedness of defence solicitors and barristers, and their neglect of their clients up to and during the trial, was strongly criticized as long ago as 1966.[27] And a critique in the mid-1990s of the performance of defence lawyers (solicitors and barristers) by a top official of the Law Society suggests that little has changed over the years.[28] Recent research indicates that poor defence service often begins at the police station, where the task of advising suspects is routinely assigned to unqualified, untrained, inexperienced and unsupervised staff and continues throughout the preparation of the case.[29] The organization of the majority of the criminal firms is in stark contrast to the rhetoric of the professional model, which promises individual, high-quality advice and case preparation, maintaining the interests of the client above the profit concerns of business. Neither do solicitors perceive the wholesale delegation of case preparation to be problematic. They do not see themselves as engaged in proactive investigation in an adversarial process, but, rather, in the routine production of guilty pleas (McConville *et al.*, 1994: 276–82). Nevertheless, the Court generally has been unwilling to consider the alleged inadequacy of legal representation as a valid ground of appeal.[30] The underlying reason was explained in its dismissal of the appeal in *R v. Shields and Patrick* (1977) at p. 281, where it observed that there was an increasing tendency to treat the trial as a preliminary skirmish and, hence:

> to be less energetic in locating defence witnesses, to refrain from calling witnesses who were available but whose evidence might in some respects be thought dangerous to the defence and then, after the trial, to claim that the verdict was unsafe because those witnesses had not been called.

The Royal Commission concurred, arguing that the Court is right not to 'encourage defendants and their lawyers to think of Crown Court trials as nothing more than a practice run which, in the event of a conviction, will leave them free to put an alternative defence to the Court of Appeal in whatever manner they please' (1993: 173).

But the Court, in refusing to offer itself as the forum for rectifying miscarriages that might have resulted from inadequate defence, invites criticism that it may be allowing defendants to be punished for mistakes made by their legal representatives.[31] However, there have been exceptions to the Court's general approach. In the Cardiff Three case, the Court criticized one of the defendant's solicitors for 'being gravely at fault for sitting passively through this travesty of a [police interview]', during which his client denied involvement in a murder over 300 times, before confessing after lengthy and oppressive questioning by the police. In *Fergus* (1994), the Court found that the appellant's original defence solicitors had 'acted in the most flagrant disregard of their duties' in failing to trace or interview named alibi witnesses. In overturning the conviction for robbery, it also criticized the defence counsel's trial performance as 'markedly short of the standard to be expected of a member of the Bar', having neglected to call alibi evidence or to invite the judge to withdraw the case from the jury due to several clear weaknesses in the identification evidence.

The Court has also been criticized for its narrow exercise of its power to consider appeals based on the ground of 'fresh evidence' (s. 23, CAA 1968), i.e. evidence not previously before the courts which, if taken into consideration, might render the conviction unsafe and unsatisfactory. This could be either new material not available at the trial or material that existed at the time of the trial which was not used, in which case its use in an appeal would have to be accompanied by a 'reasonable explanation' for its not having been presented at the original trial. Fresh evidence must also be admissible, relevant and credible (which means likely to be believable in the context of the case). Given the standards set by the Court, most appeals against conviction grounded on fresh evidence have been unsuccessful, being dismissed for failing to meet the Court's test either of what constitutes 'fresh evidence' or of what is considered a 'reasonable explanation' for evidence not having been adduced at the trial.[32]

The Court's 'excessively restrictive' attitude towards fresh evidence was criticized by the Commission, which recommended that once the Court has decided to receive evidence that is relevant and capable of belief, and which could have affected the outcome of the case, it should quash the conviction and order a retrial, unless this would be impracticable or undesirable (1993: 168–9). Providing there was fresh evidence *and* if it was in the 'interest of justice', the Court could order a re-trial. The Criminal Justice Act 1988 (s. 43(1)) also lowered the threshold for a re-trial by making the 'interest of justice' criterion alone sufficient. Nevertheless, in most cases where appeals have succeeded, the Court has preferred to quash convictions rather than order a retrial. An important reason for its choice is the issue of delay,[33] but it is also influenced by factors such as cost, the availability of witnesses and fairness to the appellant, who 'would have to run the gauntlet and the hazards and prejudice of being tried yet again' (ibid.). In light of these factors, the Commission concluded that where the ground of appeal is fresh evidence the Court should take on the jury function itself (1993: 169).

Obstacles to petitions to the Home Secretary

Where an appeal to the Court against wrongful conviction had failed, the appellant (prior to 1997) could petition the Home Secretary to have the case referred back to the Court for further review.[34] However, the system was much criticized, and the Home Secretary's role in dealing with cases of alleged miscarriages of justice was transferred to the CCRC. In order to assess whether the CCRC is likely to be effective in correcting miscarriages of justices, we will first look at the failings of its predecessor.

On average, between 700 and 800 petitions alleging wrongful conviction were received each year by the Home Office's C3 Division, which screened cases to the Home Secretary. However, since prisoners were ineligible for Legal Aid, those without private funds lacked access to legal advice and were not likely to prepare petitions sufficiently convincing to encourage investigation by C3 staff. Lacking external support, their only contact with the Home Office following submission of their petition was likely to be a notice of its rejection. Moreover, since it took the Home Office several months or longer to evaluate and reply to a petition,[35] those serving short sentences may well have completed them before ever getting a response. However, those who attracted the support of groups like JUSTICE or Liberty stood a better chance of having their cases reviewed, but this was mainly because of the external pressure brought to bear by these groups, as well as by the media and interested politicians.

The C3 Department was not proactive on behalf of petitioners. It did not conduct its own investigations, and largely confined its evaluation of cases to determining whether there was fresh evidence.[36] If a case was recommended to the Home Secretary, it could be referred back to the Court, dismissed or – where there were questions about the evidence – there could be a re-examination of the case by the police force which initially handled it, or by a different force. However, to ask the police to evaluate their own competence or honesty with regard to the process that led to the conviction under appeal was hardly a satisfactory arrangement.[37] They were more likely to attempt to shore up the case against the defendant than to provide a disinterested examination of the complaints – especially in cases where the appellant was alleging police misconduct as part of the complaint.[38] Moreover, when an investigation was ordered, the report prepared by the police was confidential to the Home Secretary, thereby preventing the petitioner and her lawyers from assessing the findings. Finally, even when a police report expressed concern about a conviction, officials did not necessarily act upon the information.[39]

This practice of using the same police force to carry out re-investigations was criticized by Lord Foot (House of Lords, 9 April 1986), who suggested that a different police force should be used. However, the Lords were told that this option was already available to C3, although rarely used. The reason, explained a Home Office minister, was that

> in most cases it seems preferable, in the interests of speed, that the police force originally concerned with the investigation should re-examine the case. It will know it well ... I do not think it right to assume that in every case where police inquiries are undertaken there has been some original police malpractice and thus it requires investigation by a new force. (*Hansard*, vol. 473, cols 278–300)

Conditioning the entire Home Office system of appeal was a concern to determine whether new evidence existed (RCCJ, 1993: 181); it did not inquire into other aspects of a case (Hill, 1996: 1553), and its report to the Home Secretary confined itself to commenting, usually adversely, on representations made by others.[40] Yet even where fresh evidence appeared to cast doubt on the jury's verdict, C3 had to be mindful of the Court's requirement that there be a 'reasonable explanation' as to why it had not been put before the trial court.[41] In practice, the exercise of this power was governed mainly by a concern to avoid even the appearance of interfering with the independence of the judiciary (RCCJ, 1993: 181). As a result, very few cases were referred to the Court. For example, in the period 1972–92, the annual average was five,[42] and these included the IRA bombing cases from the early 1970s, and a number of those involving the discredited West Midlands Serious Crime Squad.[43]

The Home Office system was also heavily criticized over the extraordinary secrecy that surrounded its handling of miscarriage cases. Petitioners were barred from seeing material taken into account in making referral decisions, particularly the results of any new police inquiries. Michael Howard (the former Home Secretary) claimed this was necessary in order to keep the process manageable and to avoid delays;[44] but the real motive for secrecy may have been to protect the Home Office from the greatly increased work that would accompany having to justify its method for winnowing down each year the substantial number of petitions where new evidence had turned up (about 25 per cent of the total) to the very few recommended for referral to the Court.[45] The effect was to deny any explanation to hundreds of petitioners whose applications were rejected, as to why their cases had not been referred (Thornton, 1993: 926–35).

In 1994, the High Court declared this practice of the Home Office system 'significantly too closed', and ordered the Home Secretary to disclose all expert advice received before deciding whether or not to refer alleged miscarriages to the Court of Appeal. The judgment[46] stated 'that fairness requires not merely prior disclosure but a substantial increase in the level of disclosures made'.[47] It also criticized Kenneth Clarke, Howard's predecessor as Home Secretary, for the 'plainly unsatisfactory' way in which he had dealt with new expert evidence in the Carl Bridgewater case. The judges ruled that the men had been unfairly denied access to new evidence held by the Home Office and successive Home Secretaries, which they believed could have thrown doubt on their convictions.[48]

An immediate result of the ruling was the referral of the appeal of the Bridgewater Three to the Court of Appeal. A judicial ruling compelled Mr Howard to disclose evidence in his possession which the men believed would cast doubt on their conviction. This included the testimony of three forensic experts, as well as documents recording differing police accounts about a confession allegedly made by Patrick Malloy (convicted with the Bridgewater Three but died in prison), which had been critical to the convictions.[49] The release of this information, hitherto excluded from examination by the convicted men and their lawyers, subsequently led the Court to quash the convictions of the Bridgewater Three, who were released in 1997.

This ruling also made it possible for 200 offenders who had made applications to the Home Secretary to receive information on why their cases had not been referred back to the Court. According to Anne Rafferty (then Vice-Chair of the Criminal Bar Association), it meant that the Home Secretary was obliged to not only disclose the reasons for his decision but also to reveal more detail about any new evidence that emerged.[50] Moreover, he was expected to disclose before and after his decision to reject a petition for a re-trial.[51] In short, the Court's 1994 ruling ended the practice of not revealing what was in the Home Secretary's files – thereby removing a major obstacle from the path of convicted people seeking to prove their innocence. It also increased support for the Royal Commission's recommendation that an independent body be created to investigate alleged miscarriages.

The sensitivity of C3 and the Home Secretary to the attitudes of the Court produced a 'reactive' rather than 'proactive' posture toward petitioners, which undermined their ability to enquire deeply into allegations of wrongful conviction. According to Sir John May (1994), the explanation for this was the wish of successive Home Secretaries not to infringe upon the prerogatives of the judiciary. At bottom was the role assigned to the Home Office by the 1968 Act: the Home Secretary's responsibility for reviewing judicial decisions violated the constitutional separation of powers between the courts and the executive; accordingly, Sir John recommended that alternative machinery be established to refer cases to the Court (ibid.). The RCCJ agreed, and recommended that the responsibility for investigating alleged miscarriages, and the power to refer cases to the Court, be removed from the Home Secretary and transferred to a newly created independent Criminal Cases Review Authority (1993: 182).

Criminal Cases Review Commission

The RCCJ's recommendation was enacted in the CAA 1995. The Home Secretary's power to refer convictions to the Court was transferred to the Criminal Cases Review Commission. The CCRC's function is to review cases where a miscarriage of justice is alleged or suspected. Where there is a real possibility that the conviction, verdict or sentence in a case will not be upheld, it is empowered to refer it to an appropriate appeal court (CCRC, 1998: 26).

Characterized as an executive nondepartmental public body accountable to the Home Secretary, the CCRC is headquartered in Birmingham, and chaired by Sir Frederick Crawford, who guides the work of 13 additional Commission Members.[52] Two-thirds of these are lay persons and a third lawyers;[53] according to the 1995 Act, at least two-thirds of the Commission Members (who should include at least one member from Northern Ireland) should have expertise in the criminal justice system.[54] During its first year, the CCRC was awarded a budget of £4.3 million to set up and pay for its operational costs. It has a staff of 61 people: 24 Case Review Managers, plus legal and forensic experts and administrative support.

The CCRC's statutory powers extend to England, Wales and Northern Ireland and include cases tried either summarily or on indictment. It combines the functions of screening and referral previously assigned to the C3 Department and the Home Secretary; however, when the CCRC decides that a case should be referred for review, it goes directly to the Court. Having become operational on 31 March 1997, a convicted person who has exhausted the normal channels of appeal may now apply to the CCRC to have her case referred for review.[55] Where the Commission concludes that a miscarriage may have occurred in a case tried on indictment, it refers the case to the Court of Appeal to review (s. 9).[56] It has similar responsibilities with regard to summary court cases, except that it refers them to the Crown Court for review (s. 11).

Despite the CCRC's broader powers and discretion, when deciding to refer cases to the Court of Appeal it is subject to the same constraints which handicapped its predecessors; and its potential effectiveness in correcting miscarriages may be equally threatened. Not only must an appeal have already been heard or refused by the Court before a case can be referred back to the Court, but in deciding whether to refer a case the CCRC must satisfy itself that there is a 'real possibility' that the conviction may not be upheld; and that this possibility must be due to argument and/or evidence not previously raised at trial or on appeal.[57] However, s. 13(2) of the 1995 Act does provide that the Commission may set aside the foregoing conditions and refer a case to the Court where it is justified by 'exceptional circumstances'.

While s. 13(2) does not alter the basic statutory subordinance of the CCRC to the Court, it does provide it with a degree of operational independence. However, whether it can withstand the dominant influence of the Court to the extent necessary to be effective will depend upon the willingness of the Court to accept and respect the separate role the CCRC is designed to play in correcting mistakes that occur in the criminal justice process. Having been in operation only slightly more than a year, it is too early to tell what kind of relationship may evolve between the two institutions. While its status as a nondepartmental public body may render it more independent of the government,[58] it is not likely to make it more willing than its predecessor to challenge the Court's authority, or less subject to its influence.

There are at least two reasons for this. First, nothing has altered the role, authority and status of the Court. Despite past criticism of its tardiness in responding to a number of serious, long-standing miscarriages, in the end it is the body that finally 'rights the wrongs'. In so doing, it is able to blame *others* in the criminal justice process – police, prosecutors, lawyers, forensic scientists, trial judges – for conduct said to have contributed to the injustice. It can express even outrage at those who have 'lied' or otherwise misled the courts – despite the fact that the Court itself may have resisted previous attempts of petitioners to have their cases re-heard. The second reason is grounded in the criteria which must govern the CCRC's referral decisions. If the CCRC is only to refer cases which offer a 'real possibility' that the conviction will be quashed by the Court, it may well be expected to look first to the Court's attitude and standard of what constitutes a wrongful conviction before making its decisions – much as did C3 and the Home Secretary in the past. It is already reported that the 'CCRC don't send cases back to the Court of Appeal unless there is certainty of success'.[59] Moreover, as though to encourage the CCRC to seek guidance from the Court, the Act provides that it may at any time refer to the Court any point in a case on which the judges' opinion is desired: having done so, the Court is obliged to consider the matter and provide its opinion to the CCRC (s. 13(3)). As the CCRC stated in its first *Annual Report*: 'The Commission has necessarily been feeling its way on the practical interpretation of terms of art in the Act affecting case review, such as "exceptional circumstances", "capable of belief", "real possibility" and "unsafe".' (p. 21) Taking this approach, the CCRC looks likely to develop a posture of subordinance *vis-à-vis* the views of the Court very much like that of its predecessors.

Moreover, the provisions in the Act which govern the CCRC's approach to referrals are more specific and restrictive than those under s. 17 of the 1968 Act, and it will be hard for the Commission to ignore them. As Clarke (1996) argues, the 'real possibility' test in the Act codifies a restrictive interpretation of CCRC powers, the result of which is likely to make it as cautious in exercising its powers as was the Home Secretary. The intent of the 1995 Act seems to be to ensure that the CCRC generally limits referrals to strong, fresh evidence cases which have exhausted appeal remedies. However, the Act's general prescriptions on referrals are qualified by the 'exceptional circumstances' proviso, which allows the Commission to refer cases where there is no fresh evidence, or where the matter has not yet been heard by the Court of Appeal, but where nevertheless there is a strong possibility that the Court would quash the conviction if the case were referred.[60] As Clarke points out:

> It has to be recognized that things go wrong at trial and on appeal, whether because of mistaken decisions by the lawyers or for a host of other reasons, so that miscarriages of justice can occur despite all the evidence being available. If there is an arguable case that justice has miscarried then the Court of Appeal should have a chance to re-examine the conviction whether or not there is new evidence. (1996: 947)

The CCRC does intend to include cases in which evidence was known about at the time of the trial, but had not been raised for any number of reasons – legal incompetence, a mistaken tactical decision, or the failure to appreciate its full significance.[61]

There are additional features which indicate that the CCRC is likely to be more effective in addressing and correcting miscarriages than were its predecessors. It is better resourced in terms of personnel[62] and technology than was the Home Office; and it has explicit statutory authority to undertake whatever further investigation it thinks necessary to determine whether a miscarriage of justice may have occurred. Section 19 CAA 1995 empowers it to require the appointment of an investigating officer (IO) to carry out inquiries. The rub for critics is that such investigations will be largely carried out by the police, who are clearly intended to play a major role in the conduct of most CCRC inquiries.[63]

But the CCRC makes the decision of whether an IO should be appointed, and has a considerable measure of control over who will conduct inquiries[64] and how they will be carried out (s. 20(4)). The IO is deemed to be under its direction and supervision, and the Commission is empowered to take appropriate steps to ensure that police investigators follow up all lines of inquiry necessary to a thorough re-examination of the case. Finally, should the CCRC be dissatisfied with the performance of the IO, s. 20(5) provides that they may have her replaced by another IO who must meet with the Commission's approval.[65] Despite the continued role of the police as investigators in miscarriage of justice cases, these provisions should enable the CCRC to overcome the weaknesses of the much criticised Home Office practice of having a case reinvestigated by the same police force that did the initial investigation and against which accusations of misconduct may have formed part of the alleged miscarriage. Thus, while one of the four IOs appointed to aid its investigations during its first year of operation was from the same force that conducted the original enquiry, three were not (CCRC, 1998: 22); nor were there complaints about the one exception.

Nevertheless, the criticism of those who insisted that the CCRC should have been given the power to select an IO from among its own staff, remain valid.[66] The issues involved in cases alleging miscarriage of justice are likely to be contentious and difficult, and without disparaging the capabilities or good intentions of the police officers or police forces who might be selected to re-investigate them, the potential influence on enquiries of factors such as the norms of police culture, the collective frustrations of the police in securing convictions and the generalized corporate loyalty of the police on the outcome cannot be dismissed. Such factors are especially likely to intrude where the focus of a police investigation is the conduct of colleagues either in their own force or others, where it is difficult for an investigating officer not to identify and emphasize with those under scrutiny. Despite this, the CCRC, like its predecessor, is left dependent upon the police to carry out investigations – even where allegations of police malpractice are made.

More encouraging is the power of the CCRC under s. 17 to obtain documents and materials that assist them in carrying out their functions; and its authority under s. 21 to undertake any other steps necessary to aid them in their inquiries. Together with its other investigatory powers, these project a profile of the CCRC that stands in sharp contrast to that of the Home Office system, where C3 only responded to representations made to it rather than carrying out its own investigations of a case or the evidence given at trial.[67] Unlike the C3, the CCRC has the means to possibly develop a genuinely proactive role in relation to cases that attract their attention.

A second positive feature is the CCRC's power to refer appeals against summary court convictions to the Crown Court; and the proviso that the Crown Court's power to increase a sentence on a normal appeal[68] (up to the maximum allowed for magistrates) does not apply to CCRC referred cases (s. 11(6)). Should knowledge of this safeguard become widely known amongst defence lawyers, it may well increase the number of applications to the CCRC from those convicted in contested cases in the magistrates' courts. Thirdly, under s. 5(1) of CAA 1995[69] the CCRC may contribute to the resolution of cases alleging miscarriages of justice. This section provides that the Court of Appeal may direct the CCRC to investigate and report to it on any matter that is relevant to an appeal being heard by the Court. During the CCRC's first year of operation, the Court referred two matters for it to investigate (CCRC, 1998: 17), although the CCRC's report does not indicate their relevance to any case of alleged wrongful conviction.

Fourthly, the review of eligible cases being conducted by the CCRC is far more thorough than those carried out by C3. After defining the issues raised by the applicant, a series of steps are taken to determine their validity. Typically, the caseworker will study CPS documents and materials, the trial judge's summing-up, the Court of Appeal file, and documents preserved under s. 17 of CAA 1995. Interviews may be conducted with relevant persons, including prisoners and (if legal privilege is waived) solicitors and counsel. Expert opinion may be sought on forensic evidence such as DNA tests, fingerprints and explosives (CCRC, 1998: 18). Where needed, the Commission may require the police to carry out further enquiries (s. 19).

Finally, the CCRC is positioned outside the criminal justice system, in the sense that it has no historical or institutional linkage with the police, CPS and FSS, and only a rather tenuous link with the Home Office. This means it should be able to pursue its work with fewer pressures from these sources than might have been the case with C3 and the Home Secretary. However, the CCRC is aware that, aside from applicants and their representatives, there are others with a stake in its activity, such as appellate court recipients of referrals, the Court of Appeal as a recipient of reports, agencies of the criminal justice system and the government; and that all are likely to have (perhaps unreasonably) high expectations about what the CCRC should deliver.

Although its workforce is nearly four times larger than the number allocated to the C3 Department to deal with referral petitions, the CCRC believes it needs at least 26 additional Case Review Managers to handle its prevailing intake of cases (roughly 4.5 per day as compared with less than three cases previously received by the Home Office) and reduce the accumulation of cases over the next few years (CCRC, 1998: 7).

It remains to be seen whether the CCRC's estimates of its needs will suffice to prevent the long delays in handling miscarriage of justice claims that characterized the Home Office system. Prior to transferring its responsibilities to the CCRC, the Home Office was taking up to two years to process referral applications, and there was a backlog of 284 cases waiting to be dealt with when the CCRC took over in April 1997 (CCRC, 1998: 17). During 1997–8, 1,094 new cases were added, producing a total of 1,380 by April 1998. However, the CCRC was able to dispose of only 308 during its first year of operation: 228 were screened out as ineligible for further consideration,[70] and 80 selected for intensive review.[71] Of these, 68 were subsequently rejected, and 12 were referred to the Court of Appeal; no referrals were made to the Crown Court. At the start of the CCRC's second year there were already 1,072 cases in the CCRC pipeline (221 under review and 851 awaiting review), and by September 1998 the number had increased to 1,805. Thus, even allowing for the proposed doubling of the number of Case Review Managers, and for the anticipated increase in operational efficiency, the goal of providing speedy yet thorough reviews of alleged miscarriage of justice cases may be difficult to obtain.

As of February 1999 thirteen of the 40 cases which the Commission referred to the Court had been reviewed, and it had quashed the conviction in eight of the ten considered on that ground and substituted a lesser sentence in two out of the three sentence referrals. The case with the longest history was that of Derek Bentley. Convicted of murdering a policeman during an attempted burglary, he was hanged in 1953, at the age of 19. The Court also quashed the conviction of Patrick Nicholls, who was found guilty of murder in 1975 and served 23 years in prison. He was released in 1998 at the age of 78 when it was established that the 'victim' had died from natural causes. More fortunate was David Ryan James, who was jailed for life in 1995, having been found guilty of poisoning his wife. He was freed in July 1998, following the discovery of his wife's suicide note in an old copy of the *Veterinary Record*. In March 1999, the infamous case of James Hanratty, convicted of murder and hanged in 1962, was referred back to the Court of Appeal.

But there is a backlog of cases awaiting CCRC attention. This may prompt the CCRC to adopt case selection criteria driven by the scarcity of resources, and increase the possibility that some miscarriages will be missed due to the apparent lack of evidence which might only be brought to light were further investigations to be conducted. Thus, fewer cases might be referred; however, this would be in keeping with the thinking of the Conservative government in passing the legislation which created the CCRC: they were expected to use their power sparingly. In the government's view, 'It would be a mark of failure in the system of criminal justice if a substantial number of cases needed to be reconsidered by the court on more than one occasion ... A "last resort" procedure should be precisely that: a vehicle for remedying miscarriages of justice, not an extra stage in the ordinary criminal justice process to be used routinely.'[72]

The 1995 Act also tackled the failure of the Home Office system to inform petitioners of the results of their applications for referral. The Act requires that in every instance where the CCRC decides not to refer a case back to the Court they must give applicants a statement of the reasons for their refusal (s. 14(6)). Thus, in the process established by the CCRC, petitioners are informed within six weeks of the receipt of their application whether they are eligible for intensive review; and where, after intensive review, it is decided not to refer a case the applicant is sent a statement of reasons and invited to make further representations. Finally, when the CCRC decides to refer a case, a detailed statement is sent to the applicant, and notice of the referral is sent to the Court of Appeal and to the CPS (CCRC, 1998: 22–3).

On the other hand, while the Act provides the CCRC with power to require that the police and prosecution produce documents, there is nothing in the statute which requires the CCRC to disclose material to the applicant. Moreover, where information is obtained under s. 25(1), a duty of secrecy prohibits the CCRC from revealing it without permission. Denial of access to new material, previously undisclosed, may handicap applicants in making further representations. When queried about the absence of a duty to disclose, a government spokesman replied that disclosure would be 'limited to what is required by the interests of fairness'.[73]

A major handicap to those seeking to have their cases referred back to the Court has always been their lack of adequate legal assistance, and this situation has not changed since the establishment of the CCRC. In June 1998, it reported that only about 10 per cent of new applicants seeking referral have been legally represented, and in these cases mainly by lawyers acting *pro bono* (1998: 18). However, the Commission arranged to have Legal Aid extended under the Legal Advice and Assistance Scheme to allow referral applicants to receive up to ten hours of legal assistance. Whether this will be sufficient given the complexity of these cases seems doubtful; however, and despite the emphasis of the Legal Aid Board on its availability,[74] many firms remain unaware of such support and are turning away referral applicants. The CCRC is presently trying to eliminate this unfortunate information deficit.[75]

A preliminary assessment of the CCRC's ability to resolve claims of wrongful conviction must consider several factors. The first is the role and attitude of the Court of Appeal, which remains the final arbiter. In acceding to a claim of wrongful conviction, the Court is obliged to overturn the verdict of the jury, and this it has been reluctant to do. Nevertheless, in recent years it has quashed a number of cases where a miscarriage was alleged (especially where there was an error in law), but these have taken years,[76] and even then the Court has quashed only grudgingly and under strong public pressure. Meanwhile, those wrongfully convicted have languished in prison, in some cases for several decades. Yet there is nothing in the 1995 Act to deal with the Court's reluctance to overturn jury decisions; nor is there any assurance that the Court's present allegedly greater willingness to consider claims of wrongful conviction will persist. Failing future strongly felt doubts in their minds about the correctness of convictions, it is highly probable that the Court will continue to uphold jury verdicts; and this will reduce the CCRC's chances of correcting some miscarriages of justice.

Secondly, while the Act substitutes the CCRC for the Home Office, the Court may still resent having a non-judicial body second-guess its decisions. The attitude it is likely to adopt will only be known after more referrals have been made by the CCRC. Meanwhile, the choices made by the CCRC must be governed by criteria set forth in the Act: foremost, that they should only refer a case where they feel there is a 'real possibility' that a conviction may not be upheld by the Court. Over time it will become clear to the CCRC, as a result of the views expressed in Court decisions, what is and what is not acceptable to the Court.

However, the Act contains provisions aimed at encouraging a working relationship between the Court and the CCRC. Thus under s. 5 the Court may direct the CCRC to investigate and report to it on aspects of an appeal case under review by the Court. In addition to simply fostering interaction between the two bodies, the results of the

CCRC's inquiry may provide the Court with the basis for quashing a conviction when a case is first appealed before it. Similarly, s. 14(3) enables the CCRC to secure the advice of the Court on any point arising from a case under review by the CCRC pursuant to an application for referral. Use of this provision might prevent the CCRC from referring a case on grounds that would be unacceptable to the Court or, alternatively, allow it to refer where it otherwise might not have, due to its uncertainty about the probable reaction of the Court.

Much of this suggests that the relationship of the CCRC and the Court may turn out to be not much different from that of its predecessor, with the CCRC's limited independence in deciding referrals further subordinated to its perception of what is acceptable to the Court. Thus the anticipated operation of the CCRC leaves the final resolution of future allegations of injustices where it has been: in the hands of the very body which for years has failed to deal effectively and consistently with miscarriages of justice. As Adrian Clarke (1996: 947) has noted, we are now, as we were before, faced with a structural problem: 'the Court of Appeal will, usually, have already looked at the conviction and found it to be safe and is, therefore, bound to be reluctant to come to a different decision second time round'. Along with Clarke (1996), one cannot help but wonder 'whether the Government's motive in creating the CCRC was to deflect criticism from the Home Office for failing to remedy miscarriages of justice rather than a sincere attempt to eradicate the imprisonment of the innocent' (p. 948).

Summary

An accessible and effective appeals process is essential to a fair and just criminal process. Trial court errors can be rectified – whether it be an error of law, procedure or the insufficiency of available evidence. Most important here is the rectification of the individual injustice of a wrongful conviction or sentence, but the moral integrity of the criminal justice process is also preserved when the system is able to correct its own errors. Unfortunately, a number of high-profile miscarriages of justice cases have highlighted the appeals process not simply as being inadequate, but as a source itself of justice miscarrying. Most famously, the Birmingham Six case was treated unsympathetically by a judiciary who declined to countenance police wrongdoing and became increasingly convinced of the guilt of the convicted men.

The RCCJ recommended the creation of an independent body to replace the C3 division of the Home Office, to be responsible for referring cases back to the Court of Appeal. The CCRC was established in 1997 under the CAA 1995. Although still in its infancy, the new body has been well received. It has a greater number of staff than C3 and does not have the criminal justice ties which had cast doubt upon the independence of the Home Office as a review mechanism. It has the power to obtain further material which may be of assistance, and where it decides that a case merits intensive review the CCRC may require the police to conduct further investigations. They are not obliged to refer the case to the original investigating force. In place of the secrecy surrounding the work of C3, written reasons are provided to those whose applications are rejected.

However, the CCRC must operate within many of the same constraints as the former Home Office arrangement. The Court of Appeal determines the outcome of cases and the CCRC must be mindful of the judges' approach in deciding whether or not to refer cases back. The requirement that there must be a 'real possibility' of the appeal succeeding serves to reinforce the practices of the Court. The independence of even an outside police force has also been questioned by critics. Those investigating may have to be highly critical of the work of colleagues in what are often well-publicized cases. Although the CCRC is better served than C3 in terms of resources and technology, it has inherited a backlog of cases from the Home Office, as well as receiving twice as many new cases for consideration. The average number of cases to be referred to the Court of Appeal annually by the Home Office was five. The CCRC made a promising start by referring 12 in their first year and 40 by February 1999.

Despite making recommendations which would strengthen the role played by magistrates' courts, the RCCJ did not commission research into aspects of summary justice. Instead, it assumed that, together with the Crown Court, verdicts were reliable and trials conducted in a manner regarded by all participants as fair. In fact, a quarter of those convicted after a contested trial in the magistrates' court appeal to the Crown Court. Appeals to the Court of Appeal are generally filtered out by a single judge, who may be inexperienced in criminal work. Decisions have been criticized as inconsistent, and JUSTICE reports an instance where the same judge erroneously considered the same case twice – firstly, granting leave (and the sentence was reduced) and later refusing it (JUSTICE, 1994c: 8) Appellants are also disadvantaged by the restricted availability of Legal Aid, since those unrepresented are much less likely to be successful. Around one-third of the appeals which survive the process of obtaining leave to appeal and are heard by the Court, are allowed – most on the ground of some error or material irregularity at trial. The approach of the Court has been criticized strongly, as being too conservative, in narrowly applying the requirement for fresh evidence and being extremely reluctant to overturn the decision of a jury. Not surprisingly, it has also been unwilling to criticize colleagues in the legal profession, whose poor defence work may also lead to miscarriages of justice. The case of Stephen Miller and Ivan Fergus revealed exceptional incompetence, and criticism could not be avoided. It remains to be seen whether an incompetent defence will infringe the accused's right to a fair trial under Article 6 ECHR which must be given effect to under the Human Rights Act 1998.

10
Concluding Comments

Injustice redefined: the RCCJ and government reform

Five years on from the Runciman Commission's report, how are we to understand criminal justice reform and policy? To what extent have the causes of the now infamous miscarriages of justice been addressed? And has a new government brought with it a new optimism for change? The establishment of the RCCJ appeared to mark a turning-point in criminal justice, a recognition that something had to be done in response to the catalogue of cases which had come before the Court of Appeal and the crisis of public confidence which they had brought about. As the chair of the Criminal Bar explained:

> In answer to criticism of the criminal justice system for producing these wrongful convictions, the Government announces that they are going to set up a Commission to look at its operation, obviously with the implicit understanding ... that it is to look at ways and means to ensure that this sort of thing doesn't happen again, that we do not get further wrongful convictions in the future. And the Royal Commission starts off on that high moral plane.[1]

But we have seen throughout the course of this book, that the recommendations made in the RCCJ's final report were of a very different hue. Those wrongly convicted had been poorly served by the criminal process, and a mass of independent research (including that carried out for the RCCJ) demonstrated that their experience was far from exceptional. The response of the Commission, however, was not to focus on measures which would better protect accused persons and avoid the kind of injustices which had been so dramatically brought to light, but, instead, to propose a host of reforms designed to make the system more 'efficient'. For example, despite the fact that inducements such as sentence discounts may produce 'the risk that defendants may be tempted to plead guilty to charges of which they are not guilty', the Commission considered that to be a risk worth running, given 'the benefits to the system' in encouraging an earlier plea (RCCJ, 1993: 111). Risks and benefits are balanced freely. Nothing is considered 'fundamental', everything can be negotiated: the right to silence, the right to jury trial, the right to know of the evidence against you, the right to a lawyer. Things hitherto considered cornerstones of due process and criminal procedure have been casually swept aside, ignoring the obvious inequality of opportunity and resources in evidence-gathering (allowing the police to benefit further from their position of advantage), as well as the numerous miscarriages of justice resulting from inadequate prosecution disclosure. Yet, the sentence discount reform was considered desirable, as the Commissioners were 'confident that the *system* will benefit overall from our proposals' (RCCJ, 1993: 100; emphasis added).

Although denying allegiance to any model or theory, the Commission's final report is resonant with the wider discourse of 'system efficiency' and 'the management of risk'.[2] This begins with the terms of reference provided for the Commission. Wrongful convictions were to be considered alongside (and soon became subordinate to) wrongful acquittals[3] and resource issues:[4] the third of these, in the form of 'system efficiency', was swiftly elevated by the Commission as the most important. Strengthening the due process rights of the accused is expensive, may result in more complex (and so more costly) proceedings and, unless public opinion is realigned, is likely to be regarded as helping the criminal, rather than the victim. More appealing are measures which streamline the processing of cases and can be measured in terms of output, rather than effectiveness – making 'success' all the more achievable.

This is part of what has been dubbed the 'new penology' – forged within the market ideology of new managerialism.[5] It is attractive to policy-makers, as it is neither aspirational nor transformative: 'It takes crime for granted' (Feeley and Simon, 1994: 173). It no longer seeks to address the causes of crime, but to manage the effects of crime. Thus, it does not appeal to external values (such as suspects' rights or crime reduction), but to its own formal rationality on the basis of which its performance can be measured easily.[6] Performance indicators are concerned with 'outputs' (what the organization does) rather than 'outcomes' (what it achieves).[7] Due process and crime control are replaced by cost-efficiency and risk management in a form of 'actuarial justice'[8] which has pervaded most parts of the criminal justice process.[9] Through surveillance and the effective production of knowledge,[10] suspect populations are 'managed' at minimal cost.[11] Brownlee (1998: 323) comments that 'The maintenance of the criminal justice system itself and the continual striving for ever greater efficiency of operation become *the* inherent values which are to be pursued. Wider social or ethical values are excluded'. However, the notion of 'risk management'[12] tends to de-personalize and de-politicize the handling of suspect individuals. In practice, it will be the police who, in most cases, are responsible for this task. Policing the risk society lends legitimacy to police ideologies of identifying problematic or suspect communities as part of their law-and-order function.

In adopting this emphasis upon efficiency and the management of cases through 'the tripartite co-operation of defence, prosecution and court' (Smith, 1994: 299), the Commission aligned itself, not with those addressing the causes of miscarriages of justice, but with the concerns of policy-makers. Yet, argue some critics, to expect anything other than this is to misunderstand the function of the Royal Commission, which is not to go beyond the system which established it: it is itself a part of official discourse and so, unable to stand outside its own socio-legal and political contexts (Scraton, 1994). It reproduces, rather than challenges, the concerns of criminal justice agencies.[13] The appointment of the Commission served initially to appease public concern, but ultimately to re-establish the credibility of the criminal process. These dual objectives are in contradiction and Scraton describes how they are reconciled through processes of denial (miscarriages are an aberration), neutralization (balancing interests) and the disqualification of knowledge (selective in the commissioning and use of research), as 'a classic deconstruction of criticism through which a new agenda is established deflecting the central issues, confirming legitimacy and reaffirming confidence' (1994: 107).

As part of official discourse, the Commission played an important role in the shift in public opinion, from horror at the conviction of the innocent to concern over the acquittal of the guilty. This metamorphosis was described by a leading criminal barrister:

> From its outset, the tone of the Commission quickly changed. Within the very short period of two years between their being set up and their reporting, the pendulum has swung and they've come down from their high moral plane. So by the time we get to their Report,

while they're still concerned to a degree with the prospect of wrongful convictions of the innocent – for example, their recommendation that we should set up this criminal appeals complaints body[14] – they have strayed away from that and into what they see as the 'wrongful acquittal' scene. And they come out with a Report which contains highly varied, even contradictory, recommendations.[15]

The Commission provided an important bridge between miscarriages of justice and the need for reform, and the government's own law-and-order agenda. It might be argued that given the crisis in confidence in British criminal justice following the miscarriage cases, only two solutions presented themselves as viable. Firstly, government may accept the lack of integrity of the criminal justice process and move to fundamental reform. Clearly, this approach had been rejected before the Commission was even in place, as the then Home Secretary, Kenneth Baker, explained,

> Our criminal justice system deals perfectly well with the overwhelming majority of cases. That should never be forgotten. The cases that are now the cause of our concern represent only a tiny proportion of the work that is carried out to very high standards. I would wish that to be clearly understood, so that we don't get carried away with the quite erroneous belief that everything in our current arrangements is flawed.[16]

In the absence of political will to undertake radical change, the government turned the tables. Realizing the need to be seen to respond in some way, they focused instead upon a second, quite different strategy: the wrongful acquittal of the guilty and associated repressive measures. Within a short time of the establishment of the Commission, the tone of debate began to shift as the shock of the miscarriage cases was replaced by increased concern over the rise in crime being reported by the media, and being experienced personally by a growing minority of the population.

The upsurge in crime was, of course, partly the result of a decade of wrenching change in the economy which left millions of people unemployed, many for long periods if not permanently. Simultaneously, these same people, together with many others, suffered from the reduction of a variety of social support programmes as a result of the government's determined objective of dismantling the welfare state. One result of these changes was the creation of a society increasingly divided into 'winners' and 'losers'. Locked in permanent unemployment and bereft of all but minimal support, many of the 'losers' were gradually transformed into an underclass for which there was no place in the British society of the late 1980s and 1990s – what Garland (1996: 461) has called the *'criminology of the other*, of the threatening outcast, the fearsome stranger, the excluded and the embittered'. Taylor and Jamieson (1998) argue that the 'continually reinforced fear of crime now works to condense a series of other interconnected anxieties about the current experience of middle class life in England' which includes the real danger of crime, but is rooted in wider social, political and economic anxieties, such as the dismantling of the welfare state and the changing culture of work. They go on:

> Inescapably associated with these anxieties (in the national popular press, local newspapers and everyday gossip) are a set of moral narratives that focus, in particular, on the underclass ... who are seen to constitute what Margeret Thatcher called 'the Enemy Within' and what urban sociologists and criminologists call 'the Urban Other' ... This is a moral narrative about the defence of existing social position (constructed in terms of categories of social difference). (1998: 173)

The members of this underclass have come to be seen increasingly as a threat to the interests of the 'winners' and, therefore, as objects that must be regulated and controlled by the forces of law and order:

> As time passed and memories of miscarriages faded, and as the crime rate went up or seemed to go up, the forces of law and order rallied themselves. People begin to think that things have gone too far in one direction ... The 1990s represent a classic example of a swing away from the liberal interpretation of events which took place following the realisation that there had been these horrendous miscarriages of justice.[17]

Public understanding of those caught up in the criminal process was unsympathetic:

> The society is now asking us in the legal profession – through the politicians and through other organs: 'Is it better that ten guilty men go free rather than one innocent man be convicted? Or is that perhaps a price which is too high to pay?' (Ibid.)

Exploiting this change in the public mood, and aimed at reinforcing it, the government began to espouse a new 'law-and-order' rhetoric.[18] It found a ready ally in the media, who have long known that crime sells well; and so the public was fed a steady and fulsome diet of crime and criminals. The top echelons of the police, recognising that the time was ripe for their views to be well received, joined the discussion with complaints of being handicapped in the enforcement of the law, due to a process that had become tilted in favour of offenders. Some officers warned that the system was reaching a point where they were no longer confident that they could contain the escalation of crime. Thus, explained a criminal barrister:

> The pendulum has swung or is now swinging away from the left to the right – back towards the more conservative end. People are becoming more and more obsessed with law and order. People are convinced that society as they knew it is breaking up; and it's all coming down around their ears. As a consequence, they are bringing pressure to bear on their political representatives; and the politicians are bringing pressure to bear on the criminal justice system. The end result is that the criminal justice system is becoming more weighted in favour of the victim, rather than in favour of the accused. In short, what we are undergoing in England and Wales is a quite fundamental reappraisal of the criminal justice system. (Interview, 1995)

This populist appeal to a divided nation was used most effectively in bringing about the curtailment of the right to silence.[19] Thus, despite the wrongdoing and abuse of authority on the part of the police, prosecution and their experts, the way was paved for measures which diminished the rights of the accused, whilst strengthening the hand of the police and the prosecution. The increasing marginalization of portions of the population – those who were portrayed as threatening to the interests of the majority – served to reinforce the perceived need for tougher laws. The CJPOA 1994 exemplifies this and Lord McIntosh of Haringey described the public order provisions as, '... an open invitation for the police and for authorities generally to interfere in the legitimate activities of people, and particularly of young people, in our country ... These are repulsive extensions of police power in our society and at some stage they will have to be removed.'[20] Government rhetoric was of 'just desserts' and 'individual responsibility', with no room for (more costly) consideration of the causes of crime.[21]

The 1997 change of government has offered little hope of a change in the thrust of criminal justice policy. With its campaigning slogan 'tough on crime, tough on the causes of crime', Labour has identified itself as the party of law and order and so embraced policies traditionally associated with the right.[22] The move from a welfarist to punishment-as-deterrent approach is seen in the 1998 Crime and Disorder Act's new juvenile justice measures which abolish repeat cautioning and provide the courts with greater powers to incarcerate children, as well as the much criticised anti-social behaviour orders – described in one commentary as 'the hybrid law from hell'.[23] The discourse of risk management also remains: for example, the CDA 1998 requires crime audits to be carried out in order to develop community safety strategies. The Criminal Justice (Terrorism and Conspiracy) Bill, for which Parliament was recalled from the 1998 summer recess, has also attracted widespread criticism, with claims that it infringes both the rule of law and the ECHR.[24] Under the Bill, the opinion of a police officer is sufficient proof of a suspect's membership of a proscribed organization, so long as it is corroborated – such corroboration may be in the form of the suspect's silence. Commentators have pointed to the danger of rushing into legislative reform in the immediate wake of atrocities, in an attempt to demonstrate 'tough action against terrorism'.[25] The Guildford Four, for example, were among the first to fall foul of the Prevention of Terrorism Act, passed after the 1974 Birmingham pub bombings.[26]

Despite promising to address the causes of crime, Labour places much emphasis on individual choice and responsibility[27] and this creates a tension between the punitive rhetoric of 'get tough' policies and new managerialism's desire for increased efficiency. Advocating harsher punishments, for example, makes non-custodial sentences appear 'soft' and so creates an insatiable appetite in the public for the imposition of prison sentences and leads to a spiralling (and so increasingly expensive) prison population.[28] Labour have attempted to marry these two conflicting approaches by appealing to ideals of restorative justice and communitarian values. Criminals will be punished, and victims and communities will have a greater say in the administration of that punishment. Given the evidence that prison is expensive as well as ineffective as a deterrent, and the current focus upon the role of the victim, this will be welcomed by some. Others will inevitably see it as justice 'on the cheap'.

As with many other areas of policy, the present government has shown itself unwilling to effect a retreat from the agendas pursued by the previous Conservative administration. Improving the efficiency of the criminal justice process remains a priority, and although reducing delay and improving communication through measures such as nationally coordinated information technology are to be welcomed, safeguarding the position of the accused remains absent from the policy and discussion papers. The overall gain to the system is the guiding objective. For example, the proposal to set up 'criminal justice units' of CPS and police staff to prepare files for trial the day following charge in straightforward matters, has been warmly taken up. This would move many cases through the process more speedily, without 'unnecessary' adjournments. A case is likely to be considered straightforward when there is an admission. Yet, this ignores the unreliability of confession evidence and the fact that suspects may give a legally inaccurate account of their conduct or intentions.[29] Lawyers will be unable to put forward detailed mitigation if instructions are taken in the pressured environment of the police station. At the earliest sign of an incriminating statement, the suspect risks being railroaded into a guilty plea without proper consideration of her position or of the evidence against her.[30]

Labour's commitment to populist policy[31] suggests that it does not have the political will to turn back the tide of public opinion. If criminal justice policy is to change direction (and it is unclear that Labour desire this), this must be accompanied (or even preceded) by a change in public perceptions of crime and criminal justice. Labour's policy documents, however, continue to talk of 'getting tough' and 'cracking down' and 'no more excuses'. There is no room within this macho rhetoric for the rights of accused persons. In the same way that public concern was guided away from miscarriages of justice and toward wrongful acquittals, the rhetoric of government policy must change in order to make acceptable a more just and humane approach to criminal justice.

Reform in the 1990s – away from the adversarial

The objective of recent reforms has been to create a criminal justice process which is administratively efficient and minimizes the 'risk' of an adversarial trial. Case resolution is being moved away from the costly public forum of the courtroom and towards a pre-trial resolution of the issues where the accused herself will play a decreasing role in decisions about the trial of her case: the 'success' of measures such as defence disclosure requirements and charge bargaining, depend upon professional representation of the accused. The accused's own role diminishes to minor participation in the formal confirmation of earlier decisions, which the trial becomes. Failure to comply with administrative procedures, such as the provision of a defence statement, may become 'evidence' against the accused. The necessary effect of these administrative goals is to undermine the rights of the accused, which can only increase the number of persons who are wrongfully convicted. In the space of only a few years the presumption of innocence until proven guilty has been eroded, with an increasing burden placed upon the accused to positively demonstrate her innocence. The obligation upon the defence to disclose the substance of their case in order to obtain further disclosure from the prosecution is not simply a 'cards on the table' approach, which will improve efficiency. In an adversarial process it strengthens the advantage already enjoyed by the police as resourced investigators (first on the scene and therefore in possession of relevant information) by allowing them to disclose less of their case; and it disadvantages the defence, by requiring them to expose their case to their adversaries before trial, on pain of adverse inferences from the court. The defendant no longer enjoys the right to see the whole of the evidence of the prosecution: they must make out a case to see that evidence. According to Robert Roscoe, President of the London Criminal Courts' Solicitors' Association:

> If they want access to undisclosed information, defence solicitors will have to show the court that the information is relevant to the case. This is a classic Catch 22 situation. Solicitors won't know if information is relevant to the defence until they have seen it, but they will only be able to see it if they can show it is relevant. This can only further imbalance the criminal system and undermine public confidence in it.[32]

Where do such fundamental reforms leave the criminal justice process? To what extent may it properly be described as adversarial when plea bargaining is formalized, silence is conditional, and the defence must reveal their hand before being allowed to see the extent of the prosecution evidence? Both research and miscarriage cases have shown defence lawyers to be insufficiently adversarial and geared towards the routine production of guilty pleas. The police and prosecution, on the other hand, have been excessively adversarial to the point of malpractice.[33] This imbalance is further aggravated by the advantages enjoyed by the police and prosecution both in terms of resources and authority.

Recent reforms which seek to 'harmonize' the functions of the prosecution, defence and courts, have further skewed roles and procedures with no thought as to how they will impact upon a wider 'process' of criminal justice. The RCCJ, the source of many of these measures, proudly claimed to reject the use of any theoretical framework,[34] preferring to make recommendations on 'practical' grounds. Yet, it also acknowledged that 'In some instances...our recommendations can fairly be interpreted as seeking to move the system in an inquisitorial direction' (RCCJ, 1993: 3).

To what extent are these moves inquisitorial in nature? And is this significant? There are now a number of procedural disincentives designed to make court resolution of the issues the exception, and for a wider range of evidence to be made available with fewer constraints upon admissibility (Dennis, 1995). Both of these trends may popularly be described as inquisitorial in nature: a wide-ranging enquiry with a more 'cards on the table' approach, unhampered by evidential restrictions. But to view them as such is problematic and raises issues which go to the heart of the approach adopted in recent law reform. There is much misunderstanding about the meaning of the term inquisitorial and whether recent reforms in England and Wales can properly be called such. The Royal Commission was presented with an ideal opportunity to rectify this, to generate a research agenda for a wider and more reflective study of other jurisdictions. This it failed to do, asking researchers simply to examine other systems with a view to their reception in this country (Leigh and Zedner, 1992: 67). In their final report, the Commission rejected out of hand the idea of any change in an explicitly inquisitorial direction, without affording it any proper consideration.[35] It appeared to be searching for the perfect bolt-on system to remedy the deficiencies of the criminal justice process – a quest in which it was inevitably disappointed.[36] No attempt was made to try to understand the wider structures of inquisitorial processes and the factors which may lead to their success or failure. Such an approach would permit more general lessons to be learned and, arguably, would better serve the Commission's purpose of exploring the viability in our own process, of the features of other jurisdictions.

It is true that in jurisdictions such as France, there may be less debate at trial around the issues in the case, but this is not the result of the defence and the prosecution working together. Rather it reflects the different role played by the public prosecutor in supervising the police investigation and reviewing the prosecution case. Problems may be eliminated pre-trial by the prosecutor directing the police to interview witnesses, to stage a confrontation between the suspect and the victim, or to release the suspect without charge because of a serious procedural error, for example. The prosecutor alone is responsible for bringing a thoroughly prepared case and once a charge has been brought, the defence have access to the whole of the prosecution file. In more serious cases, where investigation is supervised by the *juge d'instruction*, the defence may choose to provide information at the investigation stage, if it will shape the case in a way favourable to the accused. Otherwise, to require the defence to reveal any of its case to the prosecution or the *juge d'instruction* would be regarded as an infringement of the prosecutor's role in investigating the case.

As well as different procedures, inquisitorial systems have a history, structure and legal culture quite different from our own. This includes legal personnel whose title of 'police officer' or 'prosecutor' is suggestive of some functional equivalence, but whose role, training and occupational culture is often quite different. In France, for example, police investigations are supervised by either the *procureur* or the *juge d'instruction*, both of whom have a career judiciary training as *magistrats*. Thus, the *procureur,* for example, is not only a prosecutor like a member of the CPS, but has been trained for her role in supervising the gathering of evidence and protecting the rights of the suspect.[37] She, rather than a police officer, is responsible for the detention of suspects before charge. As a *magistrat*, she is distanced from the prosecution-centred objectives of the police and is able to scrutinize the evidence before deciding whether or not to charge. The prosecutor's assessment of officers' competence as investigators is part of the information upon which their promotion depends, which gives further force to their responsibilities. The police require the authority of the *procureur* or the *juge d'instruction* in many instances and once an *information* has been opened,[38] they are not permitted to interview the suspect – the *juge d'instruction* must do this.

To take isolated examples of what are presumed to be inquisitorial measures, and expect them to be put into effect by legal actors trained in, and accustomed to, an adversarially-rooted process, is inappropriate. Thus, CPS supervision of police investigations would require altering the structural relationship between the two, as well as a revised programme of training for the new roles. In any event, the Royal Commission expressly rejected the idea of the CPS supervising police investigations, not because the CPS as currently constituted may not be the appropriate body to do so, but on the ground of principle that it would remove police accountability.[39] This demonstrates the

Commission's misunderstanding of jurisdictions whose procedures it shuns: making investigating officers responsible[40] to a public prosecutor or *juge d'instruction* is central to the structure of police accountability in which inquisitorial procedures operate.

This is not to argue that the French (or any other) system is superior, or that in practice it conforms more closely to its own rhetoric than is the case here. There are concerns that only 8 per cent of cases are dealt with by the *juge d'instruction* and that delays in serious cases are unacceptable. Whist the *procureur* is responsible for the conduct of the *garde à vue* – the detention period following arrest – she is of course dependent upon the police to carry out interviews and gather evidence, albeit under her supervision. Rather, the point is that the more open approach to evidence-gathering, and the pre-trial identification of issues, is embedded in a history and a structure quite different from our own. 'Harmonizing' the roles of police, prosecution and defence, in some form of tripartite cooperation, offends against both adversarial and inquisitorial principles. At both the structural and theoretical level, we are left with a process which is increasingly disjointed.

The awful miscarriages that preceded the establishment of the Commission and those that continued after did not prompt a renaissance in due process values – neither in the Commission's final report nor subsequent government legislation.[41] In the ways documented above, quite the reverse has occurred, with public sentiment manipulated once more toward crime control values and beyond,[42] with administrative efficiency and risk management as the new discourse.[43] The measures to flow from this conservative swing in thinking about the criminal justice system span both political parties: from curbs on the right of silence[44] to a tougher regime for dealing with juvenile offenders[45] and suspected terrorists[46] and the stipulation of minimum and automatic life sentences.[47]

The extent of the damage inflicted upon due process protections is suggested in the following commentary by a very senior criminal barrister:

> I still take a very firm stance in favour of what I would call the traditional criminal justice system, in which safeguards are built in to protect the individual; but I think it would be naive not to recognize that those safeguards are being eroded. It's not a question of just **eroding** the safeguards: they are being systematically and intentionally removed in response to the actions of politicians. One sees a graphic example of that in the very fundamental abridgment of

the right to silence, which was part of our legal jurisprudence or common legal jurisprudence for centuries; and now it's gone.[48]

The presumption of innocence and the presumption of *mens rea*[49] are often described as fundamental principles of our criminal law, yet an increasing number of statutes have been drafted and interpreted in a way which dispenses with them. A recent study by Ashworth and Blake (1996) found that around half of all offences triable in the Crown Court do not require *mens rea* for all parts of the *actus reus*, and 40 per cent of offences violate the presumption of innocence.[50]

Ashworth has argued against the principal justifications advanced for this legislative trend: rather than wider police powers, more serious offences require stricter safeguards to prevent citizens from wrongful conviction.[51] Claims as to the sophistication of suspects (in keeping with the 'criminal justice process balance tipped in favour of the suspect/criminal' school of thought) lack any empirical basis, and research tends to demonstrate the reverse: that most suspects are in a weak position, in contrast to the enormous power of the police (see also, McConville and Hodgson, 1993).

Some efforts towards change have been made. Police station advisers must now be trained and accredited; the organization and structure of the CPS will change in the light of the Glidewell Report; 'ethical interviewing' has gained some currency in police circles; and the Human Rights Act will require judges to interpret UK statutes in accordance with the European Convention on Human Rights. But this is overshadowed by the host of measures which further advantage the police and the prosecution at the expense of the rights of the accused. As McBarnet (1983) argued some time ago, the police abuse of power is not the sole cause of injustices. Rather, the way in which legal rules and procedure are framed affords the police wide discretionary powers and so fails to protect suspects.[52] This continues to be the case, as citizens have their right against self-incrimination curtailed and as the nature of the burden of proof and the criminal trial itself are altered by making full disclosure of prosecution evidence conditional upon the defence revealing its response to a case of which it is not yet fully aware. Moreover, those who put their faith in legislative reform alone continue to be disappointed, as even those measures which appear to strengthen due process values are consistently undermined and subverted in practice.

The accreditation requirement, even with external enforcement and financial sanctions, has been of limited success. There is little evidence that the practices and ideologies of defence lawyers are evolving to create a legal profession which can respond to the increasing demands placed upon it by recent reform, where defendants will be judged increasingly by the conduct as much as by the content of their defence. Neither has the question of police error and abuse of power been addressed. Instead of holding officers accountable for malpractice, they have been provided with extended powers to extract evidence from suspects, formally and informally, both inside and outside police stations – based on the mistaken (but populist) premise that increasing police powers will improve the effectiveness of the police in reducing or solving crime.[53] Increased emphasis is being placed upon surveillance and intelligence-gathering as investigatory tools, despite concerns that this leaves the police less accountable and individuals without effective remedies.[54] At the same time, nothing has been offered to relieve accused persons who are the victims of police malpractice, and of inadequate legal defence at all stages of the criminal justice process. Finally, the willingness of judges to admit improperly obtained evidence at trial sends out important messages about what is acceptable police practice. These decisions are not the neutral application of law to facts, by learned experts in the Court of Appeal. Their jurisprudence reflects an ideology which permits police officers to abuse their powers and to continue their function of social control. In sum, the RCCJ and subsequent legislation have contributed to the creation of a whole culture which is unashamedly antagonistic to the accused.

Notes and References

1 The Criminal Justice System and Miscarriages of Justice in England and Wales

1. In addition to published research, we also draw upon commentary derived from 44 tape-recorded interviews conducted in 1995 by Frank Belloni with the assistance of Debra Chitton at two interviews conducted in 1947 by Jacqueline Hodgson. The interviewees were primarily solicitors and barristers with criminal law practices, but also included civil rights advocates who monitor the operation of the criminal justice system and other criminal justice personnel. Because of their willingness to share their practical experiences and considered thoughts about the criminal justice process, we feel we have a better understanding of its everyday operation. For this we are extremely grateful. Where permission has been granted, the interviewee's name is indicated in footnotes.

2. Walker, for example, suggests three categories of miscarriages: when the State abuses individual rights; when adverse treatment of individuals by the State is disproportionate to what is required to protect the rights of others; or whenever the State fails to protect and vindicate the rights of potential or actual victims. See Walker and Starmer (1993: 4–5).

3. See Kennedy (1992: 191–221).

4. Packer (1968) suggested that tendencies in criminal justice might be evaluated by means of two theoretical models: crime control and due process. In the crime control model the most important function of the criminal process is the repression of criminal behaviour: hence, the operational emphasis is on a high rate of apprehension and conviction. In contrast, the due process model subordinates these objectives to procedures which are fair, reliable and fully protective of the legal and civil rights of the suspect or defendant against possible abuses of state power (ch. 8). For objections raised against Packer's models, see Ashworth (1998: 25–9).

5. In contrast, for those with a strict crime control view, the legal acquittal of a person who is factually guilty of a criminal offence will be seen as a miscarriage of justice. Indeed, the Royal Commission on Criminal Justice were specifically required to consider this in their terms of reference. Their report not only addressed this issue, but also endorsed the perspective of the crime control advocates. For further discussion, see Hodgson (1994: 86).

6. See especially pp. 10 and 14–17. See also, Walker *et al.* (1990).

7. Fitzgerald (1993: 17) suggests the possibility that the police may simply be 'more proactive in the policing of Afro-Caribbeans'.

8. See Hall (1994: 316–17).

9. At the time of writing, Ricky Reel's case is being investigated by the PCA. See PCA (1998: 39).

10. See McConville *et al.* (1994: 211–38); and Legal Action Group (1993b: 5).

210

11. This view is echoed by LAG (1993b: 5), who also report that most solicitors and barristers view magistrates' courts as less fair and more likely than juries to convict innocent people.
12. Interview, May 1995.
13. See Jackson (1993b: 132).
14. Mistakes made in magistrates' courts can also be rectified by appeal on a point of law to the Divisional Court of Queen's Bench in its supervisory role.
15. This is discussed further in Chapter 8.
16. See also reports by organizations such as JUSTICE, Liberty and the Legal Action Group, which examine the causes of miscarriages together with details of specific cases which they have investigated.
17. Sir John May carried out special inquiries of the Maguire Seven (HC 556, 1990 and HC 296, 1992) and the Guildford Four (London: HMSO, June 1994); and a painstaking study of the Birmingham Six may be found in Mullin (1990). Discussions of a number of high-profile cases of miscarriages of justice (the Guildford Four, the Birmingham Six, the Maguire Seven, the Tottenham Three, Judith Ward and the Carl Bridgewater case) may be found in Rozenberg (1992: 91–117).
18. RCCJ (1993: 6).
19. J. Mullin, 'Shake-up "would not have freed famous cases"', *The Guardian*, 7 July 1993.
20. Detective Chief Inspector Thomas Style, Detective Sergeant John Donaldson, and Detective Constable Vernon Attwell were all found 'not guilty' of having fabricated evidence to convict the Guildford Four (*The Guardian*, 7 July 1993 and 28 July 1994).
21. *R v. McIlkenny et al.* (1991) 93 Cr App R 287.
22. This was established by ESDA (electrostatic data analysis).
23. *The Times*, 16 October 1992; and *The Guardian*, 28 July 1994. In contrast, similar media coverage did not persuade the court to drop the charge of murder (of a police officer) against Winston Silcott, one of the Tottenham Three (see *Silcott, Braithwaite and Raghip* (1993) 9 Cr App R 99). According to a report in *The Independent* (2 August 1994), before, during and after Silcott's trial, 'he was demonised by much of the press to an extent rare in the annals of crime'. His solicitor, Adrian Clarke, said that the level of vilification was such that Silcott's parents had to move house after attempts to firebomb it (A. Travis, *The Guardian*, 4 August 1994).
24. See, further, Kaye (1991). A supervised enquiry into complaints about the West Midlands Serious Crime Squad led to the convictions of 22 men being quashed. PCA (1995: 10).
25. For example, the conviction of Gary Winship was quashed following testimony that the original trial court had not been told that evidence, subsequently found questionable, had been provided by an officer then under investigation for alleged police corruption. Granting appeal, Lord Justice Henry said there were questions as to the 'character, credibility and conduct' of a police officer who had been involved in other convictions which had been successfully appealed. 'It was a matter of regret,' he said, 'that this appellant was convicted on evidence that was tainted.' After

release, Winship said: 'I've served three years for something I didn't do' (*The Guardian*, 6 July 1994).

26. The Bridgewater Four (or Three, by the time of their appeal, as one of them died in prison) was a West Midlands SCS case. In January 1998, a man was awarded £200,000 damages for five years' imprisonment for an offence (originally investigated by the WMSCS) which he had not committed (*The Guardian*, 21 January 1998).

27. Based on the usual one-third remission for good behaviour, Treadaway was released in August 1991. In the meantime, however, his children had grown up and his marriage had ended.

28. Alan Pickering, John Brown, James Price and Timothy Russell.

29. Mr. Justice Mckinnon had expressed a number of important findings in terms of 'beyond reasonable doubt' – the criminal standard of proof – by saying 'I have no doubt'. See C. Dyer, 'Judges deal DPP third blow', *The Guardian*, 1 August 1997.

30. D. Graves, '£50,000 for victim of "torture" by police', *The Guardian*, 29 July 1994.

31. Dyer, 'Judges deal DPP third blow', *The Guardian*, 1 August 1997.

32. PACE would not apply to a number of these, such as the Birmingham and Guildford cases, even if they were to occur now. They would be governed by terrorist legislation, which provides fewer safeguards than PACE for suspects detained by the police.

33. *Paris, Abdullahi and Miller* (1993) 97 Cr App R 99 at 103.

34. *The Guardian*, 23 March 1996.

35. *The Guardian*, 18 February 1992.

36. This, rather than the damage to individuals, is of concern to the judiciary and it is interesting to note their power to shape the character of future cases through robust appeal decisions. Greer (1995) attributes the ultimate failure of the 'supergrass' system in Northern Ireland to the posture adopted by Appeal Court judges. Concerned at the negative impact upon the integrity of the criminal justice system which supergrass cases were having, the courts became unwilling to give credibility to the evidence provided by supergrasses, with the result that convictions were quashed and the whole supergrass phenomenon ultimately abandoned.

37. However, this commonplace understanding of the cause of a miscarriage of justice – that it results from mistakes or errors – is rejected by some observers of the criminal justice process: they see it, instead, as the product of the deliberate and systematic use of methods and practices known to be wrong; see, for example, Hillyard (1994: 76).

38. See, McConville *et al.* (1991: 14–35) and Hillyard (1994).

39. See Chapter 6.

40. See also Ashworth (1998: ch 2) for further discussion of this, especially in relation to the European Convention on Human Rights

41. At the Conservative Party Conference in October 1993, the Home Secretary, Michael Howard proclaimed that in 'the last thirty years, the balance in the criminal justice system has been tilted too far in favour of the criminal and against the protection of the public. The time has come to put that right.' Quoted in Rose (1996: 325). Thereafter a stream of legislative proposals followed (see, for example, the Criminal Justice and Public Order Act 1994

and the Criminal Procedure and Investigations Act 1996 below) which increased police powers and in many instances actively diminished the rights of accused persons.

42. See, for example, the arguments advance for curtailing the right to silence, discussed in Chapter 5.
43. [1988] 2 ALL ER 135 at 144.
44. (1990) 91 Cr App R 150.
45. (1990) 91 Cr App R 237 at 243. For further discussion of these two cases, see Hodgson (1992).
46. This deficiency is illustrated by the need for persistence demonstrated in cases such as the Birmingham Six and Derek Treadaway. It is also discussed in JUSTICE (1989: 5–6); see also JUSTICE (1993) 'Miscarriages of Justice: The View of the Defendant'.
47. Interview with a leading member of the Criminal Bar Association, April 1995.
48. E.g., the Carl Bridgewater case. See also Hall (1994: 317). The conviction of Michael Stone in 1998 for the murder of a woman and her daughter and the attempted murder of her other daughter, is already being viewed by some as having the classic hallmarks of a wrongful conviction. (see, for example, Darcus Howe, *The Independent* 'Why the Stone conviction makes me uneasy', 25 October 1998). The murders of a woman and child took place in a country lane as they walked home from a swimming gala. The horror of the crime put the police under immense pressure to find the killer. The evidence against Stone consisted principally of admissions alleged to have been made to fellow prisoners – one of whom, Barry Thompson, claimed to have lied when telling the jury that Stone had implicated himself in the murders. There was no forensic evidence linking him to the murders (although a tourniquet was found near to the scene, and Stone is a heroin user) and he made no admissions to the police. Much weight seems to have attached to his psychopathic personality disorder, violent past, and recent fantasies and threats of killing. (see Jury and Buncombe, 'Stone gets life', *The Independent* 24 October 1998).
49. Examples include the following: the convictions of the Birmingham Six were based on police fabrication of evidence and questionable forensic tests; the conviction of Judith Ward rested on unreliable forensic evidence and non-disclosure by the prosecution; the Silcott murder conviction was based on a confession falsified by the police; the Kiszko conviction relied on unsustainable medical tests. Each of these convictions as ultimately quashed by the Court of Appeal. More recently, the case of James Hanratty, convicted and hanged in 1962 for the 'M61 murder' of Michael Gregston, was referred back to the Court of Appeal by the CCRC in March 1999. The suppression of vital information by senior police officers, a lack of disclosure of information to the defence and a flawed process of identification were given as the reasons for the decision to refer. See Duncan Campbell 'Appeal Court to review Hanratty murder case', *The Guardian* 30 March 1999.
50. Zander (1993: 1341).
51. RCCJ (1993: 7). A similar view was offered by Sir John May, in his report on the quashed conviction of the Guildford Four; see also Richard Ford and

Stewart Tendler, 'Human Failings Blamed for Guildford Four Error', *The Times*, 1 July 1994.

52. In 1989, 15 years after the imprisonment of the Birmingham Six, the Home Secretary, fearing a wrongful conviction, sent the case once again to the Court of Appeal. In the appeal process, Lord Chief Justice Lane and his co-judges made plain their outrage at allegations made by defence against the police, and dismissed the appeal; see Kennedy (1992: 8).

53. Responding to the report of the inquiry of the Guildford Four by Sir John May, Chris Mullin, the Labour MP for Sunderland South, noted that 'A record quantity of fraud and perjury was committed in this case and it was reasonable to expect that, after careful study, Sir John might have identified some of those responsible. Instead, he absolved just about everybody, except the Guildford Four – on the question of whose guilt or innocence he declined to express a view' (*The Times*, 1 July 1994).

54. Mansfield and Wardle (1993: 14).

55. Hillyard (1994: 74–5; emphasis added).

56. Evidence to RCCJ, November 1991: para. 10.

57. Interview with John Davis, May 1995.

58. '"Calumny!" was the charge that echoed through the Royal Courts of Justice on 15 April 1992. It was the cry of an endangered species, defying those who expected concern and self-criticism instead of a closed-ranks defence of the indefensible.' See Kennedy (1992: 1). Also, witness the debate in the House of Commons after the release of the Birmingham Six. Far from shame, regret or apology, members of the House were on the attack; see Hodgson, (1994: 85–6).

59. House of Lords debate, 12 December 1990; (in Mullin, Testimony, 1991: paras. 45 and 48). Ironically, efforts are being made to reduce the use made of juries on the grounds that they too often acquit the guilty. See the discussion in Chapter 6 below.

60. 'I am of the opinion', he told the jury, 'not shared by all my brothers on the bench, that if a judge has formed a clear view, it is much better to let a jury see that and not to pretend to be a kind of Olympian detached observer' (quoted in Mullin, Testimony, 1991: para. 49).

61. McConville *et al.* (1991) criticize the legal reform model for viewing the criminal justice process 'as essentially *segmental*, with each component part susceptible to separate analysis and separate reform'. In contrast, they argue 'it is essential to understand that the criminal justice process is marked by *unity* not disunity, and requires singular not separate analysis' (198–9; emphasis added).

62. Quoted in ibid.: 203.

63. This was well illustrated by the closing of ranks of the police and judiciary during the miners' strike of 1984–5 (see Belloni, 1987). See also Hall (1994: 317–8) on the inseparability of the roles of the police and the courts.

64. Kennedy (1992: 6) states that she has 'frequently weathered horrible court experiences where the defence has inevitably involved direct confrontation with or contradiction of police evidence, and the judicial wrath has poured upon my client and upon me'. In a discussion of defence strategy in the appeal case of the Guildford Four, she notes that a prime concern was how to deal with Lord Chief Justice Lane's abhorrence of the slightest slur on the

police: 'We considered all sorts of formulae which would soften criticism of the police' (ibid.: 9).

65. Ericson (1994: 139–40), for example, describes criminal justice as a surveillance system coordinated by knowledge, communication and surveillance mechanisms. To accomplish its purpose, the dominant values and emphases in criminal justice – i.e. the efficient control of crime – have been displaced by surveillance: 'the efficient production of knowledge useful in the administration of suspect populations'. Secondly, the former emphasis on suspects' rights has been displaced by 'system rights', which are required to maximize the surveillance capacity of the system.

66. According to Ashworth (1998: 3), 'discussion devoted to criminal trials, particularly trials by jury, far outweighs their numerical significance within the criminal process'.

67. It is, of course, ironic that this may and does have the reverse effect. Ashworth (1996: 227) argues for the strong maintenance of due process values, over and above that of the 'truth', which is itself a construct in the context of the criminal trial. 'The principle of integrity insists that it is self-defeating if law enforcement agents themselves flout the law'.

68. Witness the terms of reference of the RCCJ, and the way in which 'efficiency' was elevated as a central concern. See also, Ericson (1994: 113–40).

2 Policing on the Ground: Gathering Evidence

1. As Ashworth (1998: 93) explains, 'the original file put together by the police will have considerable hold. Prosecutors do not review two files, one for the prosecution and one for the defence. They are merely provided with the police file, and that may well have been constructed in a way that is selective in what it includes and excludes, that interprets certain phenomena in accordance with the investigating officer's beliefs, and that tends to present the "evidence" so as to support a particular conclusion'.

2. The constable holds a public office as an officer of the Crown. As such, she is said to exercise an original discretion in keeping the Queen's peace, and to be 'answerable to the law and to the law alone... By virtue of the office itself, a constable acts on his own responsibility when exercising his powers (unless executing a lawfully issued warrant)'; see Clayton and Tomlinson (1992: 25).

3. McConville *et al.* (1991: 2).

4. See Lustgarten (1986: ch. 1).

5. See Chapter 3.

6. See RCCJ (1993: 29); Dixon *et al.* (1990a: 130); and McConville *et al.* (1991: 44).

7. Two-thirds of prosecution barristers and half of defence barristers reported that nobody listened to interview tapes in contested cases. Judges reported that tapes were heard in court in only 11 per cent of contested cases. See Zander and Henderson (1993: ch. 3). It is likely that even fewer are listened to in non-contested cases.

8. McConville *et al.* (1991: 197) and Reiner (1992: 109). Chapter 3 of Reiner (1992) summarizes the research literature on 'cop culture'.

9. Reiner (1978: 161) indicates that a 'machismo syndrome' operates; and McConville *et al.* (1991: 26) suggest that there is a search for excitement on the part of all police officers. Also Reiner (1992) and Singh (1994: 166).

10. See McConville *et al.* (1991: ch. 2), 'Constructing the suspect population' (especially p. 35). Similarly, in all of the cases studied by Wells (1994: 53), the suspects 'were either Irish, working class or in some other way regarded as outside the broad spectrum of respectable English'. See also Smith and Gray (1983: 233); and Hillyard (1994: 69–79).

11. According to McConville *et al.*, all that is sometimes needed to make someone an official suspect is being 'known to the police.' One officer related to them that the police constable's 'stock in trade [is] recognizing people who were arrested in the past' (p. 23); thereafter, the offender's status is, for the police, enough to make the person a suspect – for something (p. 24).

12. See data from Smith and Gray's PSI Study (1983).

13. McConville *et al.* (1991: 25).

14. Ibid.: 16.

15. Ibid.: 99.

16. Ibid. 199; (original emphasis). For examples of police determination of the guilt of suspects at the outset, and of their subsequent efforts to construct the cases necessary to ensure conviction, see ibid., 201–10. But the problem is not that a small number of police officers are dishonest and fabricate confessions; it is, rather, that the culture in which police operate and the expectations that are placed on them drives them to find suspects 'guilty' (C. Mullin, 'A New Travesty is Waiting to Happen', *The Independent*, 7 July 1993).

17. McConville *et al.* (1991: 2 and 18).

18. Interview, April 1995.

19. Interview with Nick Brown, May 1995.

20. See Chapter 3.

21. In his Final Report to the Home Secretary and the Attorney-General on the circumstances surrounding the wrongful convictions of the Guildford Four, Sir John May, a retired Appeal Court judge, noted that 'where the police feel certain they have the right people, perhaps on the basis of what is regarded as reliable intelligence, but have little or no admissible evidence to prove their guilt, there may be a strong temptation to persuade those persons to confess'. (1994: 307). See, further, discussion in Chapter 3.

22. See above, n 7.

23. See McConville and Hodgson (1993); Baldwin (1993b); Evans (1993).

24. See Maguire and Norris (1993: ch. 5).

25. See McLean (1992).

26. In the Moston and Stephenson study, tape-recording was used with 93.9 per cent of the suspects interviewed in the police station (1993: 33).

27. In the course of a stop, the police also may seize goods they reasonably suspect may be stolen and/or articles the possession of which are prohibited by law.

28. COP A, paras. 1.5 to 1.7 and Note for Guidance 1A states 'Regardless of the power exercised all police officers should be careful to ensure that the selection and treatment of those questioned or searched is based upon objective factors and not upon personal prejudice.'

29. Sanders and Young (1995: 38–9).
30. See discussion of case-law in Sanders and Young (1995: ch. 2).
31. See *King v. Gardner* (1979) 71 Cr App Rep 13; and *Lodwick v. Sanders* [1985] 1 WLR 382.
32. Since April 1996, all police forces must produce ethnic monitoring data on stops, searches, arrests, cautions and homicides. See further Fitzgerald and Sibbitt (1997).
33. A study of policing in a London borough found, for example, that a black was stopped four times as often as a white. See Norris *et al.* (1992). See also Southgate and Crisp (1993). For a summary and analysis of other relevant research findings on police stops and arrests of ethnic minorities, see Fitzgerald (1993: especially 14–17).
34. Although no class analysis is attempted, Phillips and Brown (1998) found that 54 per cent arrests were of unemployed people, 27 per cent were employed and 14 per cent at school or college.
35. McConville *et al.* (1991: 35).
36. In the research of McConville *et al.* (1991: 26–9), officers cited stereotypical cues, being present in a particular situation or setting or being uncooperative that make individuals or groups 'suspicious'.
37. Smith and Gray (1983) found that 'Police officers tend to make a crude equation between crime and black people, to assume that suspects are black and to justify stopping people in these terms.' The 1996 *British Crime Survey* found that 23 per cent of black people recalled being stopped in the previous year, compared to 16 per cent of whites and 15 per cent of Asians. See analysis in Bucke (1997).
38. A Home Office study of ten police forces found that ethnic minorities are four times more likely to be searched than whites (Home Office, 1997b). A countrywide analysis of stop, search and arrest figures conducted by Statewatch, found the ratio to be even higher, with blacks being 7.5 times more likely to be stopped and searched than whites. Whilst 19 whites were stopped and searched per 1,000 of the population, the figure was 45 for Asians and 142 for blacks per 1,000 of the population. In Cleveland, the figure was 419 per 1,000 – more than 40 per cent. (Statewatch, 1999)
39. See Smith and Gray (1983) and Walker *et al.* (1990). Skogan (1990, 1994). Phillips and Brown (1998: 38) found that 18 per cent of stop and search arrests were for black people, compared to 12 per cent of other arrests and 11 per cent of all arrests being from a stop and search. Statewatch (1999) found that 70 per cent of police forces arrested four times as many black people as white people.
40. *The Observer,* 9 August 1998. The police's handling of the death in October 1997 of an Asian youth, Ricky Reel, is also being investigated by the PCA. The Metropolitan Police attributed Reel's death to accidental drowning, but his family claim that he was racially abused and attacked.
41. *The Guardian,* 14 October 1998.
42. *The Independent,* 16 October 1998.
43. See generally, ch. 5 of their report.
44. Section 67(10) provides that a failure on the part of a police officer to comply with the provisions of Code of Practice A 'shall not of itself render him liable to criminal or civil proceedings'.

45. See Chapter 4.
46. *Fennelley* [1989] Crim LR 142.
47. For example, when a person is brought to the police station under arrest or is arrested at the station, the custody officer must tell her clearly of the following: (i) the right not to be held incommunicado; (ii) the right to free, private legal advice; and (iii) the right to consult PACE codes of practice which stipulate these rights, as well as other rules which should govern police behaviour and which are intended to protect the interests of persons in police custody.
48. See Lord Donaldson, 'Beware this abuse', and A. Travis, '"Despot" Howard warned', *The Guardian*, 1 December 1995.
49. Section 81(1) CJPOA, which amends s. 13A of the Prevention of Terrorism (Temporary Provisions) Act 1989.
50. The 'sus' laws have their origin in the Vagrancy Act of 1824 which gave parish constables the power to arrest vagabonds, trespassers, and loiterers – the underclass of society – who almost automatically were suspected of intent to commit crimes. This power was passed on to the Metropolitan Police in 1829 and was used widely by street constables throughout the country – more recently against ethnic minorities and other groups disfavoured by the police. See Alderson (1992: 13–14).
51. Interview, May 1995.
52. Or indeed, any person.
53. These relate to secrecy, prostitution, taking a vehicle without authority, going equipped for theft and a number of public order offences – PACE s. 24.
54. Suspects may also be arrested for threatening, abusive or insulting words or behaviour under ss. 4 and 5 of the Public Order Act 1986 and there is a common law power of arrest for an actual or apprehended breach of the peace – *Albert v. Lavin* [1981] 3 All ER 878; *Howell* [1981] 3 All ER 383.
55. *Holgate-Mohammed v. Duke* [1984] AC 437.
56. *Christie v. Leachinsky* [1947] AC 573 at 600. Unlawful arrest, therefore, is false imprisonment.
57. For example, in Stretford the proportion of black arrestees was more than 17 times that of blacks in the local population; in Luton 13 times; and in Hackney and Croydon, five times (1998: 14).
58. Officers considered there to be enough evidence to charge on arrest in 63 per cent of cases involving whites, 56 per cent involving blacks and 52 per cent of Asians (Phillips and Brown, 1998: 44). It is of interest that charges were not made on arrival, as stipulated in PACE s. 37.
59. See McConville *et al.* (1991). In one example, a police officer explained that it 'would have been all right if he'd just gone away but he had to be Jack the Lad ... I grabbed him and arrested him' (p. 25).
60. *Wilson* [1955] 1 WLR 493.
61. The suspect must have been cautioned, but not necessarily arrested for the provision to bite.
62. Shepherd *et al.* (1995), for example, found that 59 per cent of their sample saw the caution as threatening or pressuring. See Chapter 5 for further discussion of this matter.
63. This will be subject to the court holding the conversation as admissible. See further Chapter 3 and 4, which discuss judicial exclusion of evidence.

64. See *PACE Codes of Practice*, Revised Edition 1995: Note 10.5A (a) and (b). For further details and discussion, see Wasik and Taylor (1995: 50–68 and 170–4).
65. *PACE Codes* (1995): see Code D, Note 10.5B: (a) (b) (c) (d) (e).
66. 39 per cent of suspects exercising the right to silence.
67. 70 per cent refused to respond to a s. 36 warning and 77 per cent to one under s. 37; Bucke and Brown (1997: 38).
68. Sections 54–9, CJPOA. These provisions were recommended in the *Report* of the Royal Commission (1993: 14–16); and are discussed in Wasik and Taylor (1995: 72–80). The changes are incorporated in PACE, Codes of Practice, Revised Edition (Effective 10 April 1995).
69. See discussion of forensic evidence in Chapter 8.
70. One might speculate that an additional purpose of the enhanced power of police to stop and search could well be to facilitate this method of acquiring data about the population.
71. See discussion in Creaton (1994).
72. If that person has been charged with a recordable offence or has been informed that she will be reported for such an offence or has been cautioned for such an offence (s. 63 PACE as amended by s. 55 CJPOA).
73. Section 63 PACE as amended by s. 55 CJPOA.
74. See s. 58 of CJPOA 1994, which amends s. 65 of PACE 1984.
75. Those identified in Code of Practice D(3A) 1995 as punishable by imprisonment.
76. S. 62(10) PACE.
77. S. 63A(1) PACE.
78. CJPOA 1994, s. 57.
79. Wrench, Home Office Circular, 16/95, para. 16.
80. Section 15 of the PTA 1989, as amended by paragraph 62 of schedule 10 to the CJPOA 1994; Wrench 1995: para. 19.
81. Wrench 1995: para. 20; emphasis added.
82. The Forensic Science Service has been designated as the initial custodian of the DNA Database, charged with running the system. For details on service providers, profiling of criminal justice samples and analysis of crime stains, sampling procedures and profiling (ibid.: 29–51).
83. Ibid.: para. 21 and 22; however, the existence of the national database is not meant to preclude local searches being carried out.
84. Authors' conversation with Sarah Bishop of the Home Office, 31 October 1995.
85. *The Times*, 17 March 1995; *The Guardian*, 6 February 1995.
86. *The Guardian*, 6 February 1995.
87. McConville *et al.* (1991: 16).

3   The Suspect at the Police Station

1. PACE ss. 56, 58; PACE COP C paras. 3.1, 3.15, 6.1.
2. PACE COP C para. 2.1.
3. PACE COP C para. 6.5.
4. PACE s. 37.

5. PACE COP C para. 3.9.
6. Note that although published the following year, the data in Bucke and Brown (1997) was collected more recently than that in Phillips and Brown (1998).
7. RCCP (1981) *Report*, para. 4.89.
8. See, for example, *R v. Dunn* (1990) 91 Cr App R 237, discussed in Hodgson (1992).
9. See, for example, McConville and Hodgson (1993). However, note the RCCJ's refusal to recommend a requirement that confessions be admissible only when made in the presence of a solicitor: they highlighted the fact that the presence of a defence adviser *could not* guarantee that the interview had been conducted fairly, nor that improper pressure had not been earlier applied upon the suspect.
10. Although reflecting police cultural beliefs, this misleading dichotomy was also adopted by the RCCJ (1993:8): 'there is a potential conflict between the interests of justice on the one hand and the requirement of fair and reasonable treatment for everyone involved, suspects and defendants included, on the other'. A reading of this passage would suggest that, for the Commission, justice is more about convictions than the fair treatment of accused persons.
11. Interview with Anne Owers (JUSTICE), April 1995.
12. Interview, May 1995.
13. Sanders *et al.* (1989); Dixon *et al.* (1990a); McConville *et al.* (1991). Most recently, Phillips and Brown (1998) found only one case in a sample of 4,246, where detention was refused. See also Maguire and Norris (1993), who attribute much of the failure in police supervision generally to the fact that supervising officers are subject to the same performance pressures as fellow officers and do not wish to be seen to undermine the work of colleagues.
14. Two-thirds of prosecution barristers and one half of defence barristers reported that nobody listened to interview tapes in contested cases. Judges reported that tapes were heard in court in only 11 per cent of contested cases. See Zander and Henderson (1993: ch. 3). The numbers listened to in non-contested cases are likely to be far lower. McConville *et al.* (1994) also found that defence lawyers rarely listened to tapes of interview.
15. See Baldwin (1993b).
16. See *Holgate-Mohammed v. Duke* [1984] AC 437.
17. *R v. Paris, Abdullahi and Miller* (1993) 97 Cr App R 99.
18. See also discussion in Leng (1995). Dixon (1997: 163–4) argues that he makes the more modest claim – that PACE has become a normality for many officers, albeit grudgingly.
19. Interview with John McCormick, February 1995.
20. Interview with Shawn Williams, March 1995.
21. See Sanders *et al.* (1989) who found, in their study of duty solicitors, that advice was provided by clerks in some one-third of cases. McConville and Hodgson's study (1993) found that greater use was made of non-solicitor staff (in three-quarters of cases) as their sample included own solicitor cases, where there is no qualification requirement, as well as duty solicitor cases.

22. On the drawbacks for the client advised by non-qualified staff, see McConville and Hodgson (1993: 30–4).
23. Former police officers were used in 21 per cent of cases.
24. The Royal Commission expressed its concern about the failure of some legal advisers to provide protection to suspects from unfair police practices. It regarded as 'disturbing' the findings of researchers that legal advisers sometimes remain passive whilst police break the rules by indulging in oppressive, threatening, or insulting practices; (RCCJ, 1993: 37).
25. Notably McConville and Hodgson, 1993 (examining custodial legal advice) and McConville *et al.*, 1994 (examining the organization and practice of defence lawyers). See also Sanders *et al.* (1989).
26. See Chapter 5.
27. Previously, conditional bail could only be granted by the magistrates' court. The effect of s. 27 CJPOA 1994 is to extend s. 3 of the Bail Act 1976 to police bail. The police, though, may not require the person to be bailed to a bail hostel.
28. See the recommendations of the Neary Report, Home Office (1997) and the Glidewell Report, Home Office (1998c).
29. Baldwin and Hunt (1998) examined the impact of CPS pre-charge advice to police officers. They conclude that even with prosecutors physically present at the station, pre-charge advice had little impact upon the case outcome.
30. Over half of these failed to complete any part of the accreditation process.
31. See Gudjonsson and Clark (1986); Cahill and Minghay (1986); Gudjonsson (1992).
32. Gudjonsson *et al.* (1993). The most striking finding in the study was the low IQ scores of many suspects, with a third of the sample found to be intellectually disadvantaged, having an average IQ of about 85. Another third (35 per cent) experienced extreme distress or mental disorder as a result of being in the police station; and 7 per cent were suffering from a mental illness, such as schizophrenia or severe depression. Some of the latter were actively suicidal. Ibid.: especially, pp. 23–26; see also McConville *et al.* (1991: 56 ff).
33. COP C, para. 11.16.
34. COP C, Note for Guidance 11B.
35. Although not an appropriate adult, a solicitor may be an independent person for the purpose of s. 77. See *R v. Lewis* [1996] Crim LR 260.
36. Bucke and Brown (1998: 8) found that no appropriate adult attended in one-third of cases involving mentally disordered detainees. In most of these cases, a doctor had recommended that no appropriate adult was necessary, or that the detainee was fit to be interviewed. The requirement for a doctor and the issue of fitness to be interviewed are quite separate from that of an appropriate adult.
37. Gudjonsson *et al.* (1993). Bucke and Brown (1997: 7) cite an unpublished Home Office study which estimates the numbers to be up to 26 per cent.
38. Bean and Nemitz (1995).
39. It would, of course, be open to the defence to raise the issue of vulnerability at trial and to argue for the exclusion of any confession on that basis.
40. Availability of appropriate adults varies regionally, with some areas making provision for trained individuals to attend. Bucke and Brown (1997) found

that panel representatives attended in one per cent of juvenile cases and two per cent of others.

41. See Evans (1993) and Bucke and Brown (1997).
42. See, further, Hodgson (1997).
43. For instance, a juvenile's estranged father, whom she did not wish to be present, was not an appropriate adult in *DPP v. Blake* (1989) 89 Cr App R 179.
44. The defendant's father, who was of low intelligence, almost illiterate and probably incapable of appreciating the gravity of the situation on which his son was placed, was not an *appropriate* adult in *R v. Morse and others* [1991] *Crim LR* 195; a juvenile's 17-year-old brother was not considered an adult and would be unable to provide the kind of assistance required, *R v. Palmer* (1991) *Legal Action*, September, 21.
45. Adverse inferences from failure to testify will not be drawn, only where 'it appears to the court that the physical or mental condition of the accused makes it undesirable for him to give evidence'; s. 35(1)(b) CJPOA 1994.
46. Interview with Anne Owers of JUSTICE, 1995.
47. Tape-recording on its own cannot guarantee that the contents of a confession are true, or reveal what was said or done before the tape-recorder was turned on.
48. Sanders (1993: 91).
49. McConville *et al.* (1991: 60).
50. An example is the case of the Cardiff Three, whose convictions were quashed by the Court of Appeal in December 1992: the judges were appalled by the endless repetitive questioning that the tapes revealed (see *Paris, Abdullahi and Miller* (1993) 97 Cr App R 99.
51. RCCJ (1993: 61–2). cf the RCCJ recommendations on plea bargaining and defence disclosure, where it was content to rely on the quality of defence lawyers.
52. The Home Office Research and Planning Unit examined 2,210 magistrates' court cases; McConville (1993b) examined 524 cases. See RCCJ (1993: 65). For further discussion of the corroboration debate, see Chapter 8.
53. Schedule 1 of CPIA 1996 modifies the Magistrates' Court Act 1980. The door was finally closed on the 1994 reform when the CPS advised that it would not have produced the savings envisaged since many of the cases would require court hearings for other matters such as bail or charge amendments. The new provisions abolishing committal proceedings for indictable-only offences are being piloted in six areas from January 1999.
54. For example, if the defendant is also charged with an either-way or summary offence which appears to be related to the indictable-only offence.
55. See Chapter 2 on the tendency of the police to determine the guilt of suspects at the outset of an investigation.
56. This approach typifies much of the Commission's Report. See also Hodgson (1999) forthcoming.
57. The revised Code C, para. 11.1 (effective 1 April 1991) stipulates: 'Following a decision to arrest a suspect he must not be interviewed about the relevant offence except at a police station or other authorised place of detention' unless a delay would produce negative results such as harm to evidence or persons (para. 11(a),(b),(c)).

58. Moston and Stephenson (1993: 2 and Table 5 on p. 20).
59. Ibid. Informal questioning in the police station has also been found to be prevalent by Dixon *et al.* (1990ab). According to this study, 53 per cent of the officers admitted doing so (always or often) to establish rapport with suspects.
60. Sanders and Bridges (1990: 505–6).
61. See 'Interview Records' in Code C, 11.5–11.13.
62. Op cit.: Table 11, p. 27; and p. 29. See also their discussion of the reasons why both suspects and police might engage in interviews outside the station (p. 28).
63. See the discussion in Moston and Stephenson (1993: 42–4).
64. See Bottomley *et al.* (1991), McConville *et al.* (1991), Baldwin and Moloney (1993) and Maguire and Norris (1993).
65. In not including video-taping within the cells, the Commission might have been concerned about excessive infringement upon the privacy of detained persons.
66. A number of submissions were made to the Commission in support of the video-taping of interviews with suspects. These included a joint ACPO, Superintendent's Association and Police Federation report that advocated video as 'the means to invite the court into the interview room to see for themselves the truth of what goes on'. *Police Review*, 29 November 1991: 2366, cited in Moston and Stephenson (1993: 45).
67. See generally, ch. 5 of their report.
68. M. McLean, *Identifying Patterns in Witness Interviews: An Empirical Examination of the Interviewing Behaviour of Police Officers* (Bradford and Ilkley Community College, April 1992); copy sent to authors. See also the research into police summaries of interviews with suspects: Baldwin (1991).
69. See Moston and Stephenson (1993). Moreover, Wolchover and Heaton-Armstrong (1991: 242) report that in the post-PACE period there has been a marked increase in police questioning before arrival at the station, a practice which was previously 'comparatively rare'.
70. Interview with Anne Owers (JUSTICE), April 1995.
71. McConville *et al.* (1991: 189).
72. See testimony of Chris Mullin MP, RCCJ (1993: para. 14). An example already noted (Dixon *et al.*, 1990a) is the routine fabrication of the custody records that police stations are required to keep.
73. See Smith (1994: 298) and LAG (1993: 8). According to Mansfield and Wardle, the current situation does not appear to have improved, for 'reports of police malpractice are now almost a daily event' (1993: 60).

4   Remedies for Police Misconduct

1. For example, the Birmingham and Guildford cases, Judith Ward, the Broadwater Farm defendants, the Bridgewater Four and others. In the Bridgewater case, four men were convicted of murder as a result of a confession allegedly made by one of them (Patrick Molloy). This confession was extracted after Molloy had been shown a confession reportedly made by a second defendant (Vincent Hickey). However, 18 years later the Court of

Appeal was shown an electrostatic analysis of the 'Hickey confession' which revealed that it had been concocted by two police officers, DC John Perkins and DC Graham Leeke, as well as evidence that the Molloy confession was based on a statement which had been significantly altered. See K. Ahmed and D. Campbell, 'Judgement: Crucial doubts that led to collapse of prosecution's case', *The Guardian*, 31 July 1997.

2. This is recognised under s. 77 PACE: where the prosecution case relies wholly or largely upon the confession of a mentally handicapped person, the jury is warned of the dangers of relying upon that confession if it was made in the absence of an independent party.

3. Per Auld J in *Jelen* (1989) 90 Cr App R 456 at 464–5.

4. Both ss. 76(3) and 78(1) PACE provide for the judge to exclude evidence on her own initiative, but in practice the judge will not intervene even if counsel relies on an inappropriate ground for exclusion. See *Fulling* (1987) Cr App R 136 and *Howden-Simpson* [1991] Crim LR 49. Also discussion in Sharpe (1998: 112).

5. 'It's a complicated situation. You've got to look at where the judges come from, their political background and their perception of the justice system: and also most judges in the higher echelons have prosecuted in order to become judges. You don't often get the Michael Mansfields and these sorts of people – liberal lawyers – appointed judges: unless it's to shut them up and stifle their ability'. Solicitor-advocate interview, June 1995.

6. Note, also, that s. 82 PACE preserves the common law power to exclude evidence, see *Sang* [1980] AC 402.

7. cf *Ibrahim v. R* [1914] 1 AC 599.

8. CJPOA 1994 ss. 34–8. For further discussion of case-law in this area, see Chapter 5 'The Right to Silence', below.

9. CPIA 1996 s. 11. See further, Chapter 7. In some cases, the judge must also decide whether evidence need not be disclosed to the defence on the grounds that it is not in the public interest. If this is the case, the decision must be kept under constant review by the Crown Court throughout the trial; CPIA 1996 s. 15. Whilst magistrates must also decide these issues, they are not obliged to keep the decision under constant review.

10. *R v. Paris, Abdullahi and Miller* (1993) 97 Cr App R 99 at 103.

11. See *R v. Emmerson* (1991) 92 Cr App R 284, where the officer raised his voice and used bad language.

12. cf *Everett* [1988] Crim LR 826. See also discussion of case-law in Hodgson (1997) and Sharpe (1998).

13. *R v. Paris, Abdullahi and Miller* (1993) 97 Cr App R 99. cf *R v. L* [1994] Crim LR 839 where similar pressures applied to a man of normal intelligence were held not to render inadmissible his admissions.

14. *Goldenberg* (1988) 88 Cr App R 285; *Crampton* (1991) 92 Cr App R 372.

15. cf *Everett* [1988] Crim LR 826 (vulnerable suspect); *McGovern* (1991) 92 Cr App R 228 (vulnerable suspect because of pregnancy and limited intelligence); *Souter* [1995] Crim LR 729 (soldier in highly distressed state). For further discussion of case-law, see Murphy (ed.), *Blackstone's Criminal Practice*, 1998, pp. 2173–5.

16. See *Harvey* [1988] Crim LR 241 in which a psychopathically disordered woman of low intelligence overheard her lover confessing to a murder. It

was held that her own subsequent confession may have been borne of a child-like desire to protect her lover and so it was excluded under s. 76(2)(b).

17. See *DPP v. Blake* (1989) 89 Cr App R 179, where the juvenile suspect's estranged father was held not to be an appropriate adult; *Morse* [1991] Crim LR 195 where the juvenile's father, who was of low intelligence, was held not to be an appropriate adult; *Moss* (1990) 91 Cr App R 371 where the suspect was of low intelligence, was repeatedly interviewed without a lawyer or appropriate adult present.

18. (1991) 92 Crim App R 314. Exclusion was not because of denial of access alone, but also the failure to show *the solicitor* a note of interview. See also *Mason* where the deceit practiced upon *the solicitor* had not been taken into account by the trial judge, but was emphasized by the Court of Appeal.

19. [1988] Crim LR 747.

20. See, *Quinn* [1990] Crim LR 581; *Walsh* (1989) 91 Cr App R 161; and *Keenan* [1990] 2 QB 54.

21. The first instance decision of *R v. Fennelly* seems to be the only reported case and this was later disapproved in *R v. McCarthy* [1996] Crim LR 818 where evidence from an unlawful stop and search was admitted. See, further, cases cited in Sharpe (1998: 223).

22. [1978] QB 490 at 497.

23. The police are concerned with the immediate impact of the judgment – that the evidence is admitted – rather than the wider rhetoric concerning impropriety.

24. Note also that Home Office statistics of stops and searches recorded under PACE suggest that most (between 85 and 90 per cent), while not necessarily unlawful, do not lead to arrest even, let alone trial. This excludes 'consensual' searches. The requirement of reasonable suspicion does not appear to be an inhibiting factor in police stops. See Chapter 2.

25. See *Mason* [1988] 1 WLR 139 and *Canale* [1990] 2 All ER 187.

26. See *Alladice* (1988) 87 Cr App R 380.

27. ibid.

28. (1990) Cr App R 150.

29. [1992] Crim LR 40.

30. [1988] 2 WLR 920.

31. (1990) 91 Cr App R 237.

32. [1992] Crim LR 372.

33. cf *R v. Condron (K) and Condron (W)* [1997] 1 WLR 827; *R v. Argent* [1997] 2 Cr App R 27; *R v. Roble* [1997] Crim LR 449.

34. At p. 837. See Chapter 5 for further discussion.

35. See Hodgson (1994: 90).

36. (1989) 91 Cr App R 161, at p. 163.

37. See, for example, *Menard* [1995] 1 Cr App R 306 and *Park* (1994) 99 Cr App R 270, both cited in Sharpe (1998: 213).

38. Required by Code C 11.2A.

39. Provided that there is no incitement to crime and the undercover pose is not used to deliberately circumvent the code. See *Christou* [1992] QB 979.

40. [1993] 3 All ER 513.

41. [1997] 1 Cr App R 217.

42. Interview, June 1995.
43. Sections 1 and 2.
44. The investigating officer must be of at least the rank of chief inspector and no less senior than the officer complained of (s. 85 PACE).
45. A Home Office study found that of those who felt like making a complaint against the police, 66 per cent did not do so because: (i) they believed they 'might get into trouble' (18 per cent) or (ii) they were 'afraid to do so' (10 per cent) or (iii) they felt 'it would be of no use' (38 per cent). See, Harrison and Cragg (1991: 6–7).
46. See Home Office (1998b: 4–5).
47. See Harrison and Cragg (1991: 7).
48. As Maguire and Norris point out, 'senior officers (who share similar goals of crime control) have no genuine interest in reducing at least "minor" forms of malpractice, so long as it is effectively concealed' (1993: 74).
49. This category includes complaints withdrawn or where a dispensation is granted because investigation of the complaint is not reasonable or practicable.
50. See Home Office (1998b: 4).
51. In December 1994, for example, there were 2,464 cases in progress involving complaints against the London Metropolitan Police received during the year, as well as 350 that had been received in earlier years; the figures for the rest of England and Wales were 6,625 received in 1994 and 955 received in earlier years. See Home Office, 'Police Complaints and Discipline: England and Wales, 1994': Table 7, p. 14.
52. In 1992, the police forces, CPS and PCA entered an agreement whereby the police forces aimed to complete their investigations within 120 days while the CPS and PCA each have 28 days to consider the completed investigation. The average time taken by the PCA to complete a case rose to 53 days in 1996/97, but was reduced to 31 days for 1997/98. During the same year, the police forces concluded 65 per cent of their investigations within 120 days. See, PCA (1998: 15–16).
53. See Home Office (1998b: 9–10).
54. Home Office (1998b: 6). Charges were proved against 113 officers (1998b: 13).
55. 163 'serious non-sexual assault' and 6,028 'other assault'; see PCA (1998: 13).
56. See PCA (1998: 13).
57. The report does not indicate the nature of the original complaint.
58. This percentage is the same as the previous year. It has remained under 2 per cent throughout the history of the PCA.
59. Interview with Nick Brown, barrister, May 1995.
60. Even a decision to prosecute may not survive, as is shown in the following examples during the 1990s. In 1986, Paul and Wayne Darvell were convicted of the rape and murder of a sex shop manageress and given life sentences. The Court of Appeal freed them in 1993, declaring that their convictions were based on fabricated evidence. In June 1994, three officers from the South Wales Police charged with fabricating the evidence were cleared. In October 1993 an Old Bailey judge dropped charges against three retired West Midlands detectives who had been accused of fabricating evidence in the Birmingham Six case on the grounds that the 'volume and intensity' of

media coverage following the Six's acquittal in 1991 made it impossible for them to have a fair trial. On 19 May 1993, three detectives were acquitted at the Old Bailey of conspiring to pervert the course of justice in fabricating evidence to convict the Guildford Four, whose convictions were quashed by the Court of Appeal in 1989. In December 1993, the convictions of the Cardiff Three for murdering a prostitute were quashed by the Court of Appeal. The judges were strongly critical of the oppressive questioning by police of one of the three, which included a tape-recorded interview in which the suspect had denied murder 300 times. None of the officers in the case was suspended and there was no internal inquiry. For other cases, see Emily Barr, 'Fair Cop?', *The Guardian*, 28 July 1994. Winston Silcott's conviction for the murder of PC Keith Blakelock during the 1995 Broadwater Farm riot, was overturned by the Court of Appeal when it was shown that officers had falsified the interview notes on which the conviction was based. Two officers were prosecuted and acquitted of conspiring to pervert the course of justice. Silcott was immediately paid £10,000 compensation for the time he spent in custody and for damage to his reputation (*The Daily Telegraph*, 27 July 1994). Despite police abuses so numerous that the West Midland Serious Crime Squad was actually disbanded in 1989, only two former officers of the SCS have been punished. After having been found guilty of falsehood and prevarication by a disciplinary panel they were fined an undisclosed amount by their chief constable. See, again, Barr, 'Fair Cop', *The Guardian*, 28 July 1994. In May 1995 a stipendiary magistrate decided not to proceed against a police superintendent and a Home Office forensic scientist (both retired) charged with withholding critical evidence in a murder case that led to the wrongful conviction of Stefan Kiszko, who was released by the Court in 1992 after serving 16 years of a life sentence. The magistrate was concerned that the policeman and forensic scientist could not get a fair trial because of lengthy and detailed publicity about the case. See Martin Wainwright, '"Rough justice" case halted', *The Guardian*, 2 May 1995.

61. See H. Mills, 'Insult added to Widow's Injury', *The Observer*, 27 July 1997.
62. PCA, *The 1996/97 Annual Report* , 21.
63. PCA (1998: 20).
64. See PCA, *The 1997/97 Annual Report*, 21. In response to the two deaths, *The Observer* (27 July 1997) noted that it 'is a grim fact that few of the hundreds of officers accused of brutality, using excessive force, abusing their powers or serious malpractice are ever disciplined, let alone brought to trial'.
65. See Duncan Campbell, 'Police "avoid charges by retiring early"', *The Guardian*, 11 May 1995.
66. See announcement of the Home Affairs Committee, House of Commons, *Hansard*, 23 March 1998.
67. See Parliamentary Documents, Home Affairs Committee, House of Commons, *Hansard*, 16 December 1997.
68. Data for the 1988 to 1992 period was supplied in a report to C. Mullin, MP (Sunderland South), by Charles Wardle of the Office of the Secretary of the State for the Home Department, 4 December 1992; those for 1993 and 1994 were supplied by Matthew Baggot, Superintendent Staff Office to Commissioner, Metropolitan Police Service, 14 June 1995. Copies of the reports were provided to the authors by Chris Mullin.

69. The assertion of police authority is enough and may include detention on the street during an unlawful search, as well as being held unlawfully at the police station.

70. In December 1995, Rennie Kingsley was awarded £76,000 damages plus legal costs of £25,000 from the Metropolitan Police in settlement of his claim for false imprisonment, assault and malicious prosecution. Kingsley served four months in prison before his conviction for possessing LSD was overturned by the Court of Appeal. His complaint had been investigated as part of 'Operation Jackpot', a four-year inquiry into allegations of corrupt conduct against 44 officers at Stoke Newington police station. Even though the Metropolitan Police did not dispute Kingsley's claims, the CPS did not bring charges against the officers involved; nor were they subject to any disciplinary charges. Of the 44 officers investigated, only one was convicted (see H. Mills, 'Police brought to book for drug arrest', *The Independent*, 12 December 1995).

71. *The Independent*, 2 August 1994; and *The Guardian*, 8 August 1994.

72. Thus, despite having agreed to pay £20,000 for the illegal strip-searching of two young women in a drug raid, the image of the Met was still widely discredited; see, for instance, *The Guardian*, 26 November 1994.

73. Interview, June 1995.

74. For example, while the Commissioner of the Metropolitan Police paid over £33,500 into court in settlement of a family's claim over assault and battery and false imprisonment, the police force denied any culpability. As *The Independent* noted,'When the police do any wrong their reaction is to point the finger of suspicion at anyone but themselves.' See 'Met chief attacks lawyers', 2 August 1994.

75. Communication from the Metropolitan Police Service to C. Mullin, MP, 14 June 1995, a copy of which was sent to the authors.

76. Interview, June, 1995. It is quite understandable, therefore, that some complainants remain bitterly dissatisfied with 'victory' in a civil suit when they learn that the offending officer or officers are not disciplined in any way and are allowed to continue to work.

5   The Right to Silence

1. The defence have for some time been obliged to provide the prosecution with advance warning of any alibi (CPIA 1996 and, formerly, s11 Criminal Justice Act 1967) or expert evidence (s. 81 PACE and 1987 Crown Court Rules) to be relied upon at trial. See also, Serious Fraud Office investigations under s. 2 Criminal Justice Act 1987.

2. Adverse inferences may also be drawn from the defendant's failure to account for objects, marks, substances or presence at the scene. See ss. 36 and 37 CJPOA 1994.

3. Under the *Criminal Evidence (Northern Ireland) Order* 1988.

4. See CLRC (1972) *Eleventh Report*, Cmnd 4991; Home Office Working Group (1984).

5. Although they also recommended that the defence should be obliged to disclose the substance of their case and suspects should provide samples for DNA analysis, with refusal subject to adverse inferences.

6. Cited in Leng (1998). The ACPO study is unpublished and no methodology identified.
7. For a general discussion of the various positions taken on silence, see Greer (1990).
8. See *Holgate – Mohammed v. Duke* [1984] 1 All ER 1054 where the House of Lords held that this was a legitimate reason for exercising the constable's discretion to arrest once a lawful ground had been established.
9. Gudjonsson and Mackeith (1990); McConville *et al.* (1991).
10. McConville and Hodgson (1993: 139).
11. See, e.g. *Paris, Abdullahi and Miller* (1993) 97 Cr App R 99 (discussed in Chapter 3) where the police engaged in oppressive questioning even in the presence of a lawyer.
12. 'It cannot be assumed that suspects under pressure to speak will tell the truth. They may wish to protect others, they may fear retribution, they may not wish their spouses to know where they were, they may simply not remember a sequence of events which may have taken place some time before their arrest. They will be under pressure to provide any plausible explanation. Wrong or misleading answers will damage their case...' Gudjonsson and Clare in a letter to the Home Secretary, Mr Michael Howard (14 November 1994) cited in full in JUSTICE, (1994d: 31). See also RCCJ (1993: 52).
13. This conclusion is based on JUSTICE's analysis of 89 cases in which alleged miscarriages of justice rested on disputed confessions which were obtained from suspects under conditions of distress, pressure and fear of the consequences of silence (ibid., p. 1).
14. See s. 58(8) PACE 1984.
15. *R v. Chandler* [1976] 3 All ER 105, where the court considered the legally represented suspect to be on even terms with the police and so allowed in evidence of unanswered as well as answered questions.
16. McConville and Hodgson (1993); Baldwin (1993a).
17. See Table 2.1, p. 17. Clerks were both on staff and from independent agencies, including former police officers.
18. See, for example, discussion of *Dunford* (1990) 91 Cr App Rep 150 in Hodgson (1992).
19. The RCCJ's recommendation that solicitors be tested was not followed up.
20. In the most recent figures, Phillips and Brown (1998) report 37 per cent of suspects who had been legally advised making admissions, compared to 65 per cent of those who had not.
21. See the studies conducted by the Metropolitan and West Yorkshire police forces (Home Office, 1989, Appendix C) and by Moston *et al.* (1992) and Baldwin (1992).
22. Leng (1993) reviews major studies on the extent of use of the right to silence: for example, Zander (1979): 4 per cent; Baldwin and McConville (1980): 3.8 per cent to 6.5 per cent; Mitchell (1983): 4.3 per cent; McKenzie and Irving (1988): 11 per cent to 16 per cent; West Yorkshire Police (1989): 12.3 per cent selectively silent; Moston *et al.* (1992): 16 per cent selectively silent; Baldwin (1992): 1.7 per cent no answers, 18 per cent selectively silent; McConville and Hodgson (1992): 2.5 per cent no answers, 27 per cent selectively silent. In his own study for the Royal Commission, Leng (1993) found that suspects relied

upon the right to silence in only 4.5 per cent of cases in which interviews were held (p 73). Home Office research carried out by David Brown estimated that the percentage of suspects who refuse to answer *any questions at all* is 5 per cent for those outside London and 9 per cent for those within the Metropolitan police district. The average of those who exercise their right *to some extent* is 8 per cent for those outside London and 15 per cent for those in the Metropolitan district. *The Incidence of Right to Silence in Police Interviews: The Research Evidence Reviewed*, Home Office Research and Planning Unit, unpublished; cited in RCCJ (1993: 53).

23. Neither do defendants in court appeal to the right to silence in order to avoid the perils of cross-examination (McConville *et al.*, 1994: 215).

24. The whole notion of 'ambush defences' seems to be a part of police mythology which portrays suspects as guilty and defence lawyers as crafty if not corrupt in providing 'off the peg' defences. In fact, the reverse is true. Defence lawyers frequently lack an adversarial ideology and fail to represent adequately their clients interests throughout the case (McConville *et al.*, 1994).

25. Bucke and Brown (1997) found 6 per cent of suspects refusing to answer all questions and 10 per cent refusing to answer some.

26. Compare with the Singapore experience, as dicussed in Yeo (1983).

27. Quoted in Zander (1994: 145).

28. See McConville *et al.* (1991); Choongh (1997).

29. That is, a case to answer, where there is sufficient evidence to put the defendant on trial.

30. COP C, para. 10.4. An earlier version read: 'You do not have to say anything. But if you do not mention now something which you later use in your defence, the court may decide that your failure to mention it now strengthens the case against you. A record will be made of anything you say and it may be given in evidence if your are brought to trial.' See *The Independent*, 7 December 1994.

31. Noted in JUSTICE (1994b: para. 4).

32. JUSTICE 1994a: 14.

33. Detained under the Mental Health Act in a regional secure unit.

34. The original research study, carried out for the Royal Commission by Clare and Gudjonsson (1993), showed that even the previous relatively simple caution was fully understood by only 42 per cent of suspects – although 52 per cent understood the part which advised them of the right to remain silent. The later Gudjonsson and Clare (1994) study is referred to in a letter by Gudjonsson cited in JUSTICE 1994b.

35. See Gudjonsson *et al.* (1993), discussed in Chapter 3, note 32. Another recent survey conducted by three psychologists on 109 people, suggested that on average only about half of the caution made sense to them. Eight out of ten interviewed found the 'adverse inference' element of the caution pressuring or threatening. See Shepherd, Mortimer and Mobasheri (1995).

36. It is hoped that this is unlikely, given the restrictions on questioning outside the station in COP C.

37. Reported in *The Independent*, 13 March 1998.

38. Interview with John Davis, June 1995.

39. [1997] 2 Cr App R 27.

40. *R v. Condron (K) and Condron (W)* [1997] 1 WLR 827 at 837. See Chapter 4 for a discussion of the court's generally more sympathetic attitude to vulnerable persons as 'deserving' defendants.
41. *R v. Roble* [1997] Crim LR 449.
42. Interview with John Davis, June 1995.
43. See Jackson (1995: 592). For example, in *R v. Connolly and McCartney* (NICR unreported, 1992) the court stated, 'I should not regard it as reasonable for a person being interviewed to fail to mention facts because he had been advised by his solicitor to remain silent. If that failure is objectively unreasonable, it does not in my opinion become reasonable merely because a solicitor gave his client ill-judged advice.'
44. See *R v. Condron (K) and Condron (W)* [1997] 1 WLR 827; *R v. Argent* [1997] 2 Cr App R 27; and *R v. Roble* [1997] Crim LR 449. For further discussion of the defence position, see Cape, 1997.
45. *R v. Cowan,* op. cit.
46. See *R v. Kavanagh* CA, 7 February 1997 LEXIS (cited in Pattenden, 1998: 153). Pattenden (1998: 159) argues that this is clearly wrong: 'If the admissibility of a confession, an express admission of guilt, is normally determined on the *voire dire*, the same procedure should surely apply when the admissibility of evidence capable of giving rise to an implied admission of guilt is contested.'
47. Interview, August 1997.
48. At a practical level this raises difficulties. As one solicitor interviewed commented: '...how on earth, at perhaps 3 o'clock in the morning, is a lawyer, no matter how experienced, in dealing with a serious allegation, supposed to make a quality decision as to whether his client, in a year's time, is likely to give evidence or not?' (Interview, June 1995).
49. This occurred in only 9 per cent of accredited adviser cases and 14 per cent of all advisers. See Bridges and Choongh (1998).
50. In both instances, only around one-third of all advisers did this. Ibid.
51. Again, only around one-third of advisers did this. Ibid.
52. Around one-quarter of all advisers asked about charge, and only 15 per cent of accredited advisers asked about bail. Ibid.
53. 86 per cent of accredited advisers; 77 per cent of all advisers; ibid.
54. [1998] 2 Cr App R 373.
55. Section 35(1) CJPOA 1994.
56. Unreported, 9 October 1995 cited in Jennings (1996).
57. [1997] 2 All ER 1011.
58. Quoted by Jennings (1996).
59. [1995] 4 All ER 939.
60. Defendants under the age of fourteen are no longer exempt following the passage of the Crime and Disorder Act 1998.
61. It was impossible, said the Court, 'to anticipate all the circumstances in which a judge might think it right to direct or advise a jury against drawing an adverse inference'. Lord Taylor at 945.
62. See Colvin and Akester (1995).
63. This was done in the case of *McLernon* (1990) 10 NIJB, which concerned provisions of Article 4 of the Criminal Evidence (Northern Ireland) Order 1988 which are in similar terms to s. 35 CJPOA 1994; ibid.: 1622.

64. This difference was raised in the partly dissenting opinion of Nicholas Bratza QC in *Murray v. UK*, who called attention to the dangers of allowing juries to draw inferences which are not open to review; ibid.
65. See Taylor (1994).
66. See the discussion in Chapter 4.
67. *Murray* 1991 discussed in Jackson (1995: 598).
68. (1996) 22 EHRR 29.
69. (1997) 23 EHRR 313.

6 Prosecution, Bail and Trial Venue

1. The right of private prosecution is still in force; Sanders (1986: 257).
2. See CPS, *Crown Prosecution Service in Brief* (August 1994).
3. As early as 1929 the Royal Commission on Police Powers and Procedure took note of the practice and stated that it was important to keep separate the duty on the police of preventing and detecting crime and the duty of bringing to justice people who have broken the law. It recommended the appointment of special officials to conduct prosecutions.
4. A judge *orders* an acquittal before the trial begins because the prosecution are not able to advance sufficient evidence to warrant proceeding; a judge *directs* an acquittal when the evidence is so weak that no reasonable jury could convict.
5. See Uglow (1995: 122).
6. See Chapter 3 and the role of committals as a safeguard against unreliable confessions.
7. This can be contrasted with the role of the Scottish procurator fiscal who has always been responsible for the investigation and prosecution of offences and thus has considerable powers to direct the activities of police officers, including to require further police investigations. In more inquisitorial systems, such as France, the *procureur* is responsible for supervising the initial police investigation and any detention of suspects in custody, as well as taking the decision to prosecute. The police have no power to charge. It is interesting that the RCCJ rejected such an approach in this jurisdiction, on the grounds that it would remove accountability from the police; France retains such a system for that very reason.
8. See McConville *et al.* (1991) who argue that the prosecution case is largely a police construction, the parameters of which the CPS are unable to shape or alter.
9. It is also noteworthy that, although having an important responsibility to the CPS, police targets do not relate to the quality and promptness of files passed to them.
10. The CPS, in consultation with the police, produces detailed guidance, called 'Charging Standards', to assist police and prosecutors in making the most appropriate initial charges; it also consults with the police when a charge needs to be amended (see CPS, 1997: 11).
11. This is a 50 per cent increase since 1986.
12. CPS, (1995: 24).
13. Crisp and Moxon (1994: ch. 4).

14. The police were hostile to the suggestion of CPS supervision of investigations and the RCCJ limited itself to recommending increased consultation and encouraging the police to be more responsive to CPS requests for further investigation to be carried out.
15. It accounts for 43 per cent of discontinued cases. National Audit Office (1997), *Crown Prosecution Service*, 42.
16. That is, about the same as it was at the outset of the 1980s, as reported by McConville and Baldwin in 1981.
17. In 39 per cent of cases terminated at court, the decision had been made beforehand, but was not communicated to the defendant in time to avoid a court hearing. Discussed in an unpublished Home Office study by RCCJ (1993: 76).
18. CPS (1998: 36).
19. Lord Chancellor's Department (1998b: 65).
20. However, inadequate advice from prosecuting counsel was also cited as a factor contributing to judge-directed acquittals, and the Royal Commission made detailed recommendations to deal with this type of inadequacy (RCCJ, 1993: 78, para. 39).
21. Glidewell recommended that CJUs be either a CPS unit with police staff, or a police unit with police staff, housed in or near the police station. See Law Society (1999) *Criminal Parctitioner Newsletter* (37) for details on the administration of fast track cases and the range of pathways which a case might now follow to court.
22. *The Independent*, 14 October 1993.
23. Defined in Schedule 1 of the 1976 Bail Act.
24. *Wemhoff v. FRG* (1968) 1 EHRR 155.
25. Jones (1985) found that the use of custodial remands ranged from 7 per cent to 37 per cent. More recently, Hucklesby (1997a) also found local variation.
26. According to Morgan and Jones (1992), all evidence suggests that untried prisoners endure without justification the most oppressive conditions found in the prison system. Thus, due to the increasingly overcrowded prison system defendants may be remanded in custody in police cells, local prisons or remand centres where conditions are far less tolerable than those in the training prisons. Sanitation and exercising facilities are below standard, and inmates in the remand centres and local prisons spend as little as one-third as much time engaged in activities such as work and education as their sentenced counterparts in training prisons. See pp. 36 and 49–53.
27. See Council of Europe, Committee for the Prevention of Torture and Inhuman and Degrading Treatment or Punishment, 1991, para. 57.
28. In 1975 (before the 1976 Bail Act) the proportion was only 8 per cent.
29. Section 49(3)(a) CDA 1998 also makes provision for the possibility that the justices' clerk (with the consent of the prosecutor and the accused) may extend or vary bail.
30. Given the determining influence of police bail decisions in most instances (Hucklesby, 1997b), this vigilance by the courts is to be welcomed.
31. The event of the 1984–5 miners' strike provided countless examples of the police use of their power to arrest, coupled with bail conditions cooperatively imposed on them by magistrates, to regulate the speech and behaviour of

picketing miners and other supporters of the strike. See, for example, *Mansfield Justices ex parte Sharkey* [1985] QB 613.

32. If the defendant elected summary trial, the magistrates had the power to order that the case be tried in the Crown Court.

33. The RCCJ cite the proportions committed as 52 per cent (sent) and 30 per cent (elected). The 1997/8 CPS figures are 53 per cent and 20 per cent – the lower number of elections presumably reflecting the defendant's more limited right of election, introduced in the CPIA 1996 and discussed below.

34. CPS (1998: 41).

35. Between 1980 and 1987 the proportion rose from 15 per cent to 23 per cent, although by 1992, it had dropped back to 17 per cent. See Home Office (1995) *Mode of Trial: A Consultation Document*, Cm 2908 (London: HMSO, 1). In 1997–8, 105,063 cases were comitted to the Crown Court; CPS, (1998: 41).

36. See Ashworth (1993).

37. These were common assault, driving while disqualified, taking a car without the owner's consent, and criminal damage up to £2,000 (now raised to £5,000 under the CJPOA); see the Criminal Justice Act 1988, ss. 37–9.

38. See Mode of Trial Guidelines, Practice Direction [1990] 1 WLR 1439. The guidelines were revised in 1995; and the revision is found in *Blackstone's Criminal Practice* (London: Blackstone Press, 1998: 1065–8).

39. See Bridges (1994a) and Ashworth (1993).

40. Interview, April 1995.

41. Lord Taylor, quoted in *The Times*, 28 July 1993: 7.

42. Home Office (1998a).

43. *The Guardian*, 14 October 1998.

44. This was the case in Bottoms and McClean's 1976 research and remained so in Hedderman and Moxon's 1992 study.

45. 69 per cent of defendants and 81 per cent of solicitors said that they preferred Crown Court trial because there was a better chance of acquittal. 62 per cent of defendants and 70 per cent of solicitors felt that the magistrates were on the side of the police; Hedderman and Moxon (1992: 20).

46. CPS (1998).

47. They note elsewhere (p. 111) that 43 per cent of trials fold at the last minute.

48. The average cost of a contested trial in the Crown Court (1991–2) was £13,500, compared to £1,500 in the magistrates' court. Relative figures for guilty pleas were £2,500 and £500 (RCCJ, 1993: 5).

49. See RCCJ (1993: 88).

50. RCCJ (1993: 88).

51. See Magistrates' Courts (Advance Information) Rules (SI 1885, No. 601); see also Jackson (1993b: 131 n 5 and 132).

52. See further our discussion of the Attorney General's Guidelines (1981) and the 'Guinness Advice' in Chapter 7.

53. Section 49 CPIA 1996 amends s17 of the Magistrates' Court Act 1980.

54. See the Home Office Consultation Document *Mode of Trial*, Cmnd 2908, July 1995, para. 21.

55. Hedderman and Moxon (1992) found that 51 per cent of defendants who changed their intention as to plea after the mode of trial hearing did so because they expected some charges to be dropped or reduced.

56. This will be especially likely for those at the heavier end of the offence scale who have little to gain from an early plea sentence discount; see Leng and Taylor (1996: 71).

57. 5,878 cases were committed to the Crown Court for sentence between April and June 1998, compared to 1,693 for the same period in 1997; Lord Chancellor's Department (1998a). The new provisions came into force on 1 October 1997.

58. This is typical of the Royal Commission on Criminal Justice, based upon a misunderstanding of the French system. Whilst the *juge d'instruction* investigates under 10 per cent of all criminal cases, the *procureur* is responsible for supervising (and later prosecuting) the remaining cases. This may entail requiring the police to conduct further interviews with the suspect, or to gather other forms of evidence. The dominance of the *procureur* is not a failure, but precisely what is anticipated by the legal texts.

59. Although the defendant does not have a choice, the magistrates may decide to commit the case to the Crown Court for sentence.

7 Disclosure and Sentence Discounts

1. Brownlee *et al.* (1994: 120; emphasis added).
2. The researchers in this study expressed their strong disagreement with this practice.
3. This is a very real danger given the high number of weak cases prosecuted by the CPS. See discussion in Chapter 6.
4. See also McConville *et al.* (1994), who document the guilty-plea oriented practices and culture of defence lawyers, and the low esteem in which most clients are held.
5. *Law Society Gazette,* 80, 1993: 2330.
6. 1 WLR 1318. This is further bolstered by ss. 39 and 40 of the CPIA 1996.
7. See Leng and Taylor (1996: 52).
8. 'Unused material' is understood to mean any information which has some bearing on an offence and the surrounding circumstances of the offence, such as witness statements, which is not included in the committal bundles (see *R v Saunders and others* (1989), discussed below).
9. *McIlkenny and others* (1991) 93 Cr App R 287.
10. Mullin, Testimony to the House of Commons (1991: para. 36).
11. The Attorney General subsequently acknowledged, in a letter to Chris Mullin, MP, dated 17 May 1991, that this 'oversight or administrative error was responsible for what was undoubtedly a most unfortunate error' (ibid.: para. 38).
12. The other basis was the alleged confessions of the men, which were found in 1991 to lack integrity.
13. Two of the men, Patrick Armstrong and Paul Hill, were also convicted of two murders resulting from an explosion in November 1974 in a pub in Woolwich.
14. Whilst this case demonstrates the danger in not reviewing the police file in its entirety, it is unlikely that the original interview notes would ever be

disclosed, whatever the requirements. They were not part of the unused material, but evidence of police fabrication of a confession.

15. The definition of 'unused material' (para. 1) is extremely wide and inclusive. Commenting that 'it is hard to imagine wider words than that', the trial judge in *R v Saunders and Others* held that the defence were entitled to see all preparatory notes and memoranda which led to the making of witness statements (Unreported, Central Criminal Court, 29 September 1989, transcript).

16. Reported in (1982) 74 *Cr App R* at 302. Exceptions are found in the Guidelines: para. 6.

17. 'All those parties are obliged to make full and proper disclosure, so that the CPS, on whom the duty finally rests, can decide what disclosure to the defence may be required ... The duty of disclosure inevitably raises an obligation on all parties to preserve potentially disclosable material' (*The 'Guinness Advice'*, 1992: para. 3).

18. Ibid.: paras. 1 and 3. The rulings on 'unused material' in *Saunders and Others* (1989) were upheld in *Maguire* (1992) 94 Cr App R: 133; and *Ward* (1993) 96 Cr App R: 1].

19. (1989) 91 Cr App R 226.

20. (1991) 92 Cr App R 115.

21. *R v. Taylor (Michelle Ann)*; *R v. Taylor (Lisa Jane)* (1994) 98 Cr App R 361.

22. Glynn (1993: 846–47) and Uglow (1995: 164).

23. However, the Court of Appeal in *Davis, Johnson and Rowe* [1993] 1 WLR 613 held the *Ward* judgment had gone too far, and it set a new procedure for balancing PII concerns and the interests of the defence.

24. For example, a police officer who had been disbelieved by a jury in a previous case or who had been subject to disciplinary proceedings for breach of rules.

25. Home Office Consultation Document on Disclosure (1995).

26. A recent example is Gary Winship, released by the Court of Appeal following prosecution by police of the Stoke Newington station, northeast London, which included testimony by a police officer under investigation for police corruption (*The Guardian*, 6 July 1994).

27. 93 Cr App R at 48.

28. In *Davis* [1993] 2 All ER at 643; and *Keane* [1994] 2 All ER at 478, procedures have developed which allow the prosecution to seek to withhold material on PII grounds. The PII material is placed before the court which rules on whether it can be disclosed without compromising its confidentiality. Where the PII option is used the defence must be notified by the prosecution of the category of material held and it must be given a chance to make representations. In all cases, the prosecution must err on the side of disclosing even the most marginal information – unless even this cannot be revealed.

29. *Primary* disclosure, as provided for in s. 3, CPIA 1996, is automatic and compulsory for all cases to be tried on indictment. It also applies on a voluntary basis in summary trials where the defence accepts the disclosure scheme. See discussion below.

30. Secondary disclosure involves the supply of schedules of other information held by the police and other key participants – such as expert scientific witnesses – of the investigations.

31. Discussion of the disclosure provisions in the CPIA 1996 will follow.
32. According to *The efficient disposal of business in the Crown Court* (1992), Report of the Working Party of the Bar Council (chaired by S Seabrooke), '...in the vast majority of cases the issues are apparent on the face of the witness statements or can be deduced' (para. 630). The sample contained some defences which either were foreseeable or which the prosecutor should have been prepared to counter.
33. The RCCJ stated that, under its proposal, 'a wholly new line of defence ... will become rarer than they are at present' (1993: 84). In addition to the police and the Royal Commission, some form of mandatory defence disclosure was supported also by the Home Office Working Group on the Right to Silence (1989), the Law Society (1991), the CPS (1992), and the Civil Liberty Panel on Criminal Justice (1993). See Leng (1995: 705).
34. Which (largely) embodied the recommendations of the RCCJ.
35. Quoted in Leng and Taylor (1996: 1).
36. An exception is where disclosure is deemed to be not in the public interest.
37. Including 'negative' information – which is interpreted as anything which is not consistent with the police case-theory of the offence at the time it is obtained or as soon as practicable thereafter. If the investigator has any doubt as to the relevance of material, she is obliged to consult the prosecutor to resolve the doubt (cf: paras. 4.3; 4.4; and 6.1).
38. Cf, respectively, paras. 2.1; 5.1; and 6.9. Any material which has been retained and which will not be used as evidence must be listed by the investigator on a schedule (either non-sensitive or sensitive – as exemplified in para. 6.12), to enable the prosecutor to decide pursuant to her duty of making primary prosecution disclosure what items should be disclosed.
39. Leng and Taylor (199: 39–41) suggest that breaches of the Code are likely to lead to adverse consequences for the prosecution, but given the examples they offer these must be seen as a *very* minor inconvenience.
40. However, an extensions are possible but it is entirely at the discretion of the court; and given the tight deadline it is assumed that an application for extension will be a routine matter. See Corker (1997: 961–2) and Edwards (1997: 326–7).
41. Sections 5(6) and 5(7).
42. In lengthy and complex cases, however, it is possible that a more level playing-field may emerge. Under s. 29 of Part III, the trial judge may invoke a preparatory hearing and order a prosecution case statement (s. 31(5)) which, in addition to the summary of evidence, obliges the prosecution to disclose the inferences it will invite the court to draw from it. The judge may also order the prosecution to provide further explanatory information and material (s. 31(4)(d)), to enable the court and the defendant to better understand the prosecution case. At the behest of the defence, she may order further and better particulars of the prosecution case statement (s. 32(4)(d)). For detailed discussion, see Corker (1997: 1063–4) and Leng and Taylor (1996: 53–60).
43. See, further, Chapter 8.
44. Section 7(2)(a). On the other hand, despite the possibility that further disclosure of material previously undisclosed may be of assistance to the defence, the prosecution may also apply to the court for an order to state

that such disclosure is not in the public interest. Finally, assuming there is no further material to disclose, the prosecution may produce a written statement to that effect.

45. However, to do so would appear to conflict with the prosecutor's obligation (s. 9) to continuously review and disclose unused materials in its possession (see further below).

46. The court also has the power to order prosecution disclosure without a defence application.

47. For a discussion of this matter, see Corker (1997: 962).

48. In theory, this seems to suggest that unless the prosecution's continuing duty to disclose following primary prosecution disclosure is *tied conditionally* to what the defence does, then, despite the accused's failure to provide a defence statement the prosecution, in theory, should still be obliged to continue disclosing.

49. See *Davis, Johnson and Rowe* [1993] 1 WLR 613, the leading PII case.

50. Alawi and Botmeh were sentenced to 20 years in prison in connection with the bombing of the Israeli Embassay and Balfour House in July 1994. After revelations by the former M15 agent, David Shayler, that warnings were telephoned from Israel before the bombings (and were ignored); and a claim by *Private Eye* that an M15 manager wrote a note expressing his view that the Israelis themselves carried out the bombing, the defence sought access to M15 material. This was met by a claim of PII. Interestingly, the decision not to disclose was made by the DPP, David Calvert-Smith QC, who prosecuted in the original trial.

51. Although this represents a controversial new power conferred upon the police which may potentially undercut the judicially regulated PII procedure, it is contained not in the Act, but rather in the Code of Practice. This is significant, as Parliament focussed more time and attention upon debate over the content of the Act, than the Code of Practice.

52. Section 11 CPIA 1996.

53. However, where a defence is put forward at trial which is different from that set out in the defence statement, the court is obliged to have regard to the *extent* of the difference and whether there is *justification* for it.

54. In support, he cites Steyn LJ in *R v. Winston Brown* 1995, that 'Non-disclosure is a potent source of injustice' (p. 319). Ironically, the reason given for forcing defence disclosure on the accused is the claim that it redresses the balance between the prosecution and defence in the criminal justice process.

55. See McConville *et al.* (1994: ch. 10).

56. For further discussion in Chapter 8.

8 The Trial

1. These involve serious offences, ranging from treason and murder (Class 1) to grievous bodily harm, robbery and all 'either-way' offences (Class 4).

2. However, ethnic minorities have been under-represented (Baldwin and McConville, 1979: 97–8); and the government has taken steps which have increased the prosecution's potential to influence the jury's composition

(Jackson, 1993b: 133–4) while decreasing those of the defence (s. 118, Criminal Justice Act 1988).

3. See also discussion in Chapter 1.

4. Under, s. 12 of the Magistrates' Courts Act 1980. In the cases examined by Phillips and Brown (1998), two per cent of all defendants processed by the magistrates were proven guilty in their absence (p. 157).

5. However, the CPS may voluntarily provide advance information if the offence charged is summary only; moreover, the defence may also provide information, but only on a voluntary basis.

6. Some cases are heard by stipendiary magistrates who are formally trained in the law, and whose powers were increased in the Crime and Disorder Act 1998. However, they constitute only a tiny fraction of magistrates (for instance, in 1991 there were only 76 compared to approximately 28,000 lay magistrates: Jackson, 1993b: 148).

7. Interview, May 1995.

8. While the protections afforded defendants tried in the Crown Court were acknowledged by the RCCJ, the lack of similar protections in summary court was not a matter of concern to the Commission. Thus in discussing proposals to protect against false confessions, they stated that while 'the risk of a false confession may not increase in proportion to the seriousness of the offence, the consequences for the suspect [in either way and indictable only cases] are greater and therefore the suspect should arguably be given greater protection in such cases against a wrongful conviction.' RCCJ 1993: 59.

9. However, Parliament has reduced the opportunity of defendants to elect trial by jury by reclassifying serious offences as summary; and the RCCJ (1993) proposed the elimination of the accused's automatic right to elect trial by jury (see Chapter 6). This was abandoned in the face of criticism, only to be resurrected by the government in 1998. While supported by the Lord Chief Justice, it has been sharply criticized by Lord Steyn, one of Britain's most senior judges, who called it a 'bad proposal, whose 'purpose is to cut costs. It has nothing to do with justice' (quoted in Dyer, *The Guardian*, 14 October 1998).

10. In 1997, in cases in which defendants had pleaded not guilty, less than a fourth of cases were dismissed by the magistrates (Home Office (1997: 134)), whereas 60 per cent were acquitted in the Crown Court (LCD (1998b: 66)).

11. Hedderman and Moxon (1992); see also, Chapter 6; and Phillips and Brown (1998: 164).

12. McConville *et al.* (1994: 213–15).

13. The Lord Chancellor's Department reported the following figures on the political affiliation of magistrates in England: Conservative (7,892), Labour (3,242), Liberal Democrat (2,694) and Independent (1,375). Those for Wales were: Conservative (715), Labour (664), Liberal Democrat (345), Plaid Cymru (117) and Independent (201); see LCD, December 1995: 'Political Profile of Benches' (document provided to authors).

14. Cf, Hedderman and Moxon (1992). This was also expressed to us in a number of interviews – for instance, Chris Mullin, MP, Home Affairs Committee (July 1995), and Roger Ede, Law Society (May 1995).

15. Interview, March 1995.

16. Interview with solicitor-advocate, February, 1995. Similar statements were made by other defence solicitors.
17. Interview with Anne Owers of JUSTICE, April 1995.
18. Interview with solicitor, June 1995.
19. Interview, February, 1995; original emphasis.
20. Interview, February, 1995.
21. It is claimed that this is due, in part, to a concern that lawyers will be accused of having perverted the course of justice. To do so, explained the Law Society's Roger Ede, would violate the unwritten rules that govern the conduct of the roles of defence and prosecution. Thus 'solicitors will very, very rarely interview prosecution witnesses. It's just not done' (Interview, May 1995).
22. See also, Wagenaar *et al.* (1993), who describe advocacy as narrative. Yet they found that many advocates are poor storytellers.
23. See also Chapter 9.
24. See also *McCarrol v. HM Advocate* (1949) SLT: 74.
25. (1978) *The Times*, 4 March.
26. For discussion of other relevant cases, see Gow, *NLJ*, 29 March 1996.
27. [1988], Crim LR, 109.
28. [1989] 1 WLR 497.
29. 20 December 1991; unreported CA.
30. [1993] 2 All ER 998.
31. Interview, April 1995. See also JUSTICE, 1989: 3 and 51.
32. See the Court of Appeal's reluctance to take account of the defence lawyer's advice to her client in custody when drawing adverse inferences from silence under s. 34 CJPOA. See discussion in Chapters 3 and 4.
33. Provisions in the Courts and Legal Services Act 1990 make it possible for experienced solicitors to qualify for rights of audience in the higher courts (which include the Crown Court). However, a veto given to four senior judges over the extension of rights beyond barristers in private practice has frustrated the aim of the 1990 Act. Thus only a small percentage of solicitors have done so. In 1998, The Lord Chancellor proposed plans to scrap the veto in order to facilitate extension of higher court rights to a broader segment of the legal community (Dyer, *The Guardian*, 14 October 1998).
34. However, a solicitor may appear in Crown Court in an appeal against a summary court judgment, or on a committal for sentence, provided the solicitor (or a partner or assistant member of her staff) appeared on behalf of the client in the lower court. Further, except for trials of more serious cases, solicitors have advocacy rights in criminal proceedings in the Crown Court in certain locations (Lord Chancellor's 1972 Practice Direction). Finally, under provisions of the Courts and Legal Services Act 1990, more than 500 solicitors have been granted rights of audience in the Crown Court.
35. Interview, February 1995.
36. And there are other benefits to the barrister: 'By delivering a guilty plea, defence lawyers can ... increase their credibility with both prosecutor and judge (thereby strengthening their hand in the occasional contested case)' (McConville and Baldwin, 1981: 194).
37. McConville *et al.*, 1994.
38. Ibid.: 256–61.

39. Interview, February 1995. The respondent served on the Philips Commission (which led to PACE 1984), and presently serves as an officer of the Law Society. Other examples may be found in McConville *et al.* (1994).

40. See, for example, the 1998 conviction for murder of Michael Stone, in which the testimony of prison inmates was crucial – testimony which, in the case of one witness, was later retracted as 'a pack of lies'.

41. Hall, 1994: 319–20.

42. That is, judicial supervision of police investigations, exclusion of evidence secured illegally, or the corroboration of all confessions (ibid.: 320).

43. The CJPOA s. 32 abolishes the requirement to administer a warning to juries of the danger of convicting solely on the basis of the evidence of accomplices, children or complainants in sexual offence cases.

44. Typically, this does not prevent the Commission from confusing the issues, by referring to the general trend away from corroboration requirements, as supportive of its own view concerning confessions.

45. See above, Chapter 3, for the inherently coercive nature of the police–suspect interrogation.

46. According to research carried out for the Commission by McConvlle (1993), less than 5 per cent of confession cases would have become acquittals had corroboration been required; in the remaining cases corroboration evidence could have been produced (RCCJ, 1993: para. 69).

47. For further discussion, see Chapter 3.

48. Clearly judges cannot be held responsible for the malpractice and dishonesty of police, or for unfair practices by the prosecution, or for the lack of integrity of Home Office scientists. However, critics assert that judges make their own contribution to the injustices of the system. According to Chris Mullin MP: 'The truth is that judges, both at trial and on appeal, played a large part in the most recent miscarriages of justice and there is nothing to be gained from suggesting otherwise' (Letter to *The Times*, 24 June 1992).

49. Three notable examples are the case of the Birmingham Six, Carl Bridgewater and the Maguire Seven. See Chapter 1.

50. The RCCJ also recommended the impanelling of multi-racial juries in cases involving special racial factors, as well as improvements in the jury system as a whole (p. 131).

51. For example, *Armstrong and others*, CACD, 19 October 1989 (the Guildford Four); *Callaghan and others* (1989) 88 Cr App R: 40; *McIlkenny and others* (1991) 93 Cr Appr R: 287 (the two Birmingham Six appeals); *Maguire and others* (1991) 94 Cr App R: 133; and *The Second Report on the Maguire Case*, HC 296, HMSO, 1992. *Ward* [1993] 1 WLR 619.

52. See Chapters 1 and 7 for further details.

53. See Chapter 1 for details.

54. See comments below on the research ot Roberts and Willmore (1993).

55. This was done in the search for the murderer of 15-year-old, Naomi Smith. The Warwickshire police secured DNA samples from 800 men (Jones, 1995), after which the Wetherby FSS lab found a match with the DNA of Edwin Hopkins, who was convicted and sentenced to life imprisonment (FSS, 1998: 13).

56. That is, any offence punishable by imprisonment.

57. See PACE, s. 62(2)(a) as amended by CJPOA 1994, s. 54(3)(b); and Home Office circular 16/95: National DNA Database (31 March), regarding amendments CJPOA 1994 to PACE (cf, item 8).

58. However, the voluntariness of those asked to undergo DNA testing has been more apparent than real.

59. As Ericson, 1994: 115, notes, the 'major concern of criminal justice system surveillance is the efficient formatting and availability of detailed knowledge about people in the hope that it will come in handy in future system dealings with them'.

60. Phillips, 1994. However, where the only evidence is a DNA profile, a conviction could be an error since DNA profiles, in contrast to fingerprints, are not unique. There are also other problems: the distribution of particular genetic traits varies among different ethnic populations; probability calculations assume that the population is homogeneously mixed when it may contain ethnic sub-groups; and a truly random match would require a database which includes samples of people *not* suspected of any offence (Creaton, 1994: 216–17).

61. However, this is unlikely to happen in magistrates' courts since there is no obligation to disclose the evidence on which the prosecution case is based (Leng and Taylor, 1996: 12). Here the accused has a right to disclosure only of material undermining the prosecution (ibid.: 54–5).

62. FSS, 1998: 31.

63. Roberts and Willmore, 1993: 72–3.

64. 'Too often [prosecution forensic science evidence] arrives two or three days before the trial and then everybody is running around in circles' (ibid.: 70).

65. This happened in 10 of the 37 cases included in the study by Roberts and Willmore. According to some lawyers, where delays occur they are invariably the fault of the police (see statement of Defence Solicitor G in ibid.: 68).

66. Ibid.: 69–70. Magistrates' courts, 'in pursuing their own agenda of increasing the through put of cases, employ strict criteria in assessing applications for adjournments' (ibid.: 71).

67. 'FSS Scientist P, for example, said that pre-trial conferences are a rarity, and FSS Scientist L said that conferences were becoming rarer, perhaps because the CPS were attempting to save money' (Roberts and Willmore, 1993: 58–9).

68. However, uncertainty about the meaning of forensic evidence is not confined to defence lawyers. In an FSS experiment, ten CPS solicitors were asked to explain what they understood an FSS report to mean: each one interpreted the report slightly differently (ibid.: 57).

69. Defence forensic experts are not likely to be called as witnesses unless they disagree with the prosecution expert in a way that is material to the case (ibid.).

70. RCCJ, 1993: 189: recommendations 18 and 19; see further, Chapter 2.

71. Stockdale, 1994: 304–12. He sees this as a type of summary justice orchestrated by administrators and clerks more concerned with balance sheets than with proper judicial process. Their prejudgment of cases, out of sight of the defence, judge and jury, is characterized as 'an unfair, unconstitutional, cynical and suspicious use of cash limits' which ensures that 'the scales are tilted in favour of the prosecution' (1994: 310). See also, Jackson, 1993b: 143.

72. For 1997–98, the figure for the police was 53 million pounds, as compared to 5 million for defence lawyers (FSS, 1998, *Annual Report*: 30).

73. Cf, s. 17(2) and (3)(a); unqualified by the issue of relevance.
74. However, 90 per cent of the FSS's operating revenue comes from research carried out for police authorities (1998, *Report*: 12).
75. Ibid.: 10.

9 The Appellate System and Miscarriages of Justice

1. Under the Magistrates' Courts Act 1980, ss. 108 to 110; and Rules 6 to 11 of the Crown Court Rules 1982, SI 1982 No. 1109.
2. *Practice Direction (Crown Court Business: Classification)* [1987] 1 WLR 1671 and Supreme Court Act 1981, s. 74.
3. Data suggest a consensus among both defendants and their solicitors that the magistrates' courts (where roughly 95 per cent of all convictions occur) are still strongly disposed to accept police testimony and to disbelieve the accused; mainly concerned with 'processing of defendants' (McConville *et al.*, 1994: 225–9 and 211–12); and decidedly pro-police, pro-conviction or conviction-prone (Hedderman and Moxon, 1992).
4. See McConville *et al.*, 1994; see also the discussion in Chapter 8.
5. 1.92 million defendants were proceeded against at magistrates' courts in 1996 (after discontinuances and committals to the Crown Court). Of these 850,000 were motoring offences (Home Office, *Criminal Statistics, 1996*: 134).
6. CPS (1998: 39).
7. It is not possible to give the exact percentage since the data is extrapolated from both the CPS, which reports data from mid-year to mid-year, and the Lord Chancellor's Department, which reports data on the basis of calendar years.
8. CPS (1998: 40).
9. As compared to 59 per cent in 1996: for both years, see LCD, 1998b: 66.
10. See CPS (1997: 37); and Part III, CAA 1995. This came into effect on 1 January 1996.
11. This is despite advice guidance documents created by the Court of Appeal, the Bar Council and the Law Society which state clearly that lawyers have a duty to meet with their convicted clients to offer preliminary advice on appeal.
12. To be discussed below.
13. Moreover, the acquittal rate in contested cases is usually considerably lower in magistrates' courts as compared to the Crown Court: for example, 25.5 per cent as against 40.2 per cent for 1997–8 (CPS (1998: 39 and 42)).
14. The Court consists of the Lord Chief Justice, the Master of the Rolls and 35 Lords Justices of Appeal (s. 2(2), Supreme Court Act 1981). It is divided into civil and criminal divisions. The latter is presided over by the Lord Chief Justice (LCJ) and may constitute itself into any number of courts which sit simultaneously. When hearing appeals against conviction or sentence, the court normally consists of at least three Lord Justices, assisted by High Court judges as required (s. 3(5) SCA 1981).
15. CAA 1968 as modified by s. 1(2) Criminal Appeal Act 1995.
16. However, the Court of Appeal may be expected to be most reluctant to grant leave to appeal against conviction where the appellant admitted guilt in the Crown Court.

17. For this reason, the process is described as a review rather than an appeal. See *McIlkenny and others* (1991) 93 Cr App R at 311, para. (4).
18. For 1988, see ibid.; and for 1989–97, see LCD (1997) *Judicial Statistics*: p. 12.
19. As compared to 53 in 1996: ibid.
20. LCD 1998b: 9.
21. See s. 17, CAA 1968.
22. As reflected in the words of Lord Widgery: '[This is] a case in which every issue was before the jury and in which the jury was properly instructed, and, accordingly, a case in which this Court will be very reluctant indeed to intervene' (*Cooper* [1969] 1 QB 267).
23. Yet the Commission shared the Court's view that juries are overly-inclined to acquit the accused: 'It is widely assumed – and we are in no position to contradict it – that the guilty are more often acquitted than the innocent convicted' (1993, *Report*).
24. Accounting for about 83 per cent (Malleson, 1993).
25. Some senior appellate judges did not regard Lord Widgery's interpretation as authoritative. For example, Master Thompson, Registrar of the Court of Appeal (Criminal Division), said that the 'lurking doubt' principle was not implicit in the concept of 'unsafe and unsatisfactory', and the Court had to have regard to the language of the statute (Malleson, 1993: 48).
26. See JUSTICE (1994d) and Chapter 1 of this volume.
27. *Report of the Departmental Committee on Legal Aid in Criminal Proceedings*, Cmnd. 2934 (London: HMSO, 1966: 81–2).
28. Interview with Walter Merricks, February 1995.
29. See McConville *et al.* (1994), McConville and Hodgson (1993) and Bridges and Choongh (1998) for recent improvements in custodial legal advice, and Bridges and Hodgson (1995) for a discussion of the limitations of the accreditation scheme.
30. See the discussion of court cases in Chapter 8.
31. In trying to appeal against a wrongful conviction resulting from faulty representation, the appellant is further disadvantaged since their lawyers will be ill-disposed to support an appellant's allegations of lawyer incompetency.
32. The success of fresh evidence appeals is relatively rare – only six in 1990 and four in 1991 (RCCJ, 1993: 172).
33. *Grafton* (1992) *The Times*, 6 March 1992, where the Court expressed reluctance to order a re-trial when a long period has elapsed between the original offence and the time of the appeal.
34. This could be done even in the absence of a petition, where new information cast doubt on the conviction (s. 17(1)(a), CAA 1968).
35. By the mid–1990s, the backlog at the Home Office was such that it was taking up to two years for cases to be dealt with (see Clarke, 1996: 946).
36. Thornton (1993: 927–8) and Sir John May, *Second Report of the Maguire Case*, 1992–93, HC 296.
37. See criticisms of the PCA's dependence upon the police as investigators in Chapter 4.
38. Obvious exceptions to the negative results were the professional investigations by the police of Avon and Somerset and Devon and Cornwall, which provided the evidence that ultimately persuaded the Court of Appeal to

quash the convictions in the Guildford Four and Birmingham Six cases (Mullin, 1991: para. 56).

39. See, for example, the case of *Roy Binns*, May 1977, described in JUSTICE (1993: 28).
40. An expert on the subject, Chris Mullin, MP, says he is not aware of any miscarriage that had been corrected as a result of an initiative by the Home Office's C3 Department. As evidence to the contrary, he calls attention to a long memorandum drafted by C3 shortly before the Maguire convictions were quashed, explaining why the convictions were safe (1991: para. 55).
41. Cf, *R v. Lomas* (1969) 53 Cr App R 256; and *R v. Kooken* [1982] 74 Cr App R 30.
42. JUSTICE (1993: ch. 5) and RCCJ (1993: 181).
43. Cf, Thornton (1993: 927–8), *The Guardian*, 29 November 1994, and PCA (1995: 19).
44. *The Times*, 29 November 1994.
45. *The Guardian*, 29 November 1994.
46. *R v. Secretary of State for Home Department, ex parte Hickey* (No. 2) [1995] 1 A11 ER 490.
47. Simon Brown LJ, at p. 500.
48. *The Times*, 29 November 1994.
49. *The Independent*, 14 December 1994.
50. Interview, 14 June 1995.
51. *The Times* and *The Guardian*, 29 November 1994.
52. Commission Members have fixed terms of not more than five years, renewable for a maximum of ten years: Sched. 1, s. 3(1), 1995 Act.
53. Barristers or solicitors of at least 10 years standing: s. 5(a), 1995 Act.
54. One notable point is the absence of persons who have been involved in campaigns on behalf of those claiming wrongful conviction, as well as the under-representation of experienced defence lawyers.
55. The CCRC also may be asked by the Home Secretary to investigate whether to recommend that a conviction be pardoned, and its decision on the matter is to be treated as conclusive: s. 16, 1995 Act.
56. The decision to refer is made by a committee of at least three Commission Members, after an intensive review of the case has been completed (CCRC, 1998: 22).
57. This conforms to the Court's long-standing rule that evidence could never be presented again which either had already been heard, or had not come before the jury because the defence (for whatever reason) had decided not present it. However, Baroness Blatch has argued that under, s. 13(2), the 'exceptional circumstances' provision, the CRCC can refer a case where the defence had failed to represent adequately the defence's case to the trial court or on appeal (see 15 May 1995, col. 329 HL).
58. According to Malleson (1997), the CCRC's independence is illustrated by its establishment by statute, its status as a corporate body staffed by non-civil service appointees and its physical location away from its sponsor.
59. McGrory (1998) *The Times* September 5: 19.
60. An example of how the last of these would apply is offered in the analysis of the case of Anthony Steele (Hill, 1996: 1552).
61. Malleson (1997: 1024 and n 100).

62. This advantage may be qualified by the greater demands made on the Commission resulting from its wider statutory obligations and investigative powers, and by the larger number of applications it is likely to receive. Predictions are that the CCRC will, in the long run, have an annual caseload roughly twice that of the Home Office.

63. The Royal Commission held that there was no practicable alternative to using the police to re-investigate the conduct of the initial investigation; and this view was endorsed by the government, which resisted all proposals calling for investigations to be made by the CCRC's staff. This was made clear by a Home Office minister during the final stages of the Bill's passage: 'The government has no intention of funding a team in the commission whose job would be to operate as a mini police force, duplicating work which could, and should, be done by the police or other public bodies' (HC Deb., vol. 263 cols. 1371–72, 17 July 1995).

64. For example, may veto the appointment of an officer who is not acceptable; and may reject the appointment of a particular police force, or other public investigatory body, that does not meet with its approval (s. 19(6), CAA 1995).

65. See s. 19(7). The rules the CCRC established during its first year of operation require that such decision be made by a committee of at least three Commission Members (CCRC, 1998: 22).

66. Letter to *The Times*, 15 May 1995 from Liberty, JUSTICE, the Bar Council and the Law Society; cited in Malleson (1995: 931).

67. See Sir John May (1994).

68. See s. 48(1) and (4), Supreme Court Act 1981.

69. Which modifies s. 23 of the 1968 Act.

70. The eligibility of new applications was determined generally by whether or not the applicant had failed at the relevant court of appeal. Different (unspecified) criteria were applied to the transferred cases, some of which had origins in the 1950s (such as that of Derek Bentley), and many of which were described as highly complex (ibid.).

71. Cases are ranked regularly for allocation to caseworkers, taking account of the date of receipt, the human costs of delay, and the effective use of resources. Date order generally prevails, except where age or health or evidential considerations favour immediate investigation (CCRC, 1998: 17).

72. Home Office (1994) 'Criminal Appeals and the Establishment of a Criminal Cases Review Authority', Discussion Paper.

73. Nicholas Baker, Standing Committee B, 30 March 1995 (see Clarke, 1996: 947).

74. Legal Aid Board, *Guidance: Exercise of Devolved Powers* (January 1998).

75. Interview with Jon Wagstaff, CCRC Legal Advisor, September 1998.

76. See Chapter 1.

10   Concluding Comments

1. Interview with Richard Ferguson, barrister, April 1995.

2. There are two meanings of risk, argues Ericson (1994: 114–15): those which 'pertain to threats to the efficiency of criminal justice surveillance'; and risk

as a probability statement, where '[S]uspects are made objects of knowledge in order to classify and profile them into risk categories'.

3. 'It is widely assumed – and we are in no position to contradict it – that the guilty are more often acquitted than the innocent convicted' state the Commission. And, it is when 'a guilty person walks free' that 'justice is made a mockery in the particular case and the credibility of the system in general is undermined' (1993: 2).

4. Similarly, the inclusion of the right to silence within the Commission's remit reflects not a desire to root out the causes of miscarriages, but a long-standing government agenda.

5. Brownlee (1998: 324–5).

6. Feeley and Simon (1992, 1994).

7. Garland (1996: 458).

8. Feeley and Simon (1994).

9. Raine and Willson (1993).

10. E.g. through defence disclosure or the taking of body samples, by force if necessary. See, further, Ericson (1994), Ericson and Haggerty (1997).

11. These are the words, for example, of a member of the Inner London Probation Service, who describes a recent joint initiative with the police as aiming 'to enhance the risk assessment and management of potentially dangerous offenders': Harraway (1998: 24).

12. The fragmentary nature of this has a postmodern flavour. 'The more people are risk-profiled in terms of their population identities, the more they feel individualized, fragmented, fractured, and separated from those not so identified ... Governance ... is based on an instrumentalism that extracts things from their wider social contexts and totalities'; Ericson and Haggerty (1997: 451).

13. Compare, for example, the statement of the Home Secretary (below at n 16) on the day he established the RCCJ, with one of the opening statements of the Commission in its report: 'The great majority of criminal trials are conducted in a manner which all the participants regard as fair, and we see no reason to believe that the great majority of verdicts, whether guilty or not, are not correct. ... [T]he damage done by the minority of cases in which the system is seen to have failed is out of all proportion to their number' (RCCJ, 1993: 6).

14. This is now the Criminal Cases Review Commission.

15. Interview with Richard Ferguson, barrister, April 1995.

16. 187 *HC Debs.*, col. 1109 (14 March 1991).

17. Interview with Richard Ferguson, barrister, April 1995.

18. For instance, the then Home Secretary's '27-point plan to crack down on crime', delivered to the annual Conservative Party Conference in October 1993.

19. See Chapter 5.

20. Hansard, HL, 7 July 1994, col. 1490, cited in Wasik and Taylor (1995: 81).

21. Garland argues that 'There is an emerging distinction between the *punishment* of crime, which remains the business of the state ... and the *control* of crime, which is increasingly deemed to be 'beyond the state' in significant respects' (1996: 459).

22. Brownlee (1998: 319).

23. Gardner *et al.* (1998).
24. Measures to tackle suspected terrorists operating out of the UK (rejected by the House of Commons earlier in the year when brought as a private member's Bill) were described as 'rejected authoritarian flotsam ... to be recycled as part of the Bill'; C. Gearty, 'The Bill's a Disgrace', *The Guardian*, 2 September 1998.
25. Jack Straw, 'My emergency bill is because of Omagh. And foreign crimes',*The Guardian*, 2 September 1998.
26. P. Mageean and M. O'Brien, 'Bombs and bad laws', *The Guardian*, 21 August 1998.
27. Consider also Garland's description of moving the responsibility for crime prevention to non-state agencies through 'partnerships', 'inter-agency co-operation' and 'activating communities' (1996: 452).
28. Emergency funding of £43 million has been invested in the Prison Service budget to reduce the crisis in accommodation and the building of private prisons (previously condemned as abhorrent) has been sanctioned (Brownlee, 1998: 327).
29. Typically, agreeing to legally significant assertions, such as recklessness, consent or dishonesty.
30. When, the authors raised this point with Geoff Hoon, Parliamentary Secretary at the Lord Chancellor's Department, he was dismissive of their concerns. Tellingly, he referred to people who 'plead guilty at the police station' being happy to be dealt with the next day (exchanges during the 'Renewal of Criminal Justice' Conference, Leeds, September 1998). This would indeed streamline the process if the need for an independent tribunal were to be dispensed with.
31. Law and order has proved to be a vote-winner for both the main political parties.
32. *New Law Journal*, 28 February 1997: 282.
33. There is a tension between the adversarial contest in which the prosecutor appears and her more neutrally defined role as the presenter of 'the facts'. This is heightened by the more limited disclosure requirement now incumbent upon the CPS.
34. 'We have not arrived at our proposals through a theoretical assessment of the relative merits of the two legal traditions [adversarial and inquisitorial]. On the contrary, we have been guided throughout by practical considerations which will, in our view, make our existing system more capable of serving the interests of both justice and efficiency' (RCCJ, 1993: 3).
35. RCCJ (1993: 3–4).
36. '[W]e have not...found...a set of practices which has so clearly succeeded in resolving the problems which arise in any system of criminal justice that it furnishes the obvious model which all the others should therefore adopt' (RCCJ, 1993: 4).
37. The advent of lawyers having even restricted access to suspects held in police custody (they may see them for 30 minutes when the suspect has been detained for 20 hours) was seen widely as undermining the authority of the *procureur* as guarantor of the rights of the defence.
38. This is the process whereby the *procureur* passes the case to the *juge d'instruction* to investigate.
39. See RCCJ (1993: 22–3).

40. Investigations are supervised; the *procureur* is responsible for the conduct of the detention period following arrest; and the *procureur*'s comments on officers' performance are taken into account in promotion.
41. In fact, the government appear to have pressed forward with their law-and-order policies regardless. RCCJ recommendations in line with government ideology were embraced; those, such as retention of the right to silence, which were not, were simply ignored.
42. Sanders (1994), for example, argues that the RCCJ operated a balance between due process and repression.
43. An appeal to communitarian values, though not touching so directly upon the issues of concern to us, might also be added to this.
44. CJPOA 1994 SS. 34–9.
45. CDA 1998 SS. 65–79; 97–8.
46. The Criminal Justice (Terrorism and Conspiracy) Bill 1998.
47. This is achieved through the implementation of parts of the Crime (Sentences) Act 1997.
48. Interview with barrister, April 1995.
49. '[I]t is of the utmost importance for the protection of the liberty of the subject that a court should always bear in mind that, unless a statute, either clearly or by necessary implication, rules out mens rea as a constituent part of a crime, the court should not find a man guilty of an offence against the criminal law unless he has a guilty mind': Lord Goddard CJ in *Brend v. Wood* [1946] LT 306 at 307.
50. See Ashworth and Blake (1996: 306).
51. See Ashworth (1996: 220). He also argues for a more meaningful and sustained conception of 'rights' grounded in the European Convention on Human Rights, protected in the context of their impact upon competing interests within the criminal process. See, further, Ashworth (1998).
52. As Ashworth (1998: 50) has noted, despite PACE and its Codes, as well as the Code for Crown Prosecutors and other efforts to introduce forms of guidance and accountability, 'there are still vast tracts of discretion, some of it left deliberately so as to enable flexibility, some eked out by practitioners in order to allow them to follow their preferred practices'.
53. See, for example, Dixon (1997: 81, 85).
54. See JUSTICE (1998: 18).

Bibliography

Alderson, J. (1992) 'The Police', in E. Stockdale and S. Casale (eds), 10–33.

Ames, J. (1994) 'Cost of curb on right of silence', *Law Society Gazette*, 16 February.

Ashworth, A. (1993) 'Plea, Venue and Discontinuance', *Criminal Law Review*, 830.

Ashworth A. (1996) 'Crime, Community and Creeping Consequentialism', *Criminal Law Review*, 220.

Ashworth, A. (1998) *The Criminal Process: An Evaluative Study*. Oxford: Clarendon Press.

Ashworth, A. and Blake, M. (1996) 'The Presumption of Innocence in English Criminal Law', *Criminal Law Review*, 306.

Baldwin, J. (1991) 'Summarising Tape Recordings of Police Interviews', *Criminal Law Review*, 671.

Baldwin, J. (1992) *Video Taping Police Interviews with Suspects: a National Evaluation*, Police Research Series Paper No. 1, London: Home Office Police Department.

Baldwin, J. (1993a) *The Role of Legal Representatives at the Police Station*, Royal Commission on Criminal Justice Research Study No. 3, London: HMSO.

Baldwin, J. (1993b) *Preparing the Record of Taped Interview*, Royal Commission on Criminal Justice, Research Study No. 2, London: HMSO.

Baldwin, J. (1997) 'Understanding Judge Ordered and Directed Acquittals in the Crown Court', *Criminal Law Review*, 536.

Baldwin, J. and Hunt, A. (1998) 'Prosecutors Advising in Police Stations', *Criminal Law Review*, 521.

Baldwin, J. and Maloney, T. (1993) *Supervision of Police Investigation in Serious Criminal Cases*, Royal Commission on Criminal Justice, Research Study No. 4, London: HMSO.

Baldwin, J. and McConville, M. (1979) *Jury Trials*. Oxford: Clarendon Press.

Baldwin, J. and McConville, M. (1981) *Confessions in Crown Court Trials*, Research Study No.5, Royal Commission on Criminal Procedure, London: HMSO.

Bean, P. and Nemitz, T. (1995) *Out of Depth and Out of Sight*. Loughborough: University of Loughborough: Mildands Centre for Criminology.

Belloni, F. (1987) 'Politics and the Law: Industrial Conflict in Britain', *International Review of History and Political Science*, 23, May: 1.

Bennett, R. (1993) 'Criminal Justice', *London Review of Books*, 15 (12), 24 June, 3, 5–15.

Berlins, M. 'Counsels of despair', *Spectator*, 25 November.

Bevan, V. and Lidstone, K. (1992) *The Investigation of Crime: A Guide to Police Powers*. London: Butterworths.

Block, B., Corbett, C. and Peay, J. (1993) *Ordered and directed acquittals in the Crown Court*, Royal Commission on Criminal Justice, Research Study No. 14, London: HMSO.

Bottomley, A. K., Coleman, C., Dixon, D., Gill, M. and Wall, D. (1991) *The Impact of PACE: Policing in a Northern Force.* Hull: Centre for Criminology and Criminal Justice.

Bottoms, A. E. and McClean, J. D. (1976) *Defendants in the Criminal Justice Process.* London: Routledge and Kegan Paul.

Bredar, J. (1992), 'Moving up the day of reckoning: Strategies for attacking the "cracked trials" problem', *Criminal Law Review*, 153.

Bridges, L. (1994a) 'Normalizing Injustice', 21, *Journal of Law and Society*, 20.

Bridges, L. (1994b) 'The Royal Commission's Approach to Criminal Defence Services: A Case of Professional Incompetence', in M. McConville and L. Bridges (eds) 273–86.

Bridges, L. and Choongh, S. (1998) *Improving Police Station Legal Advice: The impact of the accreditation scheme for police station legal advisers*, Research Study No. 31. London: The Law Society & Legal Aid Board.

Bridges, L. and Hodgson, J. (1995) 'Improving custodial legal advice', *Criminal Law Review*, 101.

Bridges, L. and McConville, M. (1994) 'Keeping Faith with their own Convictions: The Royal Commission on Criminal Justice', in M. McConville and L. Bridges (eds) 3–23.

Brown, D. (1997) *PACE Ten Years on: A Review of the Research.* Home Office Study No. 155. London: HMSO.

Brown. D., Ellis, T., and Larcombe, K. (1992) *Changing the Code: Police Detention under the Revised PACE Codes or Practice.* Home Office Research Study No. 129. London: HMSO.

Brownlee I. (1998) 'New Labour – New Penology? Punitive Rhetoric and the Limits of Managerialism in Criminal Justice Policy', 25, *Journal of Law and Society*, 313.

Brownlee I. and Furniss, C. (1997) 'Committed to Criminals?', *Criminal Law Review*, 3.

Brownlee, I. D., Mulcahy, A. and Walker, C. P. (1994) 'Pre-Trial Reviews, Court Efficiency and Justice: A Study in Leeds and Bradford Magistrates' Courts', 33,*The Howard Journal*, 109.

Bucke, T. (1997) *Ethnicity and Contacts with the Police: latest findings from the British Crime Survey.* Research and Statistics Directorate Research Findings No. 59. London: Home Office.

Bucke, T. and Brown, D. (1997) *In Police Custody: police powers and suspects' rights under the revised PACE codes of practice.* Home Office Research Study No. 174. London: Home Office.

Cahill, D. and Mingay, D. (1986) 'Leading Questions and the police interview', 2, *Policing*, 212.

Cape, E. (1997) 'Sidelining defence lawyers: police station advice after Condron', 1, *Evidence and Proof,* 386.

Choongh, S. (1997) *Policing as Social Discipline.* Oxford: Clarendon Press.

Clare, I. and Gudjonsson, G. H. (1993) *Devising and piloting a new 'Notice to Detained Persons,* Royal Commission on Criminal Justice, Research Study No. 7, London: HMSO.

Clarke, A. (1996) 'A painfully slow process', *New Law Journal*, 28 June, 946.

Clayton, R. and Tomlinson, H. (1992) *Civil Actions Against the Police.* London: Sweet and Maxwell.

Colvin, M. (1994) 'Miscarriages of Justice: The Appeal Process', in M. McConville and L. Bridges (eds) 287–96.

Colvin, M. and Akester, K. (1995) 'Directions for silence', *New Law Journal*, 3 November, 1621.

Corker, D. (1997) 'Maximising disclosure', *New Law Journal Practitioner*, (1) June 13, 885–6; (2)June 27, 961–2; (3) July 18, 1063–4.

Council of Europe (1991) *Report to the United Kingdom Government on the Visit to the United Kingdom carried out by the European Committee for the Prevention of Torture and Inhuman or Degrading Treatment or Punishment from 29 July 1990 to 10 August 1990.* Strasbourg: Council of Europe.

Crane, J. W. (1989) *Local Justice.* Edinburgh: T & T Clark.

Creaton, J. (1994) 'DNA Profiling and the Law: A Critique of the Royal Commissions Recommendations', in McConville and Bridges (eds) 209–18.

Criminal Cases Review Commission (1998) *Annual Report 1997–98.* Birmingham: CCRC, 18 June.

Criminal Law Revision Committee (1972) *Eleventh Report* (Cmnd 4991).

Crisp, D. and Moxon, D. (1994) *Case Screening By The Crown Prosecution Service: How and Why Cases are Terminated.* Home Office Research Study No. 137. London: HMSO.

Crown Prosecution Service, (1995) *Crown Prosecution Service Annual Report, 1994–95.* London: HMSO.

Crown Prosecution Service, (1998) *Crown Prosecution Service Annual Report, 1997–98.* London: HMSO.

Dennis, I. (1995) 'The Criminal Justice and Public Order Act 1994: The Evidence Provisions', *Criminal Law Review*, 4.

Dixon, D. (1997) *Law in Policing.* Oxford: Clarendon Press

Dixon D, Bottomley A. K., Coleman, C. A., Gill, M. and Wall, D. (1989) 'Reality and Rules in the Construction and Regulation of Police Suspicion', 17, *International Journal Sociology of Law*, 185.

Dixon, D., Bottomley, A. K., Coleman, C., Gill, M. and Wall, D. 'Safeguarding the Rights of Suspects in Police Custody', 1, *Policing and Society*, 115.

Dixon, D, Bottomley, A. K., Coleman, C., Gill, M. and Wall, D. (1990b) 'Consent and the Legal Regulation of Policing', 17, *Journal of Law and Society*, 348.

Drummand, H. 'Stands of advocacy revisited', *New Law Journal*, 3 May, 656.

Duce, R. (1994) 'Police 'fabricated evidence' in hunt for PC's killer', *The Times*, 29 June.

Easton, S. (1991) *The Right to Silence.* Aldershot: Avebury.

Edwards, A. (1997) 'The Criminal Procedure and Investigations Act (2): The Procedural Aspects', *Criminal Law Review*, 321.

Edwards, S. and Walsh, C. (1996) 'The justice of retrial?', *New Law Journal*, 7 June, 857–8.

Ericson, R. V. (1994) 'The Royal Commission on Criminal Justice System Surveillance', in M. McConville and L. Bridges (eds) 113–40.

Ericson, R. V. and Haggerty, K. D. (1997) *Policing the Risk Society*, Oxford: Clarendon Press.

Evans, R. (1993) *The Conduct of Police Interviews with Juveniles.* Royal Commission on Criminal Justice Research Study No. 8. London: HMSO.

Feeley, M. and Simon, J. (1992) 'The new penology: notes on the emerging strategy of corrections and its implications', 30, *Criminology*, 449.

Feeley, M. and Simon, J. (1994) 'Actuarial justice: the emerging new criminal law', in Nelken, D. (ed.) *The Futures of Criminology*. London: Sage.

Field, S. and Thomas, P.A. (1994) 'Justice and Efficiency? The Royal Commission on Criminal Justice', 21, *Journal of Law and Society*, 1.

Fitzgerald, M. (1993) *Ethnic minorities and the criminal justice system*. Royal Commission on Criminal Justice Research Study No. 20. London: HMSO.

Fitzgerald, M. and Sibbitt, R. (1997) *Ethnic Monitoring in Police Forces: a beginning*. Home Office Research Study No. 173. London: Home Office.

Forensic Science Service (1998) *Annual Report and Accounts 1997/98*. London: HC, 23 July.

Gardner, J., von Hirsch, A., Smith, A. T. H., Morgan, R., Ashworth, A. and Wasik, M. (1998) 'Clause 1 – The hybrid law from hell?', 31, *Criminal Justice Matters*, 25.

Garland, D. (1996) 'The Limits of the Sovereign State', 36, *British Journal of Criminology*, 445.

Gaskell, G. (1986) 'Black youths and the Police', 2, *Policing*, 26.

Gifford, T. (1986) *Where's the Justice?*. Harmondsworth: Penguin.

Glynn, J. (1993), 'Disclosure', *Criminal Law Review*, 841.

Greer, S. (1990) 'The Right to Silence: A Review of the Current Debate', 53, *Modern Law Review*, 719.

Greer, S. (1994) 'Miscarriages of Justice Reconsidered', 57, *Modern Law Review*, 58.

Greer, S. (1994) 'The Right to Silence, Defence Disclosure, and Confession Evidence', 21, *Journal of Law and Society*, 102.

Greer, S. (1995) *Supergrasses*. Oxford: Clarendon Press.

Gudjonsson, G. (1992) *The Psychology of Interrogations, Confessions and Testimony*. Chichester: John Wiley & Sons.

Gudjonsson, G., Clare, I., Rutter, S. and Pearse, J. (1993) *Persons at Risk During Interviews in Police Custody: The Identification of Vulnerbilities*. The Royal Comission on Criminal Justice, Research Study No. 12. London: HMSO.

Gudjonsson, G. and Clark, N. (1986) 'Suggestibility in police interrogation: a social psychological model', 1, *Social Behaviour*, 83.

Gudjonsson, G. and MacKeith, J. (1990) 'A proven case of false confession: psychological aspects of the co-erced – complaint type', 30 (4) *Medicine, Science and Law*, 329.

Hall, A. (1994) 'It Couldn't Happen Today?', in M. McConville and L. Bridges (eds) 313–23.

Harraway P. (1998) 'Managing risk', 32, *Criminal Justice Matters*, 24.

Harrison, J. and Cragg, S. (1991) *Police Misconduct: Legal Remedies*. London: Legal Action Group.

Hedderman, C. and Moxon, D. (1992) *Magistrates' Courts or Crown Court? Mode of Trial Decisions and Sentencing*. Home Office Research and Planning Unit Report No. 125. London: HMSO.

Hill, P. (1996) 'Finding finality', *New Law Journal*, 25 October.

Hillyard, P. (1994) 'The Politics of Criminal Injustice: The Irish Dimension', in M. McConville and L. Bridges (eds) 69–79.

Hodgson, J. (1992) 'Tipping the Scales of Justice: The Suspect's Right to Legal Advice', *Criminal Law Review*, 854.

Hodgson, J. (1994) 'Adding Injury to Injustice: The Suspect at the Police Station', 21, *Journal of Law and Society*, 85.

Hodgson, J. (1997) 'Vulnerable Suspects and the Appropriate Adult', *Criminal Law Review*, 785.

Hodgson, J. (1999) 'Comparing Legal Structures: the Comparativist as Participant Observer', in Nelken, D. (ed) *Contrast in Criminal Justice*. Aldershot: Dartmouth.

Home Office (1989) *Report of the Working Group on the Right to Silence*. London: HMSO.

Home Office (1995a) *Home Office Statistical Bulletin* (21 June 1995) 'Police complaints and discipline in England and Wales, 1994'. London: HMSO.

Home Office (1996) *Criminal Statistics: England and Wales, 1995*. Cm 3421. London: HMSO.

Home Office (1997a) *Review of Delay in the Criminal Justice System: A Report* (The Narey Report). London: Home Office.

Home Office (1997b) *Race and the Criminal Justice System*. London: Home Office.

Home Office (1998a) *Determining Mode of Trial in Either-Way Cases: A Consulation Paper*. London: Home Office.

Home Office (1998b) *Home Office Statistical Bulletin* (24 September 1998), 'Police Complaints and Discipline, Deaths in Police Custody, England and Wales, April 1997 to March 1998'. London: Home Office.

Home Office, Chaired by Sir Iain Glidewell (1998c) *The Review of the Crown Prosecution Service: A Report*. Cmn 3960. London: HMSO.

Home Office (1999) *Home Office Statistical Bulletin* (22 January 1999) 'Operation of Certain Police Powers under PACE: England and Wales 1997/8'. London: Home Office.

Hood, R. (1992) *Race and Sentencing*. Oxford, Clarendon Press.

Hucklesby, A. (1997a) 'Court Culture: and Explanation of Variations and Use of Bail by Magistrates' Courts', 36, *Howard Journal of Criminal Justice*, 129.

Hucklesby, A. (1997b) 'Remand Decision Makers', *Criminal Law Review*, 269.

Jackson, J. (1993a) 'The Evidence Recommendations', *Criminal Law Review*, 817.

Jackson, J. (1993b) 'Trial Procedures', in C. Walker and K. Starmer (eds) 130–62.

Jackson, J. (1994a) 'The Right of Silence: Judicial responses to parliamentary encroachment', 57, *Modern Law Review*, 270.

Jackson, J. (1994b) 'Trial by Jury and Alternative Modes of Trial', in M. McConville and L. Bridges (eds) 255–63.

Jackson, J. (1995) 'Interpreting the Silence Provisions: The Northern Ireland cases', *Criminal Law Review*, 587.

Jackson, J. (1998) 'Silence legislation in Northern Ireland: The Impact After Ten Years' unpublished paper presented at Journal of Civil Liberties Conference, 'Runciman – Five Years On', University of Northumbria, 15 July.

Jason-Lloyd, L. (1998) 'The Criminal Cases Review Commission – one year on', *New Law Journal*, 7 August.

Jennings, A. F. (1996) 'Resounding Silence', *New Law Journal*, May, 822.

Jones, P. R. (1985) 'Remand decisions at Magistrates' Courts', in D. Moxon (ed.) *Managing Criminal Justice*. London: HMSO.

JUSTICE (1989) *Miscarriages of Justice*. London: JUSTICE Education and Research Trust.

JUSTICE (1993) *Negotiated justice: a closer look at the implications of plea bargains*. London: JUSTICE.

JUSTICE (1994a) *Right of Silence Debate: The Northern Ireland Experience*. London: JUSTICE.

JUSTICE (1994b) *'Memorandom on the Codes of Practice under the Police and Criminal Evidence Act: 1984: THE NEW CAUTION'*. Lada: JUSTICE.

JUSTICE (1994c) *Remedying Miscarriages of Justice*. London: JUSTICE.

JUSTICE (1994d) *Unreliable Evidence? Confessions and the Safety of Conviction*. London: JUSTICE.

JUSTICE (1998) *Annual Report*. London: JUSTICE.

Kaye, T. (1991) *Unsafe and Unsatisfactory? Report of the Independent Inquiry into the working practices of the West Midlands Police Serious Crime Squad*. London: Civil Liberties Trust.

Kennedy, H. (1992) *Eve Was Framed: Women and British Justice*. London: Chatto & Windus.

Kettle, M. (1980) 'The politics of policing and the policing of politics', in P. Hain (ed.) *Policing and the Police*. London: John Calder, vol. 2, 59.

King, M. and May, C. (1985) *Black Magistrates*. London: Cobden Trust.

Lacey, N. (1994) 'Missing the Wood...Pragmatism versus Theory in the Royal Commission', in M. McConville and L. Bridges (eds) 30–41.

Law Society (1992) *Memorandum on the Future of Criminal Legal Aid: Evidence to Royal Commission on Criminal Justice*. London: Law Society.

Law Society (1993) 'Pre-trial reviews in the magistrates' courts: guidance for defence solicitors', 80, *Law Society Gazette*, 2330.

Legal Action Group (1993) *Police Misconduct*. London: LAG Education and Service Trust Ltd.

Legal Action Group (1994) *Preventing Miscarriages of Justice: A summary and initial response to the report of the Royal Commission on Criminal Justice*. London: LAG Education and Service Trust, Ltd.

Leigh, L. and Zedner, L. (1992) *A Report on the Administration of Criminal Justice in France and Germany*. Royal Commission on Criminal Justice Research Study No. 1. London: HMSO.

Leng, R. (1993) *The Right to Silence in Police Interrogation: A Study of Some of the Issues Underlying the Debate*. Royal Commission on Criminal Justice Research Study No. 10. London: HMSO.

Leng, R. (1994) 'A Recipe for Miscarriage: The RCCJ and Informal Interviews', in M. McConville, and L. Bridges (eds) 173–85.

Leng, R. (1995) 'Losing sight of the Defendant: The Government's Proposals on Pre-Trial Disclosure', *Criminal Law Review*, 708.

Leng, R (1998) *Reform of the Right to Silence*, unpublished paper presented to the *Journal of Civil Liberties* conference: 'Runciman – Five Years On', University of Northumbria, 15 July 1998.

Leng, R. and Taylor, R. (1996) *Blackstone's Guide to the Criminal Procedure and Investigations Act 1996*. London: Blackstone Press.

Lord Chancellor's Department (1997) 'Time Intervals for Criminal Proceedings in Magistrates' Courts: June 1997', *Information Bulletin*, Statistics on Magistrates' Courts, Issue 4.

Lord Chancellor's Department (1998a) *Magistrates sitting as judges: A consultation paper*, August. London: LCD.

Lord Chancellor's Department (1998b) *Judicial statistics, 1997*. London: HMSO.

Lustgarten, L. (1986) *The Governance of Police*. London: Sweet & Maxwell.

Maguire, M. and Norris, C. (1993) *The Conduct and Supervision of Criminal Investigations.* Royal Commission on Criminal Justice Research Study No. 5. London: HMSO.

Malleson, K. (1993) *A Review of the Appeal Process,* The Royal.Commission on Criminal Justice Research Study No. 17. London: HMSO.

Malleson, K. (1995) 'The CCRC: How Will It Work?' *Criminal Law Review,* 929.

Malleson, K. (1997) 'A broad framework', *New Law Journal,* 11 July, 1023.

Manning, P. (1977) *Police Work.* Cambridge, Mass: MIT Press.

Mansfield, M. and Taylor, N. (1993) 'Post-Conviction Procedures', in C. Walker and K. Starmer (eds) 163–74.

Mansfield, M. and Wardle, T. (1993) *Presumed Guilty: The British Legal System Exposed.* London: Heinemann.

May, Sir John (1994), *Report of the Inquiry into the Circumstances Surrounding the Convictions Arising Out of the Bomb Attacks in Guildford and Woolwich in 1974: Final Report.* London: HMSO.

McBarnet, D. (1983) *Conviction,* 2nd edn. London: Macmillan.

McConville, M. (1983) 'Search of Persons and Premises: New Data from London', *Criminal Law Review,* 605.

McConville, M. (1993) 'An error of judgment', *Legal Action,* September.

McConville, M. (1993b) 'Corroboration and Confessions: The Impact of a Rule Requiring that no Conviction can be Sustained on the Basis of Confession Evidence Alone'. Royal Commission on Criminal Justice Research Study No. 13. London: HMSO.

McConville, M. and Baldwin, J. (1981) *Courts, Prosecution, and Conviction.* Oxford: Clarendon Press.

McConville, M. and Hodgson, J. (1993) *Custodial Legal Advice and the Right to Silence.* Royal Commission on Criminal Justice Research Study No. 16. London: HMSO.

McConville, M., Hodgson, J., Bridges, L. and Pavlovic, A. (1994) *Standing Accused: The Organisation and Practices of Criminal Defence Lawyers in Britain.* Oxford: Clarendon Press.

McConville, M. and Mirsky, C. (1994) 'Redefining and Structuring Guilt in System Terms: The Royal Commission's Recommendations regarding Guilty Pleas', in M. McConville and L. Bridges (eds) 264–72.

McConville, M., Sanders, A., and Leng, R. (1991) *The Case for the Prosecution.* London and New York: Routledge.

McKenzie, I. and Irving, B. (1988) 'The right to silence', *Policing,* 4.

McLean, M. (1992) *Identifying Patterns in Witness Interviews: An Empirical Examination of the Interviewing Behaviour of Police Officers.* Bradford and Ilkley Community College.

McLeod, N. (1991) 'English DNA Evidence Held Inadmissible', *Criminal Law Review,* 583.

Mitchell, B. (1983) 'Confessions and police interrogation of suspects', *Criminal Law Review,* 596.

Morgan, R. and Jones, S. (1992) 'Bail or Jail?' in E. Stockdale and S. Casale (eds) 34–63.

Moston, S. and Stephenson, G. M. (1993) *The Questioning and Interviewing of Suspects Outside the Police Station.* Royal Commission on Criminal Justice Research Study No. 22. London: HMSO.

Moston, S., Stephenson, G. and Williamson, T. (1992) 'The incidence, antecedents and consequences of the use of the right to silence during police questioning', 3, *Criminal Behaviour and Mental Health*, 30.

Moxon, D. (ed.) (1985) *Managing Criminal Justice*. London: HMSO.

Mulcahy, A. Brownlee, I. and Walker, C. (1993) 'An Evaluation of Pre-Trial Reviews in Leeds and Bradford Magistrates' Courts', 33, Home Office Research Bulletin, 10.

Mullin, C. (1990) *Error of Judgement: The Truth About the Birmingham Bombings*. Swords, Co Dublin: Poolbeg Press.

Mullin, C. (1991) 'Evidence to the Royal Commission on Criminal Justice', November, copy supplied to authors.

Munday, R. (1996) 'Inferences from Silence and the European Human Rights Law', *Criminal Law Review*, 370.

Murray, C. (1996) 'Fair is foul and foul is fair', *New Law Journal*, 6 September, 1288.

Nobles, R. and Schiff, D. (1994) 'Optimism Writ Large: A Critique of the Runciman Commission on Criminal Justice', in M. McConville and L. Bridges (eds) 42–50.

Norris, C., Fielding, N., Kemp, J. and Fielding, J. (1992) 'Black and Blue: an Analysis of the Influence of Race on Being Stopped by the Police', 43, *British Journal of Sociology*, 207.

O'Conner, P. (1993) 'Prosecution Disclosure: Principle, Practice and Justice', in C. Walker and K. Starmer (eds) 101–27.

Packer, H. (1968) *The Limits of the Criminal Sanction*. Stanford, CA: Standford University Press.

Pattenden, R. (1998) 'Silence: Lord Taylor's Legacy', 2, *Evidence & Proof*, 141.

Police Complaints Authority (1995) *Police Complaints Authority – The First Ten Years*. London: HMSO.

Police Complaints Authority (1998) *Annual Report*. London: HMSO.

Phillips, C. and Brown, D. (1998) *Entry into the criminal justice system: a survey of police arrests and their outcomes*. Home Office Research Study 185. London: Home Office.

Plotkinoff, J. and Woolfson, R. (1993a) *Information and Advice for Prisoners about Grounds for Appeal and the Appeals Process*. The Royal Commission on Criminal Justice Research Study No. 18. London: HMSO.

Plotnikoff, J. and Woolfson, R. (1993b) *From Committal to Trial: Delay at the Crown Court*. London: Law Society.

Raine, J. W. and Willson, M. J. (1993) *Managing Criminal Justice*. Hemel Hempstead: Harvester Wheatsheaf.

Raine, J.W. and Willson, M.J. (1997) 'Police Bail With Conditions', 37, *British Journal of Criminology*, 593.

Redmayne, M. (1995) 'Doubts and Burdens: DNA Evidence, Probability and the Courts', *Criminal Law Review*, 464.

Redmayne, M. (1997) 'Presenting Probabilities in Court: The DNA Experience 1 *Evidence & Proof*, 187.

Reiner, R. (1978) *The Blue Coated Worker*. Cambridge: Cambridge University Press.

Reiner, R. (1992) *The Politics of the Police*. 2nd edn. Hemel Hempstead: Harvester Wheatsheaf.

Riley, D. and Vennard, J. (1988) *Triable either-way cases: Crown Court or Magistrates' Court*. London: HMSO.

Roberts, P. and Willmore, C. (1993) *The Role of Forensic Science Evidence in Criminal Proceedings*. Royal Commission on Criminal Justice Research Study No. 11. London: HMSO.

Rose, D. (1996) *In the Name of the Law*. London: Jonathan Cape.

Royal Commission on Criminal Justice, Chaired by Viscount Runciman of Doxford (1993) *Report*, Cmnd 2263. London: HMSO

Royal Commission on Criminal Procedure, Chaired by Sir Cyril Phillips (1981) *Report*, Cmnd 8092. London: HMSO.

Rozenberg, J. (1992) 'Miscarriages of Justice' in E. Stockdale and S. Casale (eds) 91–117.

Sanders, A. (1986) 'Arrest, Charge and Prosecution', 6, *Legal Studies*, 257.

Sanders, A. (1989) 'Rights, Remedies and the Police and Criminal Evidence Act', *Criminal Law Review*, 802.

Sanders, A. (1992) 'Reforming the Prosecution System', 63, *Political Quaterly*, 25.

Sanders, A. (1994) 'Thinking About Criminal Justice', in M. McConville and L. Bridges (eds) 141–51.

Sanders, A. and Bridges, L. (1990) 'Access to Legal Advice and Police Malpractice', *Criminal Law Review*, 494.

Sanders, A., Bridges, L., Mulvaney, A. and Crozier, G. (1989) *Advice and Assistance at Police Stations and the 24-hour Duty Solicitor Scheme*. London: Lord Chancellor's Department.

Sanders, A. and Young, R. (1995) *Criminal Justice*. London: Butterworths.

Schiff, D. and Nobles, R. (1996) 'Criminal Appeal Act 1995: The Semantics of Jurisdiction', 59, *Modern Law Review*, 573–81.

Scott, R. (1996) 'The Use of Public Interest Immunity Claims in Criminal Cases', 2, *Web Journal of Current Legal Issues*.

Scraton, P. (1994) 'Denial, Neutralisation and Disqualification: The Royal Commission on Criminal Justice in Context', in M. McConville and L. Bridges (eds) 98–109.

Shapland, J. and Vagg, J. (1988) *Policing by the Public*. London: Routledge.

Sharpe, S. (1998) *Judicial Discretion and Criminal Investigation*. London: Sweet and Maxwell.

Shepherd, E., Mortimer, A. and Mobasheri, R. (1995) 'The Police Caution: Comprehension and Perceptions in the General Population', *Counsel* (September–October).

Singh, S. (1994) 'Understanding the Long-Term Relationship between Police and Policed', in M. McConville and L. Bridges (eds) 162–72.

Skogan, W. (1990) *The Police and Public in England and Wales*. Home Office Research Study No. 117. London: HMSO.

Skogan, W. (1994) *Contacts between Police and Public: findings from the 1992 British Crime Survey*. Home Office Research Study No. 134. London: Home Office.

Slapper, G. and Kelly, D. (1996) *Sourcebook on English Legal System*. London: Cavendish.

Smith, D. (1985) *Police and People in London*. Aldershot: Gower.

Smith, D. and Gray, J. (1983) *Police and People in London,* London: Policy Studies Institute.

Smith, J. C. (1995) 'Criminal Appeals and the Criminal Cases Review Commission', 145, *New Law Journal*, 533.

Smith, R. (1994) 'Looking Forward' in M. McConville and L. Bridges (eds) 297–303.

Softley, P. (1980) *Police Interrogation: An Observational Study in Four Police Stations*. Royal Commission on Criminal Procedure Research Study No. 4. London: HMSO.

Southgate, P. and Crisp, D. (1993) *Public Satisfaction with Police Services*. Home Office Research and Planning Unit Paper 73. London: Home Office.

Sprack, J. (1997a) 'The Criminal Procedures and Investigations Act 1996: (1) The duty of disclosure', *Criminal Law Review*, 308.

Sprack, J. (1997b) *Emmins on Criminal Procedure*. London: Blackstone.

Statewatch (1999) vol. 9, no.1.

Steer, D. (1972) *Police Cautions*. London: Blackwell.

Stockdale, E. and Casale, S. (eds) (1992) *Criminal Justice Under Stress*. London: Blackstone.

Stockdale, R. (1991) 'Running with the hounds', *National Law Journal*, 141.

Stockdale, R. (1994) 'For Action This Day', in M. McConville and L. Bridges (eds) 304–12.

Taylor, I. and Jamieson, R. (1998) 'Fear of crime and fear of falling: English anxieties approaching the millenium', XXXIX (1) *Archives Européennes de Sociologie*, 149.

Taylor, Lord (1994) 'The Tom Sargant Memorial Lecture', *New Law Journal*, 28 January.

Thompson, S.(1998) 'Defence Statements – Weighting the Scales or Tipping the Balance on a Submission of No Case', *Criminal Law Review*, 802.

Thornton, P. (1993) 'Miscarriages of Justice: A Lost Opportunity', in C. Walker and K. Starmer (eds) *Justice in Error*. London: Blackstone 163–74.

Uglow, S. (1995) *Criminal Justice*. London: Sweet & Maxwell.

Vennard, J. (1981) *Contested Trials in Magistrates' Courts: The Case for the Prosecution*. Home Office Research Study No. 71. London: HMSO.

Vennard, J. (1985) 'The Outcome of Contested Trials', in D. Moxon (ed.) *Managing Criminal Justice*. London: HMSO.

Wagenaar, W., van Koppen, P. and Crombag, H. (1993) *Anchored Narratives*. Hemel Hempstead: Harvester Wheatsheaf, St. Martin's Press.

Walker, C. (1993) 'Introduction', in C. Walker and K. Starmer (eds) 1–16.

Walker, C. and Starmer, K. (eds) (1993) *Justice in Error*. London: Blackstone.

Walker, M. A., Jefferson, T. and Seneviratine, M. (1990) *Ethnic Minorities, Young People and the Criminal Justice System*, (Main Report). University of Sheffield, Centre for Criminological and Socio-Legal Studies.

Wasik, M. and Taylor, R. (1995) *Blackstone's Guide to the Criminal Justice & Public Order Act 1994*. London: Blackstone.

Wells, C. (1994) 'The Royal Commission on Criminal Justice', in M. McConville and L. Bridges (eds) 51–8.

Willis, C., McLeod, J. and Naish, P. (1988) *The tape-recording of interviews with suspects: a second interim report*. Home Office Research Study No. 97. London: HMSO.

Wolchover, D. and Heaton-Armstrong, A. (1991) 'The Questioning Code Revamped', *Criminal Law Review*, 232.

Wrench, P. (1995) *'National DNA Database'*, Home Office Circular, 16/95, 31, March. London: Home Office.

Wundersitz, J., Naffine, N. and Gale, F. (1991) 'The production of Guilt in the Juvenile Justice System: the Pressures to "Plead"', *Howard Journal*, 30 (3), 192.

Yeo, M. (1983) 'Diminishing the right to silence: The Singapore experience', *Criminal Law Review, 89.*

Young, R. (1991) 'DNA Evidence – Beyond Reasonable Doubt?', *Criminal Law Review,* 264.

Young, R. and Sanders, A. (1994) 'The Royal Commission on Criminal Justice: A Confidence Trick?', 14, *Oxford Journal of Legal Studies,* 435.

Zander, M. (1972) 'Access to a solicitor in the police station', *Criminal Law Review, 342.*

Zander, M. (1979) 'The investigation of crime: a study of cases tried at the Old Bailey', *Criminal Law Review, 203.*

Zander, M. (1993) 'Where the critics got it wrong', *New Law Journal*, October 1, 1338–41.

Zander, M. (1994) 'Abolition of the Right to Silence, 1972–1994' in D. Morgan and G. Stephenson (eds) *Suspicion and Silence: the Right to Silence in Criminal Investigations.* London: Blackstone, 141–55.

Zander, M. and Henderson, P. (1993) *The Crown Court Study.* Royal Commission on Criminal Justice Research Study No. 19. London: HMSO.

Index*

---

* Where 'n' appears, the page number is the page where the note indicator appears, *not* the
  note itself.